Involvement
and
Detachment

Norbert Elias

Involvement
and
Detachment

German editor Michael Schröter
Translated by Edmund Jephcott

Basil Blackwell

Complete English edition first published 1987

Basil Blackwell Ltd
108 Cowley Road, Oxford, OX4 1JF, UK.

Basil Blackwell Inc.
432 Park Avenue South, Suite 1503
New York, NY 10016, USA

British Library Cataloguing in Publication Data

Elias, Norbert
  Involvement and detachment.
  1. Sociology
  I. Title II. Schröter, Michael
  III. Engagement and Distanzierung. *English*
  301   HM51

  ISBN 0-631-12682-1

Library of Congress Cataloging in Publication Data

Elias, Norbert.
  Involvement and detachment.

  Includes index.
  1. Sociology. I. Schröter, Michael. II. Title.
  HM24. E385 1987   301   87–6347

ISBN 0–631–12682–1

Typeset in 11 on 12 pt Times
by Alan Sutton Publishing Limited
Printed in Great Britain by
Billing & Sons Ltd, Worcester

Contents

Introduction

Part 1

1   The point of departure for the enquiries that follow was an enduring concern with the nature of sociological knowledge, with knowledge of human societies. Why are human societies more resistant than non-human nature to a successful exploration by human beings, and thus to a more adequate handling of their self-made dangers and possible catastrophes? And why is it that almost everybody seems to take it for granted that this must be so? Why do most people appear to consider it both impossible and undesirable that human beings might learn to rid themselves of the dangers they constitute for each other and for themselves, in the same way they learned to get rid of, or at least to contain, many of the dangers with which non-human nature threatened humans in former days? Those dangers were at least as uncontrollable as the human-made dangers that threaten them today. Is it not true that the threat of a new epidemic caused largely by non-human agents is today immediately countered by the mobilization of scientists in many parts of the world? Everybody assumes as a matter of course that it is not beyond the power of human beings to find an explan-ation and then perhaps also a cure for the deadly menace. In the case of wars or revolutions, however, which are in no way smaller and often even greater human disasters than great floods or epi-demics, few people would look to social scientists for help and advice; and if they did these scientists might come up with advice which few were ready to accept or even listen to.

   To be sure, three or four centuries ago, in the case of natural

I am very grateful to my two assistants, Rudolf Knijff and Jan-Willem Gerritsen for the help they have given me during our work together on this introduction.

catastrophes too, few would have turned to or listened to scientists for help and advice. In fact at that time many people might have spurned the very idea that human beings, thanks to their own capacity for producing reality-congruent knowledge, could have the power to prevent natural disasters from killing thousands of people. Not so long ago it might have seemed laughable and naïve to believe such a thing. Now, for the time being, the course of humanity in dealing with disasters brought about by humans themselves, appears to have been arrested in a condition not unlike that which, for thousands of years, also prevailed in the case of dangers resulting from non-human nature. Once upon a time there was nothing one could do but wail about the frequency with which women died in childbirth, or little children died in the first year of life. Now there is nothing one can do about social disasters, such as wars, revolutions and other forms of human violence which shorten further the already short life of great masses of people, and inflict crippling injuries on thousands of others.

As things are, one may even fail to recognize violent action between or within states as a human-made catastrophe. Social scientists have not yet succeeded in demonstrating convincingly that killing is no answer to killing, whether in a good or in a bad cause. Nor have they succeeded in making it more widely known and also better understood that cycles of violence, whether they are kept in motion by integration or by hegemonial struggles, by class conflicts or by interstate conflicts, have strong self-escalating tendencies. War processes, for example, are difficult to stop even if they are still in the preparatory state of reciprocal threats of violence creeping towards its use. They almost invariably breed professional killers of one kind or another, whether these killers have the social character of dictator or general, of freedom fighter or mercenary. Their impulses and their actions are geared to mutual suspicion, hatred and violence; as levers of human catastrophes they are to be feared no less than the plague which once seemed to humans equally uncontrollable.

2 There is another example which may help to illustrate the weakness of the social sciences in relation to their task. Quite a number of people are inclined to believe as a matter of course that the natural sciences in general, and physics in particular, are to blame for the danger of a nuclear or maybe a chemical war which hangs over our heads on a very thin thread, like the infamous sword of Damocles. War processes, however, are

closely linked to specific social institutions. Almost all governments, and certainly those of the more powerful nations, maintain as a matter of course military forces as large as they can
afford and often larger. In their unending rivalry for power and
status, they all try to secure for their own nation the highest
position within their reach. Many of them, however, and particularly the most powerful states or blocks of states, by trying to
maximize their own security, automatically optimize the insecurity of rival or enemy states and thus in fact their own.

The explanation of the danger of war cannot be found in the
form of a stationary cause. It lies in an ongoing, self-perpetuating
social process without absolute beginning, though – like cholera –
possibly with an end. The institutional and the habitus tradition
associated with this long-term process makes not only a country's
security but also its prestige, and thus the pride and self-love of
many of its citizens, dependent on the power potential of its
military establishment. More often than not a large section of a
nation's population rejoices in the strength and prowess of its
military establishment. Hence, by continually threatening each
other, militarily interdependent rival states drive each other in an
endless spiral towards the development of even tougher and
better-trained troops, of even more deadly weapons, and thus, in
a world with more and more people, towards wars where
mounting numbers can sacrifice their lives. The difficulty is that it
cannot be of any help at all to change attitudes one-sidedly or to
advocate such a change on behalf of either small or large sections
of a country's population.

3   Whoever pays the piper calls the tune. Once upon a time
armoured knights were the principal exponents of the age-old
tradition which induced people to regard it not only as legitimate
but also as praiseworthy to settle certain types of conflict by
reciprocal attempts at killing or maiming. The smiths who, in a
rising spiral improved, now the swords and other weapons of
attack, now the armour and other means of defence, were not the
reason why kings and their warriors went to war against each
other. When at one stage a well-known spiral of violence resulted
in the dominance of firearms, when even the heaviest knightly
armour could be pierced and even the thickest fortress walls
shattered, there was an outcry at the barbaric destructiveness of
the new weapons. But the interstate rivalries and thus the war
process continued. Knights and fortress walls disappeared, but

the spiral of interstate violence went on, without halting in its un-
checked – and so far uncheckable – course towards the invention
and use of more and more destructive weapons and the employment of more and more resources for the preparation of war.

The arms race did not start yesterday. However, with or
without a big bang, it may now be nearing the end of the road.
Smiths were not the originators of endless wars between knights;
nor are scientists and engineers who apply their professional
knowledge to the improvement of weapons the reason why
nations go to war. They are usually nothing more than servants or
advisers of party politicians and other ruling groups who are the
leading players in this game.

Nor is the reason for war to be found in weapons of one kind or
another. It can only be found in groups of human beings
themselves perceiving, and bound to, each other as rivals or
enemies. These groups, nations among them, delight in their own
superiority over each other, particularly their military superiority, past or present. They are deeply affected by its decline.
They continue to live in the shadow of their greater military past
and go into mourning for it, often generation after generation.
The history books of nations, particularly those destined for
children, are full of battles won and enemies defeated. Indeed,
the handing on of this information from one generation to the
other can hardly be avoided; for it forms an integral part of the
knowledge that is needed for an understanding of the formative
period in the development of nations and other survival units,
and thus of their own identity. That some of the peoples of this
world, in cases of conflict, try to coerce each other by violent
means and that victories gained in the course of mutual woun-
dings and killings are a source of collective pride and rejoicing has
thus become part of a firmly entrenched tradition, with roots
deep in the social habitus of individual members of these groups.

In our age, moreover, the concept of a just war, a kind of moral
rehabilitation of the use of violence as a means of settling
interstate conflicts, has been extended to the settling of conflicts
within states. Partly thanks to the work of Marx and his followers,
revolution has become a praise word. The reciprocal violence of
groups of people in the course of a revolutionary process or any
other kind of long-drawn-out civil war is as great a human disaster
as a war between states. That revolutionary processes often start
from a condition of one-sided violent oppression has often been
mentioned. It is less often mentioned that they also quite

frequently end with one-sided violent oppression. If one ceases to consider revolutions in an historical manner, that is, as short-term events, if one sees instead such violent explosions as phases of a long-term process, it becomes clearer that they too form part of a cycle and often a spiralling cycle of violence, which may go on smouldering for a long time after the overt revolutionary violence has died down.

The self-perpetuating propensity of long lasting cycles of violence can be observed as much in the processes of class revolutions or ethnic and other forms of civil war as in those of interstate war. In all these cases violence breeds violence, often generation after generation. It may take a long time before the impetus of such a process exhausts itself. As for the alternative, it requires a higher level of detachment, of self-restraint, and of patience, and a gradual toning down of mutual dislike, suspicion and hatred. The threat of war, in the last resort, has it roots in the relationship of groups of people with each other, in their attitudes towards and their feeling for each other. None of these can be changed at short notice. Yet people often act as if that were the case: their emotional make-up induces them to expect and to demand that their political aims and ideals be realized in their own lifetime. Perhaps it is necessary to say explicitly that work towards the fulfilment of many of these aims, and certainly that of outlawing the use of violence as a means of settling interstate conflicts, is likely to require the patient work of many generations united in their uncompromising adherence to the paramount goal and ready for many compromises on detail.

A rather neglected aspect of the dangers human groups constitute for each other deserves some attention here – their emotional aspect. Human groups seem to take a strange delight in asserting their superiority over others, particularly if it has been attained by violent means. The area one enters here has not been much explored. In referring to the pleasure people derive from the feeling that one of the groups to which they belong is superior to other groups, one touches on the emotional aspects of group relations and the dangers inherent in them. Part of the self-love of individuals, it seems, can attach itself to one of the groups with which they identify themselves, most of all to nations and other types of survival groups. The feeling of group superiority appears to provide members of that group with an immense narcissistic gratification. It is strange to observe that all over the world groups of people, great and small, huddle together as it were, and, with a gleam in their eyes and a nod of intimate understanding, assure each other how much greater, better, stronger they themselves are than some particular other groups or maybe even all other human groups. Secretly or not, they all have a self-praising vocabulary and a corresponding denigrating vocabulary directed against other groups. It depends on the balance of power between the groups concerned whether the denigrated groups can retaliate in stigmatizing terms of their own.

The unselfish aspects of people's attachment to groups, of their we-identity, have found some consideration. Praise words such as patriotism or national pride and self-esteem bear witness to the fact. The narcissistic component of these feelings, understandably, attracts less attention. Yet if one wants to know why the unrelenting drift in that direction continues with undiminished force – even now when another war threatens to destroy a large part of humanity, including the participant nations themselves – the lure of the narcissistic gratification of victory and group superiority, the hegemonial ecstacy associated with the prospect of continental or even global leadership and supremacy, provide at least part of the answer. People in power can usually count on a warm response of approval and often of affection or love from their compatriots whenever they praise or add to the glory of the social unit they all form with each other. The remarkable propensity of people for projecting part of their individual self-love into specific social units, to which they are linked by strong feelings of identity and of belonging, is one of the roots of the dangers which human groups constitute for each other.

It is not too difficult to recognize the ambivalent and the paradoxical character of the various types of group self-love. In many cases, people expect support, protection and help in distress, from their We-group, especially from a survival group, as well as the indispensable gratification of their self-esteem; and yet at the same time they may be ready to risk their lives for the sake of their group and its distinct values and beliefs. It is a remarkable blend of self-love and altruism, of narcissistic gratification and devotion to a collective, which one encounters here. The paradoxical situation is closely connected with the fact that the human self is an I-self as well as a We-self.

The vocabulary at one's disposal in this context is marred by its lack of detachment, by its emotional partisanship for the We-group. It shows clearly the black and white design of dominant involvement. According to this design, self love which leads to narcissism in human beings as individuals or as groups is bad, while love of others and even gratification of collective self-love are usually associated with strong positive evaluative undertones. The possibility that human beings may experience love for a group to which they themselves as well as others belong is one of many instances which show that a simple polarity between feelings of self-regard and of regard for others, of egotism and altruism, or even of good and bad, may not always fit the observable evidence. Moreover, the self-esteem of nations and other survival groups need not be undeserved: they may have achievements to their credit which are of great benefit to humanity. The praise people give to the affection they feel for themselves as a collective can be entirely realistic. But their self-praise may go far beyond their real merits. Often enough the virtues which such collectives attribute to themselves are dominated by communal fantasies. Nations feast on imaginary virtues, or on the virtues and merits of their forefathers which are no longer shared by themselves. In all these cases it is a question of balances, which requires exploration and recognition, rather than a black and white design, of a polarization of good and evil. Yet the pictures people have of themselves and each other are mostly of the latter type. They are often astonishingly simplistic. Their self-representation, characteristic of their cognitive involvement and their narcissism, is often uniformly good, while rivals or enemies tend to have no merits at all; they are bad all round.

A good example of the peculiar blend of reality-congruence and fantasy that one encounters in the self-images of survival units is the recurrent confusion of a higher power ratio with a higher human value in those endowed with more power and, correspondingly, the attribution of a lesser human value to those who are less powerful. I have alluded before to the profound traumatic effect on peoples' social habitus, to the wounding of their self-love which tends to follow a marked change for the worse in their nation's fortune. In just the same way, a decisive military victory, in present times as in past ages, has often been experienced by the victors as a reward from the gods for being more virtuous than their opponents, or, in human terms at any rate, superior to them. Thus the members of nations, even in our own time, experience the descent of their nation from the highest to a secondary position in the global power – and status – hierarchy of states as a fall from grace, as a lowering of their own human value. Their self love suffers. The loss of power is tacitly experienced as a loss of their value as human beings. As their pattern of self-restraint was formerly sustained and rewarded by the narcissistic enjoyment of their nation's power and pride, a decline in power can easily lead to a loosening of restraint. The lessening of a people's love for itself which before had a strong integrating function may turn into self-denigration if not self-hatred. For a while, a people's mourning for past greatness can thus have a de-civilizing effect.

I have shown in some detail a few of the reasons why human groups in so many cases constitute a threat and a danger for each other. It is not unusual to assume that the all-pervasive danger of violent action in the form of war or civil war, with which human groups threaten each other, has mainly what we call 'rational' reasons. However, violent struggles between human groups are a standing feature of the period we call history and presumably also of prehistory. It is in many cases hard to discover any reason for them that we might call rational today, any reason, that is, apart from an increment of wealth and power, from the gratification of collective self-love and the *Fata Morgana* of perfect security enforced by violence. Yet in spite of this age-old tradition and its visible perpetuation by the military institutions of our age – now grown on both sides of the great divide into powerful military industrial establishments – many people are inclined to assume that the day has dawned when this powerful tradition, with its roots deep in the feelings and attitudes of human groups towards each other, has come to an end. They tend to assume that realistic knowledge of the unprecedented destructiveness of warfare in our age, or in other words rational reasoning alone, is enough to break the impetus of the self-perpetuating tradition of war between survival groups, while the institutions and above all the collective feelings and attitudes of such groups retain their traditional character. This is quite a good example of people's involvement, in this case their wishful thinking, gaining the upper hand over a more detached view – of short term feelings displacing a long term diagnosis oriented towards facts, however unwelcome.

The stronger the hold of involved forms of thinking, and thus of the inability to distance oneself from traditional attitudes, the stronger the danger inherent in the situation created by peoples' traditional attitudes towards each other and towards themselves. The greater the danger the more difficult it is for people to look at themselves, at each other and at the whole situation with a measure of detachment. This is an example of one of the key problems which, in more general terms, this book tries to explore.

4   One difference between a more detached and a more involved approach, which one may notice if one looks at this example, is a difference in the time perspective. A highly involved approach to the present danger of a big war has a short-term perspective. In this case people's attention is focused on the likelihood of a great war here and now, on the danger of contemporary war only. A more detached view entails in this case a different time perspective. If one takes into account the fact that organized group violence in the form of war is part of a long tradition and that this tradition is strongly represented by contemporary institutions, by the stereotyped sentiments and attitudes of different human groups in relation to each other, the danger of contemporary war appears in a different light. A long-term perspective raises the question of whether the tradition of settling conflicts between states by means of violence, in the form of war, can be brought to an end while the traditional institutions, group feelings and attitudes directed towards warfare remain unchanged. In other words, a long-term perspective shows the situation of the moment in a different light. No doubt a long-term perspective demands a greater capacity for distancing oneself for a while from the situation of the moment. But it also opens the way towards greater detachment from the wishes and fears of the moment, and thus from time-bound fantasies. It increases the chance of a more fact-oriented diagnosis. In terms of an old French proverb, it is a case of '*reculer pour mieux sauter*'.

In some cases different sciences show marked differences in their time perspectives. In the contemporary theories and research projects of sociologists, for example, a short-term time perspective prevails. I have spoken elsewhere of the sociologist's withdrawal to the present. It may well be that the disregard of long-term social processes and the narrowing of the focus of interest to present times is symptomatic of a period in which many of the countries where sociologists are at work are undergoing great changes and, more often than not, are faced with great difficulties and dangers. A spurt towards the greater involvement of the knowledge produced and used in these countries is certainly not confined to sociologists. But it is not unrewarding to compare their time perspective with that of some of the natural sciences.

The work of many sociologists is entirely concentrated on present times. In that respect their outlook resembles that of society at large. Their comprehension of the fact that what we call the present time has a point-like character, that it forms but a moment within an on-going process, appears to have lapsed. The fact that present social conditions represent an instant of a continuous process which, coming from the past, moves on through present times towards a future as yet unknown, appears to have vanished. That is all the more surprising as the tempo of change in many areas of our social life has noticeably increased. For people involved in the affairs of the moment, this may well mean that what happened yesterday has passed away and can be forgotten. However, the facts with which sociologists and other social scientists are concerned can hardly be understood, and certainly not explained, if the experienced difference between present and past is not projected on to them – if present times are perceived, as it were, in isolation. The reconstruction, in the form of models, of the processes leading from the past through the short days of those who are still alive towards the future is thus an indispensable task of sociologists. Evidently it requires a relatively high level of self distancing, of detachment. Times of growing danger and thus of growing involvement may well not be favourable to the advance of the social sciences in general and of sociology in particular. They exert pressure towards a shortening of the time perspective.

Compare this condition with that of the natural sciences such as cosmology. For sociologists, processes and structures of the nineteenth or the eighteenth century often appear as events of little significance for what happens today. What happened one thousand or two thousand years ago may appear to many contemporary sociologists not worth speaking of, something of no interest whatsoever for sociologists. Cosmologists, on the other hand, may well be equally interested in what happens today and what happened millions of years ago. They see clearly the connection between past and present. They are able to perceive such events together as aspects of a unitary process. Their time perspective, in other words, is dictated not by their personal involvement but by the facts themselves, whose connection which each other they try to unravel and to represent by means of testable theoretical models, mostly of process models. If the time perspective of sociologists too were fact oriented, they too would have the task of bringing to light the processes connecting past events with each other and with present times. But the subject matter of cosmologists, by and large, represents no danger for those who study it. They can explore it in peace. Sociologists, in that respect, are in a different situation. They participate in the facts they study. They are personally exposed to the dangers which the objects they study represent for themselves. It is understandable that in their field a more involved approach prevails.

5   What suggests itself here, no doubt as a long term proposition, is a break with the tradition, in terms of international law as well as of many state laws, which legalizes the use of group violence between states while outlawing individual violence within states. It should be recognized as a basic human right that human beings can live out their individual lives to their natural limits if that is their own wish, and that people who use or advocate and threaten the use of violence as a means of shortening other people's lives have therefore to be regarded as criminals or as insane. The proposal may seem trivial because, given the present tradition of interstate relations with their closely guarded frontiers, it is unrealizable and unenforceable, or else it may seem too daring. In actual fact, the outlawing of war or any other form of group violence, given the frontier-transcending nature of present-day weapons and the likelihood that they may change for the worse the terrestrial habitat of humanity, is simply common sense.

Another much smaller break with tradition which suggests itself and which is of immediate relevance here has also the advantage that it can be implemented. The text which follows may be regarded as a beginning. I am referring to a break with the philosophical tradition of knowledge, theories of and a beginning of sociological tradition of knowledge theories.

The philosophical tradition started from the assumption that the acquisition of knowledge is universally the same for every human being. This is assumed to occur irrespective of the time in which a human being lives, or in other words, of the stage in the development of knowledge in which a human individual acquires knowledge through learning, and irrespective of the changing relationship between human beings themselves as those who know, and the world of objects including themselves as that which they know. If the acquisition of knowledge is treated as universally the same, it is not possible to account for two basic characteristics of human knowledge, and this disregard must vitiate any theory of knowledge from the outset. Under this theory, one cannot account for the fact that human knowledge can be transmitted from one generation to another, that, in other words, every human being starts acquiring knowledge from other human beings through learning. And one cannot account for the fact that knowledge, individually as well as over the generations, can grow and decline. One cannot help saying that philosophical theories of knowledge, by neglecting the fact that individual knowledge in the first instance is – like language, – always learned from others, wrongly attribute to the individual person an absolute autonomy. No human being possesses such an autonomy. Every person is for years and in fact throughout life dependent on others for knowledge, and of course not for knowledge alone. The image of human beings on which the whole fabric of philosophical epistemology rests is unsound. An ideal, that of a totally independent individual, of an 'I' without 'you' and 'we', the ideal of a passing period, is presented as if it were a timeless and universal fact. Descartes gave the signal: '*Cogito ergo sum.*' What can be more absurd! Merely in order to say it, one had to learn a communal language; and why say it if no one was there to listen, to accept or to reject it? The man of straw presented by Descartes has lately acquired some fig leaves, such as 'intersubjectivity' or 'validity for all human beings', providing the lonely subject of knowledge *a posteriori* with some shadowy company. They do little to save it from its basic solitude, or transcendental theories of knowledge from their built-in solipsistic tendency.

Sociological theories of knowledge have to break with the firmly entrenched tradition according to which every person in terms of her or his own knowledge is a beginning. No person ever is. Every person, from the word go, enters a pre-existing knowledge stream. He or she may later improve and augment it. But it is always an already existing social fund of knowledge which is advanced in this manner, or perhaps made to decline. These theories of knowledge can thus accommodate the observable fact that knowledge, like the language in which it is couched, is group specific, even though the same knowledge can be symbolically represented by different languages.

By and large, the social funds of knowledge of societies at different stages of development have a different range and different structural characteristics. Philosophical theories of knowledge confine their attention almost exclusively to scientific knowledge and above all to knowledge of the natural sciences, that is to knowledge at a relatively high level of reality-congruence. This limitation alone is enough to explain the fact that the philosophical tradition of theories of knowledge is unsuited to the exploration of the knowledge produced by sociologists and by other representatives of the human sciences, which are less reality-congruent or, in the terms of this enquiry, are representatives of a higher level of involvement. As a rule, philosophers have done little more than to present the knowledge of the natural sciences, and especially of the physical sciences, as a model and an ideal. Their approach to a theory of knowledge has not helped to clarify the obvious differences between the provision and the advance of knowledge at different levels of integration. Neither have they devoted much attention to the problem, highly relevant to social scientists, of the influence which differences in the object of research – and thus in the problems confronting scientists – must have on the provision of more reality-congruent knowledge about them. A hardened philosophical tradition has largely obscured an obvious fact: that the scientific study of human beings, as individuals and as groups, may make different demands on those who undertake such studies from those made on scientists studying lifeless pieces of matter, such as atoms and molecules, or simpler organisms, such as amoebae or fieldmice. All that representatives of the philosophy of knowledge have usually done is to present the scientific exploration of lifeless matter as the ideal model for the provision of fact-oriented knowledge and to say categorically, 'This is the model of a scientific enterprise, take it or leave it.' If you have difficulty in adopting for the exploration of human societies the models provided by those whose task is the exploration of lifeless pieces of matter, so much the worse for you.

The venerable philosophical tradition, from Descartes to Husserl and Sartre, is revered by many and, generally, still commands great authority. A good number of sociologists who, in terms of their discipline, are newcomers of lesser authority in the academic world, have tried, as newcomers often do, to follow the authoritiative philosophical imperatives. They have rarely been very successful. The voices among social scientists which clearly say that these imperatives are false, and that the prescriptions they contain are only to a very limited extent applicable to the human sciences, are still few and far between. The emancipatory movement among sociologists, which takes from the physical sciences what can be adapted to their own ends and, for the rest, allows sociology and the human sciences in general to find their own way, is still in its early days. The text presented here is a contribution to this movement.

Sociological, like philosophical, theories of knowledge are concerned with universal versions of knowledge. Unlike philosophical theories, they take into consideration that a learnt social fund of knowledge is the point of departure for all varieties of individual knowledge and that this is, indeed, a universal characteristic of knowledge. Sociological universals, as one may see, differ fundamentally from philosophical universals. They are not idealizing abstractions, such as the model of a scientific method abstracted from classical physics and often presented as a normative universal of all sciences. Nor are they metaphysical speculations, such as the assumption that cause and effect connections and other learned characteristics of a stage in the development of knowledge exist as parts of some transcendental realm. They are universals of processes. The reconstruction of the process, in the course of which human beings from a condition of not-knowing arrived at a condition of knowing, or alternatively from a condition of knowing plunged into that of not-knowing, always holds the centre of the stage. Universals of sociological theories of knowledge have the cognitive status of auxiliaries indispensable for the construction of the knowledge process in the form of a testable theoretical model.

Among the universals of the knowledge process which are of special relevance in this context is the directional character of this process. Two directions, polar and complementary, are always linked together. Spurts in the two directions can follow each other or can be present simultaneously in the form of an even or uneven balance. Thus a tribe of hunters and food-gatherers transforming itself step by step into a group of more or less settled agriculturalists may gradually forget some of the knowledge required for hunting animals, while expanding the fund of knowledge required for the successful cultivation of the plants that can facilitate the survival of a human group. Yet the simple statement that knowledge is lost as well as gained in this case can be deceptive. For in terms of human mastery over the processes of non-human nature, and thus in terms of human control of possible dangers from that side, knowledge of the skills of agriculture, compared with the antecedent stages, represented a change with the directional character of an advance.

6   The fact that the directions of knowledge processes are one of their universal characteristics is of special relevance in the context of this book. Involvement and detachment, whatever their other functions, serve as complementary indicators of the direction of knowledge processes. The text tells more about the specific directions of the processes to which these two concepts refer, but it may be worth stating explicitly that they are not bound to any specific epoch or time perspective. They an be used, for example as indicators of differences of social and natural sciences in the twentieth century, and also as indicators of differences in the relationship and development of magic-mythical and reality-congruent knowledge from prehistoric times on. In the latter case the time span is of course much larger. In the former case one may say, for instance that on balance the level of detachment, represented by sociological knowledge in the short time of its existence, has remained, much lower than that represented by physical knowledge.

This means, among other things, that the standard of physical and also of biological knowledge, at present, leaves scope for a very much longer time perspective than that of sociological knowledge. For physicists, it appears that models of the evolution of the universe are becoming a significant frame of reference. Thus it is for them a perfectly meaningful statement to say that, according to present knowedge, the universe where humans live came into being about 4600 million years ago. For biologists, it is equally meaningful to say that hominids emerged within the evolutionary process about two million years ago. For sociologists it is, under present conditions much more difficult to tear themselves away from their involvement in present affairs. As one may see, involvement also contains references to the focus of interest and to the affectivity of knowledge. In the case of sociologists the focuses of scientific interest and of their extra-scientific interest are not very clearly isolated from each other. The affectivity and particularly the emotional partisanship spill over quite easily from the latter into the former. One may even discern a narrowing of the focus of interest of sociologists during this century. For Max Weber, to give an example, events in the seventeenth and eighteenth century were still sociologically relevant. He recognized, too, the sociological significance of events in Chinese or Roman antiquity.

The powerful spurt through which we are passing, a spurt towards greater danger at the level of human society and greater emotional involvement of people's knowledge about society has resulted in the case of sociologists in an extraordinary narrowing of the time perspective. To many, perhaps to most of them, only what happens here and now appears to be of sociological relevance. What happened in the societies of former centuries appears as something of historical interest. Sociologists who, like many earlier representatives of the discipline, include in their study past ages are dubbed historical sociologists, as if concern with sociological problems of the past were a specialism within sociology and could be separated from the study of contemporary sociological problems. And as the focus of interest of sociologists has largely narrowed to their own century and perhaps only to its last ten years, their scientific concern easily fuses with their extra-scientific political concern. Physicists or biologists who could allow their political, religious or any other extra-scientific partisanship to colour the theories and concepts they present or use in their scientific work would soon lose the respect and the trust of their fellows. Sociologists allow their extra-scientific beliefs and ideals to colour their scientific theories and research as a matter of course. The theory of knowledge of which the following exposition of problems of involvement and detachment forms part may illuminate some of the difficulties with which, under these conditions, sociologists and indeed most other social scientists have to contend. This text may help to explain some of the differences which one can observe between the natural and the social sciences in the standards of involvement and deta- chment, and also in those between prescientific knowledge and scientific knowledge of human nature itself. They may contribute, too, to an understanding of the reasons why human knowledge is not uniformly the same. The different types of knowledge, for which different balance between involvement and detachment are used here as one of the criteria, are thus placed in a wider context. Different types of knowledge are correlated with specific differences in the situation of the soceieities where these types of knowledge are used and produced.

This, as one may see, is one of the differences between theories of knowledge in the traditional philisophical manner and non- reductionist sociological theory of knowledge. The former work with the human image of a subject of knowledge, a knower, in a vacuum – of an 'I' without 'we', 'you' and 'they'. The latter work with a knower in a group as a subject of knowledge. No-one can know anything without acquiring knowledge from others. Without starting from a group of knowers sharing a common fund of knowledge and, as part of it, a group-specific language as a medium indispensable for acquiring any other knowledge, a theory of knowledge remains an artifice that is bound to mislead.

To take into consideration the fact that every human being as subject of knowledge, and indeed in order to be human, must be able to say 'we' as well as 'I', is one step in the theoretical re-orientation suggested here. Consideration for the overall situation in which the knowledge-carrying group finds itself in relation to other human groups, as well as to non-human nature, is a further step in that direction. There are various criteria one can use in order to come to grips with the different situations of human groups that are of relevance to the distinguishing structure of their knowledge, and thus to comparisons between knowledge of different types. I have used as a chief criterion the danger level and so also the social level of fear inherent in a group's situation. In an earlier part of this introduction I have referred to the different conduct of contemporary human groups in the face of dangers from non-human agents such as floods or epidemics and in the face of dangers from other human groups. One step towards explaining the different levels and patterns of involvement and detachment in the natural and the social sciences, I suggest, is the difference in the social level of danger and fear which, in our age, non-human nature on earth represents for human beings, compared with the social level of danger and fear which prevails in the relations of humans as individuals and societies. That cosmologists and biologists are able to handle concepts of evolutionary processes with a time span of millions of years, that their theories at the present time are most fact-oriented and less self-centred, more neutral emotionally and less affective, in short more detached and less involved than those of sociologists and other representatives of the social sciences, is related to the fact that people are at present to a much higher extent exposed to dangers from human beings which they experience as uncontrollable – and which are in fact at present largely uncontrollable – than they are to dangers from non-human nature on earth.

However, one cannot stop here. Neither the situation of natural scientists nor that of social scientists is stationary. They represent a phase within a condition of flux, a stage of an ongoing process. Unless it is understood that concepts such as danger level or involvement-detachment balance refer to moments of a social process, one may mistake the relationship between events to which these concepts refer for causal relationship. However, one cannot do justice to process-sociological enquiries as long as one limits explanations to those of a static, causal type. Causal explanation always implies a beginning. On closer inspection, one can easily discover that events presented as a cause and thus as a beginning always require on their part explanation in causal terms answering the question of how and why they themselves began, and so on *ad infinitum*. Processes can only be explained in terms of processes. There are no absolute beginnings. The circularity which one encounters here is not that of an argument, – it is a type of circularity characteristic of the events themselves. In the sphere of non-human nature, dangers have lessened as knowledge in that field advanced in the direction of greater detachment and reality-congruance, and changes in the involvement-detachment balance in favour of the latter were in turn made possible by a lessening of the danger level in non-human nature. As far as the natural sciences are concerned, the problem that one encounters here is still largely hidden from sight because philosphical theories of knowledge simply start from a condition of relatively high detachment, from a condition where the approach we call scientific had already gained the upper hand over prescientific, more involved forms of knowledge, those of the magic-mythical type. Philosophical theories of knowledge, moreover, represent the scientific type of knowledge as if it were a human universal, as if it could have or perhaps even as if it had existed at all times.

One of the major flaws in these traditional theories of knowledge is their total neglect of the condition of not-knowing. In any specific case the condition of not-knowing precedes that of knowing. Without the reconstruction of the former, of the condition of not-knowing, the condition of knowing and thus the knowledge process itself must remain incomprehensible. The difficulty is that once a specific item of knowledge has established itself as highly reality-congruent in a society, people acquire this knowledge as children and it appears obvious to them. They forget that it came to them as a heritage from ancestors who did not and could not know, or did not know clearly, what they themselves know as a matter of course. The heirs can no longer understand how it was possible not to know what appears to them as self-evident. That is what I mean when I say 'philosophical theories of knowledge take the existence of natural science for granted'. They fail to reconstruct the condition of not possessing the highly reality-congruent symbols characteristic of a scientific approach to nature.

Yet without the reconstruction of the condition of not-knowing, that of knowing and thus the knowledge process itself must remain incomprehensible.

That traditional philosophical theories of knowledge simply take the existence of a scientific, highly reality-congruent type of knowledge for granted has disguised the character of this knowledge as a relatively late stage in a continuous process, and as the result of a breakthrough as the phase within the movements of the involvement-detachment balance at which detachment permanently gained the upper hand. The reconstruction of this process must be left to another book. But one can see enough of this knowledge process, even without a more detailed investigation, to say that it was a very long and slow process. In its course, human mastery over non-human nature gradually grew to a point where the dangers which non-human nature constituted were sufficiently curbed for humans to learn to approach physical events with less fear, with greater detachment. This in turn helped them to advance the control, to lessen the dangers in that field, which once more helped them to curb their fears, to control their involvement in gaining knowledge, and with greater detachment to gain greater mastery of the non-human levels of nature.

With regard to the dangers which human groups constitute for each other, humanity is still very much in the trap of higher involvement of knowledge about societies which steers their actions reinforcing the danger of humans for humans, and of the high level of danger in turn reinforcing highly involved forms of knowledge. Living in the middle of a process of this kind makes it difficult to perceive its structure and even to notice its existence. Perhaps one can regard it as a hopeful sign that it is possible to calm one's involvement sufficiently to make the problem of involvement and detachment visible. Among the characteristics of high involvement I have so far omitted to mention is fear of the unknown and thus of innovations. One has sometimes the impression that in recent times sociologists no longer expect that one can make basic discoveries in their field of work. For physicists and biologists, making discoveries at both the theoretical and the empirical levels is a well-established aim. Sociologists appear to have lost sight of the fact that advances in knowledge or, in other words, discovery and thus innovations in knowledge, great or small, are a central task of scientific research.

A high level of involvement paralyses the capacity for encapsulated discovery. It produces a fear of innovatory changes, of continuous advances in knowledge. In that respect the social sciences contrast sharply with the natural sciences. Exploration of the physical and biological levels of nature is conducted at a relatively high level of detachment. The dominant position of fact-orientation and emotional neutrality in natural science enquiries is firmly established. It is constantly increased by the advanced technicization of specialized scientific experimentation and by the advancing technicization in society at large. The means of orientation about social life show the same high level of involvement in social science enquiries as they show in society at large. In the same way, in the field of non-human nature is characteristic at the physical and biological levels a high level of detachment is characteristic both of scientific enquiries and of approaches to, and the handling of, these levels in everyday life.

No such division of knowledge existed or exists in societies at earlier stages of development, although intimations of it can already be found in the classical periods of ancient Athens and Rome. If one goes back far enough one encounters the standard experience of a world which is more or less animated throughout. At these stages no ontological differences exist in human experience between the relations of human groups with each other, with animals and plants, or with earthquakes and thunderstorms. Human beings in that case experienced the world in which they lived as a unitary world. One can perhaps represent this experience by saying they perceived the world as a society of spirits, some of which were more powerful and thus potentially more dangerous than others. This unitary conception of the world was still dominant in the European Middle Ages. But compared with earlier stages, the dominant medieval European image of the world quite unmistakably conveyed signs of the coming split. The distinction between revealed knowledge and knowledge derived by means of observation and perception foreshadowed the emergence from the dominant involved knowledge, whose guardian was a highly centralized and unified church, of a knowledge which individuals could acquire on their own through experimentation and observation. Throughout the Middle Ages, involved knowledge, based on whatever the powerful spirits had revealed to human beings, dominated the knowledge scene. The breakdown of the unity of the Church was certainly one of the factors which, in the centuries-long sturggle, opened the way for the rise and finally the dominance of more detached, more reality-congruent knowledge of non-human nature.

However, as one can see, the breakthrough during the period we call the Renaissance was only a partial breakthrough. It ran its full course only in the case of knowledge now called physical or biological. In the case of social or human knowledge it advanced a little, but not very much, in the direction of greater detachment and fact-orientation. The social level of danger and of fear, too, did not change in the field of non-human nature and of human society in the same manner and to the same extent. If one is able to handle a long-term perspective, one can recognize a very powerful spurt in the direction of more detached, more reality-congruent knowledge in the field of non-human nature and of greater control of danger in that field. For about 500 years, more fact-oriented knowledge of non-human nature advanced and expanded steadily and continuously within the network of European countries. The impetus has not diminished; it still continues to advance and to expand at an ever increasing rate. We are now in a phase in which the knowledge of how to advance reality-congruent knowledge at the physical and biological levels systematically in the form of a continuous process – the process of scientific and technical advance – is rapidly spreading from its European homeground to reach more and more sections of humanity. Together with the advancing scientific knowledge of these levels of nature, people's capacity advances to manipulate and to control natural processes at these levels for their own ends. Thus at these levels the circular interdependence between the advances of more detached and more reality-congruent knowledge, and decreases in the social level of danger and fear, is clearly recognizable.

Hence, the absence of an analogous process at the human levels stands out in full relief. The contrast between the relationship of humans with a multitude of manifestations of non-human nature and the relationship of humans with each other, is impressive and one can hardly lose sight of it, once one has reached the point where it becomes visible. The relationship between the levels of danger and fear on the one hand and the involvement-detachment balance in human knowledge on the other hand, is not simply causal. It is circular and spiral in character – it is a process relationship. The balance of power between humanity as part of the natural universe, and the non-human levels of the universe has been gradually changing. In the last two centuries it has reached a stage where the balance of power, at least in the terrestrial orbit, has definitely changed in favour of humanity. The diminishing threat to humans within the terrestrial context shows more starkly the unyielding dangers which humans as groups and individuals constitute for each other and for themselves. They bring once more into focus the circular interdependence between the social level of danger and fear and the level of involvement in knowledge. Once more, the dangers which humans constitute for each other stand out in clear relief.

7 It is useful to remember that human beings, in a long succession of struggles, have established their rule over the other levels of nature on earth. The rule of one of the species over all the others – apart perhaps from some bacilli and viruses – and over the non-living earth is a milestone, both within the evolutionary process (since it has fundamentally changed the conditions of evolution) and in the development of human societies themselves. The fauna, the flora and the surface of large parts of the earth are no longer nature in the raw, but nature transformed by human beings in accordance with their own needs and aims. The long sequence of struggles between the various groups of human beings and the other manifestations of nature has culminated during the last three centuries or so in a breakthrough, in a basic change in the balance of power between terrestrial nature and human societies, and the change is in favour of the latter. Most of humanity's non-human enemies have been tamed or annihilated. More and more dangers from non-human sources on earth have been brought under human control. In its terrestrial surroundings, humanity has established its supremacy.

Lack of a long time perspective and the prevalence of involvement in people's conception of nature and of themselves have to some extent obscured this situation. The awareness of humanity's supremacy on earth demands reflection about the manner and aims of its rule. As yet, the awareness is dim. The prevalence of unending competitive struggles between human groups themselves has induced a chaotic and self-defeating utilization of human power over non-human nature, an employment of power which is dictated entirely by the short-term and sectional aims of the competitive struggles between human groups, regardless of the conditions of non-human nature on which, in the long run, human survival depends. In this vital field, people's involvement of thought and action clearly outweighs detachment. From the relative pacification of non-human nature stands out all the more starkly the untamed ferocity of the struggles between human groups themselves.

A high-level synthesis of this kind may make it easier to perceive at least one of the factors which account for differences in the development of the knowledge, in particular of scientific knowledge, about non-human nature and human society. Dangers from non-human nature to which humans are exposed have diminished; those to which they are exposed from each other have not done so, or not to the same extent. The involvement-detachment balance in the two fields of knowledge differs accordingly. Detachment has gained the upper hand in human knowledge of non-human nature; involvement remains high in people's knowledge of human society, which in turn helps to maintain a high level of danger and fear in that field. Examples are obvious and well known. Some physical events on earth and in its surroundings are totally interdependent within the global context. Human beings, however, have started to apply their supremacy over non-human nature by producing changes within this network of physical interdependencies in a manner which is wholly dictated by parochial sectional interests. Humanity is at present divided into a great number of nation states, while their natural habitat is one and indivisible. Various states of humanity produce within their territory more or less far-reaching changes of non-human nature, some of which affect its global layers and are likely to reverberate sooner or later on the whole of humanity. So far no central agency has emerged which is able and authoritative enough to survey and control, in humanity's own interest, its chaotic rule over non-human nature, which cannot speak for itself though it can blindly hit back in many of these cases. Knowledge representing a high level of detachment and reality-congruence is used in the service of knowledge characteristic of high involvement.

This is one of many examples of the practical consequences which differences in the development of knowledge of nature and knowledge of society can have for human beings. It is not the advance of natural sciences as such which accounts for the high social level of danger confronting humanity, but the way in which powerful social agencies – particularly governments, sometimes elected by a country's population, and business corporations – steer and utilize research. The combination which one encounters here, or more detached and reality-congruent knowledge in the service of people whose knowledge represents a high involvement, is instructive. Class interests as a condition of knowledge have been widely discussed. By comparison, national interests as a condition of knowledge have claimed less attention. In fact, the production of knowledge in the service of sectional interests is widespread, while the consistent use of humanity as a frame of reference is still rare.

The fact that knowledge is produced and used in a social context does not mean that it can be reduced to something extraneous to itself, to something which is not knowledge. More fact-centred or more fantasy-centred knowledge is still irreducible. Whatever its cognitive value, it has a recognizable structure. The diagnostic statement that under present conditions the involvement–detachment balance is tilted in favour of detachment in the case of knowledge of nature, in favour of involvement in the case of knowledge of human society, is a case in point. It is a statement about specific differences in the structure of knowledge. It can also illuminate the fact that the point of departure of individual knowledge is the social condition of knowledge at the time at which an individual enters the knowledge process. Knowledge of nature did not always have the high standard of reality congruence and detachment it has today: knowledge of society need not always show as much fantasy orientation and lack of detachment as it does today.

8 It is not a conventional view that the social fund of knowledge available in a society is the point of departure for theories of knowledge. Nor is it usual to relate the characteristics of a social fund of knowledge to the social levels of danger and fear and thus of security prevailing in a society. Even less conventional is the proposition that the relationship between the levels of danger and fear and the type of knowledge dominant in a particular field is not a simple causal relationship, but circular or spiral. Both levels of security on the one hand, and the involvement-detachment balance represented by people's knowledge and actions on the other, are, potentially or actually, in a condition of flux. They form part of a continuous process in one direction or another. What one might consider as a cause is

also an effect, and what might be considered an effect may in turn be a cause.

Cause and effect models can have a useful purpose in process-reducing studies and even in the study of processes of relatively short duration. They are of less use in the study of long-term processes. The social standard of knowledge on the one hand, and the social standard of danger on the other, and also the whole relationship of 'subject' and 'object' do not have a stationary causal character. In terms of the intergenerational process of society and thus of knowledge transmission, they are always on the move. A highly involved form of knowledge may well contribute to the perpetuation of a relatively high danger level, and a high danger level in turn may contribute to the perpetuation of more highly involved forms of knowledge. In the earliest stages of the development of humanity for which we have any evidence, the scope of relatively detached and reality-congruent knowledge was comparatively narrow, the danger and fear level comparatively high; and the growth of detached knowledge was very slow indeed. At that stage the subject–object relationship, particularly in terms of its main concern in knowledge – that is in terms of knowledge of dangers such as human and other enemies, or of objects needed such as food – may well have appeared to the people concerned as stationary and unchanging. Yet, through the millennia, fact-centred knowledge grew and the relationship changed between the human subjects of knowledge and the non-human objects. In its philosophical form the subject-object relationship apppears as unchanging and universal. Yet what is considered in that form is a relatively late stage of a long development, a stage at which the objects of nature have become more or less pacified and passive objects of human exploration.

However, the knowledge process, like that of society, is not rigid. It can change direction; it can accommodate currents in different directions, different stages of development at the same time. From steadily expanding, it may reverse its direction and shrink or decline. From a dominant direction towards detachment and reality congruence, it may change to that of involvement and fantasy-orientation.

To experience, in practice, the use of the terms involvement and detachment may make it easier to perceive their function and meaning. But implicit discovery of the unfamiliar meaning of more or less familiar terms can be usefully assisted by a brief, explicit, introductory presentation of terms.

9　Present-day languages such as English are rich in words which refer to specific aspects of human beings. It is possible to say that people 'feel', 'speak', 'act', 'think', or 'know'. There are substantives such as 'sentiment', 'drive', 'emotion', 'action', 'speech', 'thought' or 'knowledge' to assist the analysis. If one tries, however, to express how all these various aspects of human beings cohere, how they are connected with each other, one may be at a loss – it may not be easy to find the right words. Synthesis lags behind analysis. The unitary identity of a human person may well be taken for granted, but the fund of words referring to it is comparatively limited. In that respect our current vocabulary and thus our fund of communicable concepts is divisive rather than integrative.

'Detachment' and 'involvement' belong to the not very large group of specialized concepts referring to the whole human person. Human beings as such, as whole people, not their actions, their ideas, their experiences or feeling alone, stand at the centre of sociological research. Their relations with each other, those of people in the round, form the subject matter of the social – or human – sciences generally and thus the frame of reference for any specific investigation in these fields. That is why the two concepts of involvement and detachment have been welcomed here, why their use, to some extent, has been enlarged. One can speak of more involved or more detached forms of knowledge or of action. But it is understood that those to whom such statements refer as knowers, as actors, or in whatever capacity, are human beings as such, that is, people in time and space. If one speaks of social levels of involvement and detachment, one is referring to characteristics as well as to the situation of the human beings who form the societies concerned. One is referring to human beings, including their movements, their gestures and their actions no less than their thoughts, their feelings, their drives and their drive control. One is referring, in short, to their self-regulation, including that which is regulated. Basically the two concepts refer to different ways in which human beings regulate themselves. In their self-regulation people can be more detached or more involved. Social standards of individual self-regulation can represent a higher detachment or a higher involvement. So can their knowledge or, for that matter, their art. All statements about involvement and detachment are comparative.

Examples may facilitate the understanding of these concepts and the problems with which this book is concerned. As the second part of this introduction, therefore, I present a series of such examples, some taken from the field of art.

Part 2

1 My first example refers to one of the human activities which more than any other is often thought to distinguish human beings from animals, the fact that human beings make tools. Most certainly tool making, fashioning raw materials of some kind in such a way that they can serve human ends, is a unique human gift. 'Man the tool-maker' is a well-worn phrase. It is also rather a euphemism, for many of the early human tools were above all weapons – they were designed as a help in the human hunt for meat. 'Man the weapon-maker' does not sound nearly as nice as 'man the tool-maker'. But tool or weapon, the production of these human artefacts raises a question usually left unasked and thus also unanswered. The question is: which distinguishing characteristics of their mental structure enabled our early ancestors, on the road to humanisation, to produce with a will and a purpose weapons and tools of their own, in addition to those which, like fingers, teeth or nails, formed part of their natural constitution?

The inadequacy of our present linguistic and conceptual equipment makes it a little difficult to speak and to think clearly in this matter. Single features of their biological constitution which enabled human beings to fashion materials into utensils for their own ends are of course well known. Upright posture, the unusual development of the forefeet from what were once primarily instruments of locomotion into those uniquely flexible, multipurpose instruments the hands, and the recession of the snout as a condition of fully developed bifocal vision, have often been mentioned in this context. But the enumeration of these and other details of the human structure, which are the biologists' main concern, is not enough to account for the uniqueness of human beings. Without the ability to co-ordinate these various distinguishing characteristics of biological organization, or in other words without the capacity for an integrating activity at a higher level, physical details such as flexible hands or bifocal vision would be useless.

The conceptual difficulty one encounters here has its roots in the fact that the common-sense tradition represented by ordinary language does not provide for a clear distinction and an adequate model of the connection between different levels of integration and co-ordination in a human being. At the most, this conceptual condition offers its representatives terms for integrating functions at the higher levels of the human organism, terms which give the impression that these levels represent a totally different mode of existence from the lower levels of integration. Thus the former are often characterized as 'mental properties of people', in a way which makes it appear that these higher levels of integration do not form part of the biological and in that sense of the 'physical' organization of human beings. The flexible fingers of the human hand may in that way be classified as a physical characteristic of human beings, the co-ordination of these fingers or of eye and hand in making tools, by contrast, as a mental characteristic. However, the simple juxtaposition of two concepts such as mental and physical is a rather unsatisfactory conceptual device. Every co-ordination of fingers by a person who is making a tool demands a cerebral or mental activity, and the co-ordinating activity of the cerebrum would be rather useless without the existence of physical details such as fingers. It might seem obvious that an inquiry into the distinguishing characteristics which have enabled human beings to learn how to make tools or weapons cannot stop at cataloguing single details of the human organization. The distinguishing characteristics at the higher integrating levels which are a condition of tool-making have also to be taken into account.

The making of tools presupposes a very specific cerebral make-up. It can in no way be considered as a here-and-now event. It did not result from a sudden illumination of one of our hominid ancestors who suddenly discovered the usefulness of a stone, smoothed and rounded by streaming water, as a ballistic missile with which one could kill or injure and weaken an animal desired as food. The transition to the use and the gradual improvement of human-made artefacts as tools resulted in the early days from the interlocking and blending of two distinct types of process, a biological and a social process. The slowness of the early advances in tool-making was in all likelihood to some extent due to the slowness with which the biological capacity for learning advanced in the early Palaeolithic societies. But the biological process at this stage, again in all likelihood, intertwined and blended with the social process of increasing knowledge which was at this stage probably equally slow. It is one of the characteristics of the early stages in the development of human knowledge that the biological and the social aspects of the process of growth cannot be clearly separated from each other. The biological capacity for learning grew and went on increasing far beyond the learning capacity of any other species and that which had to be learned by young humans from their elders, the social fund of knowledge handed on from one generation to another, and as part of it the knowledge of making and using tools, also grew as time went by. Like the biological capacity of learning, the social fund of human knowledge and thus the knowledge of making and using tools increased for a long time, probably for several million years, extremely slowly. At some time, however, the biological capacity for learning, for storing individually acquired knowledge and for acting upon it, had attained the very wide scope which is now characteristic of the only surviving genus of hominids, that of human beings. The biological capacity for learning had become so great that it could accommodate without further biological changes a social fund of knowledge which was steadily growing, which in fact with the help of all kinds of auxiliary techniques and in spite of many regressive movements was growing at a steadily increasing rate.

If one looks at the making of tools with a narrower focus, one can discover some other cerebral faculties apart from the learning capacity which are of relevance in this context. Above all, tool-making requires the capacity for distancing oneself from the situation of the movement, for remembering a past and for anticipating a possible future situation where the work of one's hands, the weapon or tool, might be of use. All these operations are essentials of the variety of self-regulation described here as detachment. In order to produce a tool, human beings have indeed to detach themselves to some extent from their immediate internal or external situation. If they are hungry, making a tool or a weapon does not still their hunger. They take the trouble of making the instrument in the hope that it will make it easier to fill their empty stomachs at some later time. For the time being, making the artefact requires that they restrain their hunger. Producing a tool means in fact making a detour which, for the moment, leads away from the desired goal of drive satisfaction. Humans make the detour of producing tools in the hope that it will eventually lead to a safer, fuller, perhaps even greater satisfaction of the restrained drive than that which they can expect if the desired goal of drive satisfaction is pursued directly, and without interposing, between the drive and the direct pursuit of its satisfaction, any intermediary activities which promise a higher or safer drive reward. If one goes beyond drives in their most animal form to human needs in general, one can perhaps see the cultural, economic, technical and many other aspects of social development as fulfilling functions of this kind, functions as intermediaries between human needs and their satisfactions. In its primeval form, tool-making was a very elementary example of self-distancing and detachment. But the reminder may be of some help in demonstrating that the capacity for detachment is a human universal.

Looking at the tools found at Choukoutien, a cave often described as the habitat of Peking man, where an ancestral form of hominids known as *homo erectus* dwelled for more than 300000 years off and on, one is still struck by the haphazard way they are made. They look as if they were mostly made shortly or just before they were needed for use. The restraint was short-lived. The capacity for making a detour via detachment, for interposing an intermediary activity between drive and drive satisfaction, was still very limited. And so was the capacity for learning and for innovation. If one compares the earliest with the latest layers of refuse, and as part of it the tools, left by occasional inhabitants of these caves, one can discover some technical improvement, but over a time span of several hundred thousand years it was very small. Change at that stage was extremely slow.

There is another aspect of the life of these pithecanthropi, our probable ancestors who for hundreds of generations found a refuge in Choukoutien, which appears to indicate that their capacity for a long-term view, for detaching themselves from their immediate concern here and now, was still rather limited. Like many other ancient cave dwellers, they made no effort to clear away whatever they left behind from their meals or from any other aspect of life. Thus the rubbish accumulated, the heap grew higher and higher. In some caves it almost reached the ceiling, thus preventing people from using it as a dwelling place. This too is an example which shows that aspects of the human self regulation which one may consider as self-evident and which require today no special effort are neither obvious nor easy.

2 If I were asked for an outstanding example which could illustrate the breakthrough from the dominance of involvement to the dominance of detachment in human knowledge, I would

probably suggest the transition from a geocentric to a heliocentric world picture. I have referred to this in the text of the book,[1] but it deserves some supplementary comments.

The dominant tradition of our time makes it appear that this change can be adequately explained in terms of an exceptionally gifted individual, Copernicus; that is to say, in terms of an I without we. The tradition suggests that Copernicus proclaimed and proved to an astonished world the innovatory idea that it was not the sun which moved around the earth but the earth which moved around the sun. The explanation of this change in people's vision of their position within the universe in terms of the innovatory idea of a single individual implies that a scientific theory, if it fits the evidence better than any previous theory, is bound to command automatically the acceptance of other scientists as well as acceptance in society at large. But that is not the case. With great regularity, major innovatory scientific theories are rejected and attacked with all the means at their disposal by representatives of the antecedent traditional doctrine. Galileo nearly lost his life for defending Copernicus' heliocentric theory. In this case it is relatively easy to understand the strength of the opposition against the rising new theory. For the acceptance of that theory did not only depend on the weight of the evidence supporting it; it also depended on people's capacity for greater detachment and, as part of that, their capacity for accepting knowledge about this world which runs counter to their wishes and their self love.

The suggestion that, in order to understand advances in knowledge, one has to put oneself first into the position of those who did not yet know – of not-knowing – is of some use in this context. The geocentric conception flattered human self-love, as highly involved knowledge generally does. It represented the primary impulse of human beings, still observable in little children, to consider themselves as the central frame of reference for everything they experience. It was this primary egocentricity of human experience which accounts for the fact that, as a matter of course, they perceived the relationship between sun and earth as one where they themselves, and together with them their own habitat the earth, formed the unmoving centre around which the sun travelled during the day, rising in the east and disappearing behind the horizon in the west. This unreflecting self-centredness still dominates the experience of the relationship between earth and sun in our daily life. It is only if one restores as an integral part of one's knowledge the dominance of an involved view in one's experience of the relationship between the earth and the sun and, indeed, the other stars as well, that one can understand the enormous effort of detachment that was necessary, not simply to conceive the idea that it was not the sun which moved around the earth and to replace it by the idea that the earth was moving around the sun, but also to gain acceptance for this view from the public at large. The reorientation that was necessary for the acceptance of a heliocentric view included the unwelcome realization that neither humans nor the earth form the centre of the universe. It demanded the enactment of a move towards greater detachment at a high level. For it presupposed the capacity of humans to perceive themselves from a distance, as it were, to put themselves into the position of looking down from the sun at themselves – at humanity – and of seeing from that distance humanity and the earth moving around the sun. To perform such an act of detachment, of self-distancing, requires very special conditions and a social attitude in individuals which includes a relatively high level of stable self-restraint all round. Without it, one of the major conditions of perception and cognition at a relatively high level of detachment is lacking.

Perhaps one can fully realize the strength of this social spurt of greater detachment, necessary to conceive and accept a world view which, as the heliocentric view did, ran counter both to the daily evidence of one's senses and to one's self-love, if one remembers that a heliocentric theory had been presented by more than one great man in antiquity and that it found at that stage of social development no acceptance. Ptolemy of Alexandria himself not only knew the heliocentric theories suggested, admittedly on slender evidence, by Aristarchus and others; he even knew that it would greatly simplify one's mathematical calculations if one could accept a heliocentric world picture. He apparently could not find it acceptable because it was too unlikely, too contrary to the observable movements of the sun. The level of detachment which was necessary in order to see oneself and the earth from a distance, as it were, was at that stage still beyond people's reach.

The ascent to a higher level of detachment, one of whose characteristic manifestations was the transition from an earth-centred picture of our cosmic neighbourhood, was not confined to knowledge of the physical universe. The emergence of a sci-entific, more reality-congruent approach to nature was one manifestation of a comprehensive change in the personality structure of people which found expression in many other spheres of their life. The compartmentalization of research into human societies, its differentiation into numerous specialisms without a common theoretical frame of reference, can make us forget that the changes which took place during the period we are used to calling the Renaissance must have had certain common structural characteristics. We tend to represent different aspects of social life by different names, such as art, science, religion, politics or economy. We often perceive changes in each if them, and these movements are either considered in isolation, or reduced to or explained in terms of changes of another aspect, which is considered as the cause and thus as the explanation of changes in all other spheres. The changes in that aspect are thus presented as self-generating and self-explanatory; that is, as absolutely autonomous and without outside cause.

Perhaps one need not consider the by now somewhat routine and traditional scheme of social compartments as the last word. It represents different aspects of the social life of human beings, who, as artisans, believers in a particular religion, artists, military personnel or scientists, are different, but who are all human beings and in that respect the same. The same people may even belong to several of these spheres at the same time. They may be interconnected with each other as members of the same society or of interdependent societies. The traditional form of concep-tualizing the specialization of human beings, to which we refer in terms such as science or economy, can easily obscure the fact that they refer, in the last analysis, to human beings living together and thus interconnected in the form of societies, perhaps of societies at different stages of development and thus with a different structure. The knowers have to earn their living and thus are bound to the economic sphere, but the economic sphere in turn is not autonomous. Its progression or regression is dependent on the progression or regression of knowledge. Without the knowledge process the economic process is dead, and vice versa.

To remember that standard concepts such as science, economy or society refer to human beings living in groups, to people who can say 'I' as well as 'we', 'you', as well as 'they', is one of the basic propositions of the kind of sociology for which I am hopefully trying to lay foundations, and to which I have given the name of process sociology. I feel uneasy to have to say that, but at a later stage it may well seem obvious that sociology is concerned with the study of social processes. We, my friends and I, had to toil and to labour in order to overcome the inertia of a process-reducing sociology. To keep alive the memory of the not-knowing and of the struggle in which new knowledge gained the ascendency is a duty which must not be shirked. It took almost half a century before process sociology found resonance in society at large.

The difficulty is understandable. If I were asked to illustrate the change by means of a simple and indeed simplifying example, my choice would be a comparison of the necklace model and the staircase model. The necklace model of knowledge places one idea, one paradigm, one ideology – in short, one item of knowledge – next to the other, not necessarily in any particular order. The staircase model evokes an ascent or descent of human groups from one level to another. One may think of an ascent from one level of a mountain to another, or on the stairs of a building. Under no circumstances is it possible to ascend to the tenth floor of a building without passing through the antecedent lower levels. The ascent or the descent may be faster or slower, but even if one ascends to or descends from the tenth floor by an elevator one always has to pass through the levels below it. One cannot reach the level of the tenth floor without having passed the levels of the antecedent floors; nor can one return from the level of the tenth floor without passing, however quickly, the intermediary levels. The sequential order of a social process has comparable characteristics. The historical or historistic approach to knowledge represents different sets of ideas, different doctrines, as if they were all characteristic of the same level of detachment, or more generally of the same stage in the development of the involvement-detachment balance. But that is not the case. What is often registered simply as different types of knowledge, among them the magical-mythical and the scientific types, are connected with each other in the form of a clearly recognizable sequential order of ascent or descent. They represent different phases of a process, different stages in the development of the involvement-detachment balance.

If one is not misled by the traditional distinction represented by such concepts as science or art, if one remembers that the human beings to whom these terms refer may be connected as members of one and the same society or in some cases may even be identical, one can expect to find that the ascent to a higher level of detachment represented by the gradual acceptance of a heliocentric instead of a geocentric world picture was not confined to the scientific knowledge of nature. One would consider it as likely that changes in the same direction occurred in other spheres of Renaissance society. That was in fact the case.

3   I will use as an example one other sphere, the development of painting. The example is all the more appropriate since a long line of well-reputed sociologists have suggested that art and in a wider sense culture, in contrast to science, technology and other facets of civilization, are exempt from the sequential order of a development up or down the staircase. In this sphere, they have suggested, it is appropriate to apply the historistic necklace theory. Each culture has to be considered as a human manifestation in its own right. Greek art and medieval art, ancient Egyptian religion and contemporary religions – these and other products of human culture do not undergo development; they cannot be fitted into a staircase order.

More often than not, in theories of this type two aspects of the same societies, 'culture' and 'civilization' – the one seen as a process, the other not – are conceptually placed side by side without a clear account of their connection. The doctrine is probably due to a confusion of fact and value. In terms of their value as human manifestations, as works of art, one cannot place Greek temples and Gothic cathedrals in a sequential order. The same can be said of the religious beliefs which they served. But if one studies them as social facts, it is not only possible but indispensable to consider them as manifestations of different stages in the development of human societies. Thus if one is aware that the European Renaissance is marked not only by the breakthrough of a long antecedent movement or change in the direction of a more realistic, less self-centred picture of the physical universe, but also by the breakthrough of an antecedent movement in the manner of painting (often characterized as a change-over to a perspectivist manner of painting), one might expect men and women of learning to ask whether the scientific, artistic and other related changes characteristic of that period had in common some basic changes in human characteristics, in the social habitus of the people of that period. That was in fact the case. The change – after a considerable struggle – to a growing acceptance of a heliocentric image of the sun-earth relationship, and the change – also not without a struggle – to a perspectivist style of painting, are both symptomatic of a human change, of the ascent to a new level and pattern of detachment. Both the movement to the Copernican world system, as Galileo called it in contradistinction to the older Aristotelian world system, and the movement towards painting in realistic perspectives denoted a change in people's experience of the world in which they lived and their own position within it.

One of the most significant expressions of this change was the widening acceptance of the concept of 'nature', in the modern sense of the word. In many contemporary societies, the term 'nature' is used as a matter of course for a type of order which, like the social order of human beings, is characterized by specific laws, but laws of a different type – laws not made by human beings, but autonomous and independent of humans – the laws of nature. In most of the societies where the word 'nature' is used in that sense, this appears self-evident. It is tacitly assumed that all other human beings experience their surroundings automatically in the same way that one experiences them oneself – that is, that they experience them as nature. Not so long ago the beliefs of simpler societies were sometimes called 'nature religions'. One tried to explain these beliefs to oneself by assuming as a matter of course that the people who held them basically experienced nature in the same way that one experienced it oneself, but in their ignorance represented it as gods or as the work of gods. As in other cases, if one knows the solution to a problem it is difficult to reconstitute for oneself the experience of those who did not yet know that solution. Many societies of our age have a highly reality-congruent fund of knowledge of the nexus of events we now call natural; but their fund of knowledge is the result of a very long social process of knowledge growth. It was by no means a straight-line process: advances of knowledge were sometimes followed by periods of knowledge decline.

There is a wider problem, which need not be answered in this context, as to the conditions in European societies which made possible the breakthrough to greater reality congruence of knowledge and thus to the conception of nature as an autonomous nexus of events. A few words must be enough as a help towards the reconstitution of the stage preceding the breakthrough to the scientific stage. They may make it easier to realize how difficult was that transition to the conception of the world as 'nature', in the sense in which this word is now commonly used.

The conception of the universe as centred round the earth was only one aspect of the elementary and primary tendency of human beings to experience events with reference to themselves. Preceding the experience of the universe as an autonomous nexus of events, as nature, there is, therefore, everywhere a vision of it as a multitude of events indicating intentions or purposes in relation to human beings. The primary questions to which human beings tried to find an answer were questions such as: what is the intention behind it? Or what is its purpose? The purpose of the sun was obviously to provide light for human beings; the purpose of goats and geese was obviously to provide food, or perhaps leather and feathers, for human beings. Aristotle and the medieval Aristotelians, Galileo's chief antagonists, for all their philosophical sophistication, still continued this pre-scientific, teleological tradition of knowledge. In contrast to Galileo, their conception of the movements of inanimate bodies was, in the last analysis, still determined by the assumption that such movements had an aim. Galileo was a leading figure in the struggle not only against the geocentric concept of Aristotelians but also for the concept of the universe represented by the now dominant meaning of the word 'nature'. He has often been represented as a pioneer of what is now called the scientific method of research. It is not always clearly seen that the method of research is closely bound up with the overall picture of the level of the universe which one tries to explore. Galileo's method of research was made possible by a determined break with the teleological world-view of the Aristotelians. He was one of the leaders on the road towards a new conception of nature.

The common-sense character and above all the reality-congruence of that picture often make us forget how enormously difficult it was for human beings to arrive at such a conception. It implied that this vast universe, although it has recognizable regularities or, in traditional language, it obeyed laws, had no inherent purpose and meaning for human beings. The conception of nature as a self-regulatory nexus of events, obeying its own laws but without any purpose for human beings, is now easy to understand. But because it is easy, and because its reality-congruence very obviously enables human beings to extend their dominion within it, it is difficult to reconstitute for the living generations the human effort of detachment that was necessary to accept the fact that all the events in the heavens and on earth which could harm or help human beings did so blindly, automatically and obeying their own laws, but in complete indifference to human beings. In terms of their immediate emotional satisfactions and thus of their personal involvement, human beings had to pay a high price. But what they lost on the swings, they gained on the roundabouts. In fact, they probably gained more. The breakthrough to a picture of nature which, though emotionally unsatisfactory, was reality-congruent, increased their power within the natural universe with quite unforeseeable consequences.

To make this effort of detachment also implied an increase in the human capacity for observing nature, for exploring its connections and regularities for their own sake. By distancing themselves in that manner from nature, and, at the same time, by controlling and mastering natural events better and better, human beings gained from them new sources of enjoyment. The heightened detachment brought within reach of humans new secondary forms of involvement. The development of painting can serve as an example.

In this case, too, it is useful to reconstitute for one's own understanding not only the manner but also the function of painting prior to the perspectivist breakthrough. One can see a gradual movement in that direction, a movement towards a more lifelike, more realistic pictorial representation, if, starting from Byzantine paintings and those of the school of Duccio di Buoninsegna in Siena, one moves on to Giotto's paintings of the fourteenth century, which are already less formalized, and then moves on to the art of the fifteenth century. But it is difficult to understand the innovations of the fifteenth century without a brief reconstitution of the experience underlying the tradition of painting which preceded the breakthrough. The great majority of traditional paintings were not only religious in character, they also had the primary function of involving those who saw them directly in a religious experience. Appreciation of their aesthetic qualities was not lacking, but their function as media of a religious experience took pride of place over other functions. To be lifelike or realistic was therefore not among the primary aims of paintings during that period. Their main task was that of allowing visitors to participate in events known to them from the teaching of the Church, and thus to be drawn more directly into its cult and its rituals.

To some extent the changeover to the new, more lifelike perspectivist style in painting was due to a change in the painter's aim, in the expectation of the painter's potential public, and thus, altogether, in the paintings' function. In the new style of painting one encounters a move in the same direction as that of the development of scientific knowledge, a move towards the recognition of nature as a nexus of events in its own right. The religious function of paintings did not disappear, but another function besides that of providing a spiritual experience, an aesthetic function, gained the ascendance. One can refer to it simply by saying 'it was the function of providing an experience of beauty'. That is, in fact, the term which most easily represents the secondary involvement to which I have referred before. An aesthetic appeal to the viewers' feeling, the aesthetic involvement of the viewers now became more a painting's function and perhaps its main function. But it was achieved by representing the painter's sense of detachment, by appealing to the viewers' capacity for it. The new mode of painting, by providing the illusion that one looked into space and that what the painter presented were three-dimensional objects – were, in fact, part of nature – allowed these objects to speak for themselves. It was their own quality, it was the beauty of the human form, of its architectural surroundings and, step by step, also of non-human nature, which the painter tried to represent on canvas and through which the painter expected to move the viewers' feelings. The more secular type of involvement presupposed that the viwers entered into the painter's game, that they picked up the clues which the painter had provided for creating the illusion of three-dimensional space on a two-dimensional canvas. Only by thus stepping back and distancing themselves from the painting could the viewers secondarily become involved in the aesthetic qualities of the ensemble presented there.

However, the realism of the paintings presented by Renaissance painters was not realism in the sense in which this word was understood generations later – in the sense which this word has assumed now. It was not nature red in tooth and claw that the main painters of that period tried to represent. Perhaps it is characteristic of the Renaissance concept of reality and nature altogether that it was a specifically selected, a rather idealized form of reality which they presented in their paintings. The developmental road of scientific knowledge shows a similar sequence. The realism of scientific discovery, which in the sphere of art was modified by a quest for balance and harmony, was tempered in science by the stress on the inherent regularity and orderliness of nature. Galileo's blend of realism and idealism has sometimes been attributed to the influence of Plato. But the very idea that nature, like a good citizen of a state, obeys laws, culminating in Newton's theory, speaks of the same tendency. Perhaps a less selective picture of nature, in the earlier days of its systematic discovery, would have been too harsh and thus unbearable for human beings; perhaps they had for a time to seek compensation for the recognition of nature's unwelcome indifference by a selective attention to aspects of nature which could evoke warm feelings, which humans could welcome. The fact is that humans allowed themselves only step by step to face up to the ugliness which exists side by side with the splendours of nature. But for the pioneers of Renaissance painting themselves, the aim of achieving greater realism, greater likeness to nature than had their predecessors, certainly played a leading part in their work. Thus looking at nature by first distancing themselves from their objects, by observing them for their own sake, or in other words the strategy of detachment, of 'reculer pour mieux sauter', was as much a condition of their innovatory work as it was for the pioneers of science.

Masaccio (1401–28) is known to this day as one of the main representatives of the breakthrough, of the purposeful transition to perspectivist painting. Vasari, writing about Masaccio a century or so later, has left us in his 'Life of Masaccio' what is probably a fairly representative account of the aims of painters at that time. He named Masaccio, together with Uccello and other Florentine painters, as one of the pioneers who 'rid themselves of the rude and rough style in vogue until then'. Vasari clearly considered the paintings of his own time as works of the highest perfection. The painters of Masaccio's time appeared to him as the great predecessors who had not yet reached that perfection, but who by their innovations and discoveries made that perfection possible. It may be agreeable to read his own words, at least in translation:

For the good style of painting we are chiefly indebted to Masaccio. Desiring to acquire renown, he reflected that, as painting is nothing more than an imitation of all natural living things, with similar design and colouring, so he who should follow Nature most closely would come nearest to perfection. This idea of Masaccio led him, by dint of unceasing study, to acquire so much knowledge that he may be ranked among the first who freed themselves of the hardness, the imperfections and difficulties of the art, and who introduced movement, vigour and life into the attitudes, giving the figures a certain appropriate and natural relief that no painter had ever succeeded in obtaining before. As his judgement was excellent, he felt that all figures which do not stand with their feet flat and foreshortened, but are on the tips of their toes, are destitute of all excellence and style in essentials, and show an utter ignorance of foreshortening. Now, although Paolo Uccello had devoted himself to this question, and had achieved something towards smoothing the difficulty, Masaccio did his foreshortenings much better, varying the methods and taking various points of view, achieving more than any of his predecessors. His works possess harmony and sweetness, the flesh-colour of the heads and of his nudes blending with the tints of the draperies, which he delighted to make in a few easy folds, with perfect nature and grace. This has proved most useful to artists and for it he deserves as much praise as if he had invented it. For the things made before his time may be termed paintings merely, and by comparison his creations are real, living and natural. (*The Lives of the Painters*, London (Everyman) 1927, Vol. 1, pp.263ff)

Masaccio's paintings, like those of Uccello, offer some good examples of the way in which the painter's aim of producing in a non-spatial medium the illusion that one was looking at a scene in space, at an event in the distance, contributed to the feeling of a really existing distance between the viewer and the painted event, between subject and object. A characteristic instance is his representation of the Trinity, painted for the church of Santa Maria Novella in Florence. A religious theme was here represented with an almost scientific exactness. The painter's detached observation enabled him not only to contrast the serene face of the father above the crucifix to the face of the crucified son expressing temperate sadness and suffering, but also to succeed in giving the impression of roundness and heaviness, of the real corporal existence of the crucified person. Yet the central event is placed in a characteristic achitectural setting, in the painting of a barreled vault divided into squares which are full of bosses. This design, through the painter's exact perspectivist skill, leads the eyes into the depth of the painting and thus heightens the impression that the cross occupies a position in space which continues behind it. It also contributes to the feeling that one is watching an event which occurs in the distance. It is possible that in some cases the price one had to pay for the heightened reality content was a loss in the magic of a painting, of its appeal to feeling and fantasy.

Masaccio died very young, in his twenty-seventh year. He was without doubt a great painter. A specific social constellation contributed to his success. In his lifetime, the social climate of Florence made it possible, in some cases, to breach the social barrier which traditionally separated artisans who worked with their hands and people of learning who did not. The former, painters among them, were usually separated by a language barrier from the relatively advanced mathematical knowledge that was to be found in Latin texts. Some of this knowledge, of great help to a painter who tried to create the illusion of spatial reality on canvas, became available to Masaccio and other experimenting painters through collaboration with one of the leading Florentine men of learning, who was himself an architect and was interested in the visual arts. His name was Leon Battista Alberti. His Latin education, and his great interest in the theoretical aspects of perception and thus of perspectivist paintings, combined with the practical skill of inventiveness of craftsmen painters such as Masaccio. That the social development in this case made close co-operation possible between men of such different rank, and thus between in theory, men of learning interested and practitioners of the art of painting, was another factor which can help to explain why knowledge we now classify as scientific and knowledge of painting developed at this time in the same direction, towards a new level of detachment.

Vasari, in his 'Life of Masaccio', mentions one other item that is of interest here. He reports that Masaccio, in one of his frescoes about the life of St Peter which he made for the Brancacci chapel in Florence, painted a self-portrait. He gave one of the apostles his own face, in the words of Vasari, 'with the aid of a mirror'. Mirrors played their part in the technical equipment which made the development towards a more lifelike form of painting possible. Once the step by step development in that direction reached the point where selective similitude between the three-dimensional reality and the two-dimensional painting became a dominant aim of painting, mirrors could play an important role in serving as a model, for that was precisely what they did – they showed a two-dimensional likeness of what in reality happened within a three-dimensional space. Measurements made on mirrors could be used as a guide to the painter's foreshortening technique, which played a central part among the discoveries of the Florentine perspectivist painters. The use of a mirror as a means of painting one's self-portrait shows particularly well that at the root of the new style of painting was also a new attitude of people towards themselves. A mirror shows one to oneself in a manner which one can never achieve without such a technical aid. It shows people to themselves in the manner in which they are normally only seen by others. The ability to see oneself through other people's eyes, and also the aim of so perceiving oneself, presupposes the ascent to a fairly high level of detachment. In order to achieve it one has, as it were, to go away from oneself and then again look back at oneself from a distance. Perspectivist painting represented the arrival of societies at a new level of distancing themselves both from the objects and events of this world and from themselves. I leave open the question of why a marked spurt in that direction occurred at that time, and also of why Florence, in the case of scientific knowledge as well as that of art, was one of the main centres of this movement.

4　A movement in the same direction, perhaps not unconnected with the Burgundian court, found expression in the work of Jan van Eyck, partly produced in co-operation with his more shadowy brother Hubert. Shortly before the experimenting masters of Florence found and demonstrated a way to produce in their paintings the illusion of spatial depth, Jan van Eyck found another way to the same end. Both Masaccio and van Eyck relied on thorough explanation and experiment; but the former, and the whole circle of artists to which he belonged, achieved their aim by theory and thus by mathematical calculation. They attained the illusion of continuous space, of measurable depth, by their knowledge of the quantitative rules of foreshortening. They scaled all their objects according to their distance from an imaginary point representing the spectator's eye. They could shape their figures and their objects in accordance with the position in relation to that point which they wished to give to the objects in their painting.

Compared with them Jan van Eyck was more purely an empiricist – it is said that he learned a good deal from the smaller scale manuscript illustrations of the French school. He greatly advanced the technique of painting with oil. As against the traditional painting with a mixture called 'tempera', which was still used by his Italian contemporaries, the binding of pigments with a special type of oil allowed painters to reproduce the minute differences of colour and texture they observed in their objects, and at the same time to give the appearance of unity to the great mass of details by transparent films of colour. Nuances of colouring also played a great part in the way he created the illusion of depth in his paintings. Compared with Italian painters, van Eyck, like most northern artists, showed less inclination to be selective in favour of formal harmony and beauty. His famous picture of the Italian merchant Arnolfini with his bride, now in London, is an example. The face of the man is unflattering, his hat grotesque; the voluminous wrappings of the young girl somehow give the impression of premature pregnancy. Yet it is a great and striking picture. The earnestness of the gesture seems to solemnize the betrothal. The skill with which the eye is led into the depth of the room, and above all the artistry with which numerous small details offered for the spectator's delight are bound together so that they make a convincing whole, a unitary picture – all this contributes to the high rank which the picture has attained over the years. Among the details which are difficult to forget is the ugly little dog standing in front of the couple, perhaps the lapdog of the bride, painted, as one might say, hair by hair. And, at the other end of the room, a mirror in which one discovers, on closer inspection, not only the backs of the couple but two figures, of which one may be that of the witness and the other is believed to be that of the painter himself.

One cannot forget that the development of European painting, whatever its other characteristics may be, also has been a learning process. Van Eyck's Arnolfini painting tells us something of the joy of discovery which painters and public must once have felt when it was an innovation, an unexpected adventure in space, to find that people could conjure up on a flat panel not only human figures, but also small things like a flower in the window, and even one's own picture in a mirror. As I have said, it required a specific attitude towards a painting, as well as in the painting itself, to take this delight in perceiving on a wall, recreated by the hand of a human being, what one might easily encounter in real life without paying special attention to it.

In the fifteenth, sixteenth and seventeenth centuries, as in the nineteenth and twentieth, one encounters some of the most telling examples of an aspect of art development to which I have referred before, of the learning process and thus of the sequential order in which innovations in painting make their appearance. Changes in the power structure and the manner of living of societies helped to create new demands on painters and a receptivity for innovations. Exceptionally gifted painters experimented with innovations. They had to discover for themselves new ways of seeing the world which delighted and excited them. If they were lucky, if the overall development went in their direction, the public would stimulate them to make innovations and would learn from them to see the world in new ways if they offered innovations. If they were unlucky, their innovations remained without response. One can easily forget how often painters who were sensitive to new ways of seeing, or were sensitive to new possibilities offered them by changes in society at large, developed their art accordingly, and how their public stimulated and learned from them new ways of perceiving their world and themselves within it which they enjoyed.

The Arnolfini portrait is a good example of such a milestone. One can only surmise that the Italian merchant who, with his young bride, is represented there ordered the painting to be made or at least allowed the painter to use him as a model for it because he liked his manner of painting. Or maybe his reputation was great enough for Arnolfini to prefer a painting by him to that of an Italian painter. One can also still feel the patience as well as the enjoyment with which Jan van Eyck pursued his way towards representing human beings and a room in depth with numerous small details one could discover in the room. There were small fruits on the table. A few green leaves could be seen through the window. Arnolfini and his wife had taken off their sandals for the ceremony; they were shown lying on the floor. The wooden planks of the floor, through a form of foreshortened representation, help to give the spectator the feeling of looking into a three-dimensional space, and so does the foreshortened representation of the window and of the ceiling. But one cannot be sure whether all the various clues designed to give the viewer the feeling of spatial depth match each other. Van Eyck had a clear aim in mind: he wanted to present reality as he saw it. But he was still learning to achieve his aim.

Perhaps the mirror which one sees on the wall behind the couple shows best how deliberate the painter was in his aim of discovering new ways to represent the world and please the eye. The mirror not only shows the backs of the couple and two human figures standing in front of them, it also shows a reflection of the window suitably curved. It was, as far as is known, the first pictorial representation of a mirror. But how did Van Eyck do all this? One clearly recognizes that there was a person at work who saw the world in a new way, who delighted in what he saw and showed it lovingly in his picture. But little appears to be known of the way he learned to do all this, of his actual manner of work. Did he actually take part in the betrothal ceremony which he painted? Did the couple pose for him in his study, or did he go to what appears to have been either Arnolfini's bedroom and living room or that of his bride, and make a few sketches there as a memory aid? He aimed at realism, so it is quite possible that a mirror such as that we see in the picture was really hanging on the wall of that room. But from seeing and observing it there, how did he actually transfer its image from the object he had seen in all its complexity to his picture? Did he do his painting in the room itself? Did he carry all the pictorial details in his memory from the room to his study? Or did he perhaps, in his study, make experiments with a mirror, using it, as Masaccio is said to have done, as a welcome aid for a kind of painting that aimed at being a mirror image of reality?

Whatever the answers are, it is easy to recognize in this case too an illustration of the heightened detachment which this kind of painting demanded, linked to a secondary involvement. A painter who aimed at this kind of realism could no longer rely on painting conventions alone, on a fantasy image of the object to be represented and on his aesthetic sense. He had to be detached enough to allow his objects to speak their own pictorial language, to take his cues from them as independently existing objects; and he had then to get involved in the task of selecting and composing the observed shapes and lines and colours in such a way that they fitted each other, that they formed with each other a unitary picture which spoke a language of its own and could thus communicate with those who saw it, could elicit from them an emotional response that was in some sense enjoyable and perhaps exciting.

5   A particularly striking illustration of the complexities of the involvement-detachment balance is the famous picture by Velazquez, reproduced as the cover of this book. The picture is now known under the name *Las Meninas*, referring to the ladies of honour of the little Infanta Margarita, who, together with her ladies, is represented there – but there are a number of other people to be seen in the picture, among them Velazquez himself. It is highly improbable that the painter would have accepted this

as an appropriate name for his painting, but no knowledge of any name he devised for it appears to have survived.

At first glance it is not entirely easy to see what made him assemble the various people one can see there and present them together. But the question as to what was in his mind when he painted this picture has been overshadowed by the immediate impression one receives on seeing it of its excellence as a painting. The unusual composition as well as the tempered colouring, the calm yet varied activities of the people represented there, hold the spectator's attention, and the slight touch of mystery, of something implied there but not directly stated, merely enhances the attraction of the painting. It is easy to see or to guess what each of the different people or groups of people one discovers in the picture is doing, less easy to say what binds them together, why they are all together there in the picture. The pictorial unity of the painting is established with ease and subtlety. The distribution of nuances and contrasts of light and shade plays a part in it. But each group or person seems to go about its own business without much reference to the others. What is the picture's story, its subject matter, its overall scene? That is, at first sight, not immediately clear.

The present title *Las Meninas* – the maids of honour – was a nineteenth century invention. It filled a gap. For the name of a picture can provide an important clue; it can help the public to understand what the painter perceived as the main theme of his or her painting. However, if Velazquez revealed his intention in painting this picture by giving it a name, it has not survived. Perhaps in his own view it needed no name. One should not lose sight of that fact. It was obviously destined for the royal apartments, not for an anonymous public. The king and the queen and a few other members of the royal household who might see it needed no name for it; they knew most or all of the people represented there. Originally the painting now known as *Las Meninas* was a sign of Velazquez' devotion to Philip IV and his queen and to the peculiar conjunction of social inequality and personal intimacy characteristic of his life in the household of an absolute monarch. The need for a name first made itself felt when Velazquez and his royal master were dead. In a catalogue made of the royal collection in 1666, after the death of Philip IV, the painting was described as *The Empress with her Ladies and a Dwarf*, and in 1686 as *A Portrait of the Infanta of Spain with her Ladies in Waiting and Servants by the Court Painter and Palace*

Chamberlain Diego Velazquez who Portrayed Himself in the Act of Painting. The shorter title *Las Meninas* gained currency when the painting was transferred from the royal palace to a museum and thus changed its function. It became an exhibit in the great collection of the Prado Museum, to be seen and admired exclusively as a work of art in an impersonal and detached way by a mass of transient visitors. In that setting, too, the problem of the painting's subject matter, of its overall theme, gained a new urgency.

Many paintings of former days have a subject matter that is clearly recognizable at sight or with the help of a short commentary. Velazquez' painting is not one of them. It shows in the foreground the figure of the little infanta, daughter of Philip IV, King of Spain, with her attendant court ladies holding central position. It is an exceptionally large painting: a guess one might say that it must have taken Velazquez a year and perhaps a much longer time to complete it. One of its attractions is that it challenges the viewer's imagination, that it does not provide an easy answer to the question 'What is it? What is it meant to show us?' And the challenge is all the greater since the placing of people and of all the other objects to be seen in the picture has been obviously planned with great care and subtlety. The eye is led unmistakably from the figure of the artist himself, standing upright and half shaded at the left side of the picture as the spectator sees it, in a strong movement to the lower head of one of the *Meninas* shown in profile, to the still lower figure of the infanta herself. She is almost but not quite in the centre of the foreground figures, looking full face at the spectator or, as has been suggested, at her parents, who watch from outside the scene shown in the picture. The infanta's head forms the lowest point of a half-circle movement leading from there via the head of another of her ladies curtseying. The movement continues its upward course on the spectator's right-hand side through the heads of other figures, thus leaving ample room for a second dominant movement represented irregularly by a second group of people. Among them is a half-figure potrait of the royal couple themselves, shown as it were reflected in a wall mirror, and, most strikingly, the picture of a man shown in the very brightly lit frame of an open door and apparently leaving the room while looking back almost full face at the scene within it. A near contemporary, Palomino of the court of Philip's successor Charles II, who saw the picture in the royal palace, identified this as a small but unmistakable portrait of the palace marshal of Philip's wife, Queen Mariana.

It is a wonderfully balanced picture with its contrasting shades of colour and light. But it does not directly answer the question as to what the various peeople are doing there together. The fact that it contains a portrait of the little princess with her ladies and her living toys, her dwarfs and her dog, is of course immediately obvious. So is the fact that it contains a portrait of Velazquez himself at work. Far less clear is the connection between these two portraits. It is not easy to guess what the man standing in the open door and looking back is doing in the picture, and other figures too require explanation. Thus the problem, the need for interpretation, is inherent in the composition of the painting itself. The widely agreed solution to the problem – that it is intended to show Velazquez himself painting the royal couple, while their daughter with her attendants has come to amuse them – can be regarded as a good hypothesis.

It is a nice story, but some doubt has been voiced as to whether the picture of the king and queen is really their reflection framed in a mirror and not, perhaps, a small painting of them. Its frame is not different from that of other paintings which can be seen hanging on the wall of the studio. It has been said that this is unlikely because no double portrait of Philip IV and his queen is known to exist and Velazquez was too genuine a painter, too much inclined to paint what existed, to put into his picture a double portrait on the wall of his studio if no such picture existed in reality. It is a curious argument, because according to the interpretation that this is, therefore, a reflection, the picture shows Velazquez painting a double portrait of the king and queen. It is difficult to disregard the possibility that what one sees at the back of the studio was a mirror reflection of the royal couple standing outside the space depicted in the painting. Why should one suggest at the same time that the picture was intended to show Velazquez painting a double portrait of king and queen, and that the picture of king and queen at the back of the studio cannot have been a portrait because no such portrait is known to exist? My feeling is that one could do more justice to the picture if one did not obscure its slightly enigmatic character, and thus deny that it contains a challenge, that it asks for interpretation. The story that the royal couple visited the studio and that this is suggested by their reflection in a mirror can be regarded as possible, but not as proven.

One of the aspects of Velazquez' painting that one cannot easily forget is the fact that it is a self-representation of Velazquez. It shows at the same time his pride and his humility. It shows how he saw himself and how he wanted to be seen by others, especially by his royal master. I believe one can understand it best if one assumes that he painted it as an intimate picture for the enjoyment of the royal master to whom he was linked by an unflagging devotion, for the enjoyment perhaps of a few other people belonging to the inner circle of the royal household, and for his own enjoyment. Not the least significant aspect of his self-portrait is that he represented himself not as an isolated individual but as one person within a small group of people holding similar rank within the innermost circle of the royal family's private life. The queen's marshal, the leading ladies looking after the little princess, and Velazquez himself taking care as painter and as chamberlain of some of the king's needs – they all belonged to the inner circle of the royal entourage. It is more than likely that they were all devoted servants of the royal family and personally very well known to its members. The painter's problem was that of designing a composition that contained recognizable portraits of some representatives of this group as well as of himself without losing its unity.

Perhaps one should remember that Dutch painters of the same period were sometimes confronted by a similar task. The ways these problems were solved, however, were very different, and that was to be expected. Rembrandt and Velazquez were very different people: both men, each in his own way, were great painters, and it would not be a very fruitful exercise of brain power to argue about the question of which of them was greater. Greatness in the kind of art represented by the form of painting which gained dominance in the fifteenth and sixteenth centuries, highly individualized greatness, was hard, perhaps impossible, to attain without a very high capacity for distancing oneself from one's objects as well as from oneself, and then again, secondarily, for involving oneself personally with all one's strength in one's painting or whatever artistic activity one chose to undertake. Yet, while a comparison between the two near contemporaries can show easily enough the imprint of very different individual personalities on the blend of detachment and secondary involvement one discovers in their paintings, some essential element in the understanding of their work is missing if one leaves it at that, if one is not able to perceive the imprint on their work of very

different social experiences and thus of the different social setting
of which they formed part.

Velazquez and Rembrandt both painted pictures of human
groups. *The Night Watch* and *Las Meninas* are examples. Both
contain portraits of individual people who presumably posed for
them. It is a measure of greatness of the two men that both were
able to free themselves from the compulsion of the pose. They
observed and kept in mind how the people who were posing for
their portrait behaved and looked when they were unobserved,
when they were not posing. It was a measure of their capacity for
detached observation that they were mostly if not always able in
their group portraits to break free from the stiffness and the
other distortions which the self-consciousness of posing can
easily introduce into a persons' posture and expression. Both
were mostly able to present in their paintings people at ease;
they mostly showed people behaving as if they were unobserved,
with gestures and expression that were, as we say, 'natural' to
them. This gift for detachment, for portraying people unaffected
by their momentary relationship with the painter or by the
painter's ideals, showed itself with special force in their self-
portraits. Rembrandt in particular has left us some pictures of
himself in old age which appear to say. 'I do not care what you
think about me. The face of a broken old man eaten up by drink
and sorrow? But I have still the strength to produce this likeness
on canvas, quite unadorned and yet with an intensity which
makes you feel "this old man – there but for the grace of God go
I" It required a great strength of self-distancing, of stepping
outside oneself and of looking back at oneself from a distance, to
look into the mirror and to transfer onto the canvas without
self-pity the shape, the colour, the play of light and shade as his
perception showed it.

But if one stands in front of one of Rembrandt's last self-
portraits, or for that matter of Velazquez' self-portrait in *Las
Meninas*, one is faced with one of the central problems of art
generally. The old face of Rembrandt that looks at us from his
late self-portraits was not particularly attractive. If one had
encountered the man in person at that time, one might have
experienced a slight feeling of revulsion on seeing the person and
the face of a great painter, who in his heyday looked fresh and
attractive, how visibly decayed and disintegrated by the eroding
power of aging, by those cares and worries of life which have a
habit of mounting when people get old, and perhaps also by too

much drink, the consoler of the aged and their destroyer too. But why should a face that might seem slightly repulsive if one encountered its owner in real life make a great painting if it is portrayed without any attempt to conceal the decay and shown on a canvas in two-dimensions?

There are two aspects to the answer. The encounter with the real person focuses attention in a way very different from that of the painting. The real person speaks to us, however short the encounter and however much our feelings may go out to the decaying old man, either selflessly with sympathy and pity or selfish with revulsion and the wish to get away from the unpleasant encounter; the real face tacitly appeals for our help. Willy-nilly we are involved. The face on the canvas does none of these things. It does not elicit any personal involvement. On the contrary, it demands for a fuller understanding a high level of detachment. The red face has been transformed by the painter's imagination into a shape within a composition of colours and light, and it is as part of that composition that it speaks to us silently. As a human-made facsimile of a human-face, it speaks to us with greater intensity of the human condition than the face of a person could do if we encountered the owner in the flesh. If it is the work of a great artist, the transformation of the real face into a painted pattern and the passage through the artist's imagination which this transformation requires give it a quality of timelessness which contrasts sharply with the transience of the real face.

In the seventeenth century, the painter's learning process and thus the development of painting had gone a little way beyond the great discoveries of the sixteenth century without abandoning them. In the sequential order of art development, the innovatory advances of the fifteenth and sixteenth centuries were an indispensable precondition of the further advances of the seventeenth century. Masaccio, van Eyck and their contemporaries discovered that one could represent in two dimensions people and objects as one really saw them in a three-dimensional space. In the seventeenth century, some painters – among them Rembrandt and also, in some of his paintings, Velazquez – recognized that the perspectivist painters of the fifteenth and sixteenth centuries did not really paint people as they saw them. They painted them largely as they knew or believed they knew them. Van Eyck discovered the joy of a real bowl of fruit, the real weddinggown, as they could be seen in the even and cold light of day, as if that were the only form of light in which humans or objects could be seen. The painters of the seventeenth century were able to go one step further in their detachment. They recognized that what we know of the shape of things if we see them in the clear light of day is not necessarily identical with what we see in the light changing from day to night and from night to day. Thus Rembrandt and, to a lesser extent, Velazquez not only allowed their imagination to reproduce in their paintings, objects as they knew them to be or as they appeared to be if they were always seen in the same light. Through a further act of detachment, they were able to notice that in various shades of light and darkness the sharply defined boundaries of objects as we know them shade into each other, often imperceptibly. The discovery that the sharp contours of known objects were not really what one saw, or what early Renaissance painters believed they saw, had far-reaching consequences.

Renaissance paintings are usually very clear with regard to their subject matter. Portraits of the period show the sitter as individual; they show the picture to the world firmly circumscribed in the clear light of day. Piero della Francesca's portrait of Frederico de Montefeltro is a good example, one of many. It is not a beautiful face. The eyes are hard. The sharp crooked nose stands out without mercy. An accurate and a true picture of himself was obviously what the person represented in the portrait really wanted. A very powerful man did not stand in need of any embellishment. He could afford to show himself as he really was. Everyone could recognize him. If others thought his face ugly and hard, who cared what they thought?

For Rembrandt and his contemporaries, the accuracy of a portrait including that of a self-portrait, was no longer a problem. They may have used mirrors like Masaccio as a means of self-distancing, of seeing themselves as it were from outside in the same way that others did. But accurate rendering of nature in the harsh light of day was no longer their principal problem. For Rembrandt in particular, but also for Velazquez, the pictorial aspect of a face and a figure, the way shades of light played on it, the manner in which it fitted into the composition of the picture now played a much greater part in the enterprise. Hand in hand with this went a feeling which was rarely expressed but which nevertheless must have given impetus to their work, that minute imitation of nature and the accurate rendering of its form on canvas was no longer enough for a good picture. It deprived a figure and a face of some of its qualities. In real life, people showed themselves clearly in their gestures and actions, and faces were animated. To express this animation in a picture was not easy. Perhaps one should call this aspect of a face its open-endedness. A living face varies like the person itself. It goes through different moods. It is, one might say, a process, on the one hand always identical, always recognizable as the face of that and only that person, yet at the same time also changing. One can by no means always know where it is going. In a way, a face is always the visual expression of a mystery. Fifteenth century painters advanced to the point where they could represent most convincingly the surface of a human face. Leonardo in his famous picture of Gioconda, was one of the few sixteenth century painters who succeeded in putting on canvas intimations of a face's mystery. So, in the seventeenth century, did Rembrandt, especially in some of his late self-portraits. It seemed that he tried to discover himself, and of course there was no end to it.

Evidently such a development would have been in vain if it had been a development only on the painter's side and not, sooner or later, on the side of the public too. If a portrait and more generally a painting was open-ended and indeterminate, it left scope for and indeed presented a challenge to the spectator's imagination. It made demands on the viewer's own fantasy. I have raised earlier the question of the relationship between the real face and the painted face. That the latter can represent a challenge to the spectator's imagination is one of the answers.

There are a great number of paintings which show the quality to which I have referred as open-endedness and which, through their intimation of something not known, stir the viewer's own feelings – sends them off in search of an answer. Van Gogh's *Sunflowers* and Watteau's *Embarquement pour l'Ile de Cythère* are other examples, and there are many more. Velazquez' *Las Meninas* is one of them. It is indeterminate in quite a different way from Rembrandt's self portraits. But it does make very clearly a demand on the viewer's imagination. I have said already that there are quite a number of people to be seen, some standing fairly still, some visibly moving, but with restraint. It is not an agitated picture; in fact, given the number of people in the picture, it shows a remarkable stillness. One of the infanta's dwarfs puts her foot on the back of the quietly dozing dog, which goes on dozing; a standing woman, perhaps a nun, appears to have a very quiet conversation with the male person next to her;

the infanta appears to stand quite still looking straight at the spectator. Many aspects of what is shown in the picture are not shown in it. The painter does not clearly explain the sources of the light in the painted room and so the distribution of light and shade in the picture. He does not explain the full glare of light on the staircase shown behind the open door at the back of the painted room. Above all, Velazquez very clearly and with obvious deliberation conceals from the viewers of his painting what it is he himself is painting in it. What he shows in his picture is part of an enormous easel, almost as large as his painting itself. On the easel he shows us part of the back of his canvas.

Thus the open-endedness of this painting is to some extent deliberate. In this case, the painter wants his viewers to know that they are not to know what he is painting. In order to show himself in his painting, he presents himself as stepping slightly back and to the side of his canvas. This allows him to portray himself full figure, standing slightly behind the curtseying *Menina*, brush and palette in hand. In the development of European painting, it is one of the earliest pictures in which a painter presents himself painting a picture. It is thus a good illustration of a step on the road towards greater detachment. It does not appear to be certain what technique Velazquez used in order to produce his likeness on a canvas; perhaps it was a mirror showing his picture to himself that he required for his selfportrait. A step in that direction plays a central part in all movements towards greater detachment. He took a step towards perceiving himself more clearly as he might be perceived by others, a step towards distancing himself from himself.

I have already mentioned that the public acceptance of a heliocentric instead of geocentric world-view presupposed a step in a similar direction. So did the hypothesis which played a dominant part in the traditional philosophical theories of knowledge, the assumption that the point of departure for all theories of knowledge is a subject–object relationship. This hypothesis too demands that people can distance themselves sufficiently from themselves to be able to perceive themselves as people acquiring knowledge about objects existing outside, and apart from, their own persons. I have tried to show that this step towards greater detachment does not go far enough. It represents one to oneself as if one existed in isolation, as a '*wirloses Ich*' – an 'I without we'. If one does not go beyond it, the subject-object hypothesis makes it appear that an individual person – oneself – can acquire adequate knowledge about objects alone and single-handed, without learning knowledge from other human beings. It requires yet another step of self-distancing to integrate into theories of knowledge the awareness that every individual step of enlarging the social fund of knowledge presupposes the acquisition, by the individual subject concerned, of a social fund of knowledge, including knowledge of a language, from others. One cannot know when the self-centredness of the subject-object hypothesis as point of departure of knowledge theories and much else besides will become public knowledge, for that always depends to some extent on the overall course and direction of the development of human societies. Meanwhile, the inadequacies of a paradigm starting from the human image of an individual without a group – an 'I without we' – show themselves clearly enough in many fields, not only in the agonies of an epistemological tradition which has long ceased to bear new fruit, but also in many forms of the study of literature or the human past and other aspects of human societies.

In that respect, too, Velazquez' painting can serve as an illustration. Among the long series of painters' self-portraits, Velazquez' large representation of himself in the painting we call *Las Meninas* is one of the strangest. It is unusual not only because the painter paints himself at work with the utensils of his craft, but also because he paints himself as part of a group together with many other people. It is difficult to think of any other large self-portrait of a painter where he himself takes, as Velazquez does in this case, a markedly prominent place but in no way the most prominent, the most central place. The famous Dutch painters of the seventeenth century, as far as one can see, painted group portraits where they themselves were not represented, and self-portraits where, in the great majority of cases, they alone were represented. One encounters here, in societies of a different type, marked differences in the painters' social position and in their I-and-we balance. The group portrait which Rembrandt painted in the picture now called *The Night Watch* was the portrait of a number of wealthy burghers of Amsterdam who formed or led the city's militia in case of need. They had themselves painted in their best uniforms, which were obviously quite expensive. Rembrandt was very definitely their social inferior. He would not have dreamt of including himself in their group portrait and they, in all likelihood, would have returned the picture to him and refused to pay for it had he done so. When he felt like painting a portrait of himself, he showed himself, with very few exceptions, alone, and rarely if ever at work. Perhaps one notices the unusual character of Velazquez' self-portrait in a group only if one compares it with other seventeenth-century self-portraits, most of which appear to show the painter alone, and very few – Vermeer among them – the painter painting. What kind of group was it as a member of which – as a prominent but not as *the* most prominent member – Velazquez represented himself in this painting?

It is not altogether easy to answer this question, because human groups of the kind one encounters here existed in the absolute monarchies of the seventeenth century, but have since disappeared, although it is imaginable that here and there remnants of such groups can be found in a dictator's household. But the absolute monarchs of the seventeenth century had the advantage over present-day dictators that not only they themselves but also a considerable part of their people believed in the legitimacy of their hereditary rule. They believed in it sometimes with an almost religious fervour, and the Churches supported this belief particularly in Spain. Thus by their rank and position the king and the queen of Spain were elevated far above all other people in their country. Even in other countries, the royal couple of Spain had few equals. The little Hapsburg infanta portrayed in this picture with some of her ladies was destined to marry a Hapsburg Holy Roman Emperor. The king of Spain, Philip IV, and his queen, in accordance with the rigid etiquette of their tradition, had few if any friendly human contacts outside the innermost circle of their household. Perhaps one should remember that the king, the queen and even their children, including the infanta of this painting, had separate households.

The people portrayed in this picture are thus leading members of three royal households. It is likely that the king and the queen were personally acquainted with all of them and may have regarded one or the other of them as friends, as far as they could have friends among people far below their own rank. It is as if the king on visiting Velazquez' study one day said to the painter: 'Why don't we have a painting of our little circle, of the few people I really enjoy seeing?' And Velazquez might have agreed; but he arranged the many individual portraits together as a unified composition in a manner satisfying his taste. (Of course the Spanish king would never have used the phrase 'Why don't we' with its democratic flavour, with its use of the pronoun 'we' in a way that puts all the people present on a par. He would have given an order or his consent to the painter's prayer for permission to paint what was after all a fairly intimate picture of the royal family's domestic staff.)

However it was, Velazquez evidently produced this painting, which showed portraits of some of the leading figures in the households of the royal family together with their small daughter, mainly for the king's and the queen's pleasure. As a matter of course he grouped these people, including himself, with due regard to their rank and their standing in the king's and queen's favour. Such a project, however, raised a problem characteristic of that period. Velazquez could not possibly paint a group portrait of leading royal servants without indicating that the royal couple was at the centre of the group, was in fact its *raison d'être*. At the same time, it would have been impossible to show the king and queen in person together with people who, although perhaps the only closer human contacts of the royal couple, were immeasurably inferior to them in rank. Velazquez solved that problem by showing a rather vague but still clearly recognizable portrait of the king and queen, or perhaps their reflection in a mirror hanging high on a wall of the room represented in the painting. In that way they could still be in the centre of the whole scene though not there in person. However, to realize that idea convincingly required a good deal of forethought and of experiment. It required something more than the representational painters' usual stance of stepping back, of distancing themselves from their painting in order to compare it with the objects to be painted and to see the emergent painting itself from a distance, and then stepping forward again to the easel to see the painting from nearby and continue work.

Velazquez' involvement in his task is shown very clearly in that he allotted to himself the largest full-figure portrait in the foreground of the painting. Yet he did not place himself in the centre of the stage: that belonged to the infanta. He gave himself a prominent place on the side of the scene where he stood unobtrusively in the half-light He showed himself not only as court painter, but also as a leading man of the king's household, as palace chamberlain, with the key as sign of his office. It was a nice touch that he tried to maintain some balance in relation to the man who was probably his counterpart in the queen's household, the palace marshal. He portrayed him as a small figure at the opposite side in the background of the picture, but his prominence was underlined by the full glare of light in which he was shown – the viewer of the picture could not easily miss him. That might have made up for the prominent position Velazquez gave to his own portrait in the picture. It has been noted before that only someone who was certain of the king's favour could allow himself to take up such an important position in a picture of this kind. But he knew his place. The full light plays on the figure of the infanta, while his own figure stands more in the shade, where he can be seen in a low-key posture and with a look on his face that is perhaps a little dreamy. It is at any rate open-ended and thus open to one's own imaginings.

That can be said of the whole painting. One need not know any of the facts I have just mentioned in order to enjoy it, for the painting as such is open-ended – it allows spectators to let their own imagination play about it. That is a sign of Velazquez' greatness as a painter. A work whose immediate aim was so confined and so time-bound is now ranked among those great masterpieces of the visual arts that are often called timeless. It is also symptomatic of his detachment. He was confronted with a task which intimately involved most of the personal relationships affecting his life, including his relationship with the royal family. To produce it he may have had to make quite a number of individual portraits or at least sketches of such portraits, including his own. He succeeded in welding all these details together into a unified pictorial vision. It retains its impact on the viewer even if he or she has no idea what kind of people are shown in the painting and what position Velazquez held within that group or what episode the painting is assumed to represent. *Las Meninas*, like Rembrandt's *The Night Watch*, contains portraits of a specific group of people, but we are not told all this with a loud voice. There are many halftones; much is left unsaid or said *sotto voce*.

This picture's relative autonomy in relation to its period, its timelessness, is an example of Velazquez' great gift for perceiving people as part of a painter's vision and if necessary of inventing a pictorial vision into which they could fit. (The vision, though on the whole realistic, did not lack idealizing touches. Velazquez was in his fifty-sixth year when he painted *Las Meninas*, but there, in his self-portrait, he looked more like a man in his forties.) A near contemporary of Velazquez predicted that the painting would remain well known because the infanta was in it. The social value of monarchy was so high and its timelessness through the ages appeared so assured that a ray of eternity seemed to fall on anyone closely connected with the royal persons. As it turned out, art had a higher survival value than monarchy. Velazquez' pictorial vision, embodied in this picture, lived on even though the names of the people portrayed there, perhaps including the name of the king's daughter who became an empress, have been forgotten. Now the infanta is probably best remembered because she was portrayed by Velazquez.

Today his self-portrait is perhaps less well known than are Rembrandt's. It is, however, one of the few self-portraits in which the artist showed himself in a prominent but not in the most prominent position; one of the few, moreover, in which the artist showed himself not as an isolated individual, but as one among others, as a member of a group to which he belonged in real life. To perceive and to represent oneself as such required a high capacity for seeing oneself from a distance as one might be perceived by others. I have already indicated that this self-representation of Velazquez as one among others was closely connected with the characteristics of a court society. For members of such a society it was more difficult than it is for members of industrial societies to forget that individualization has its limits, that every human being is almost continuously dependent on others. In contemporary industrial societies many people experience themselves as a little sun around which the universe revolves. It is much more difficult in these societies to find full understanding for the fact that individual identity is closely linked to a group identity. For members of a court society it was far easier to recognize that an I-identity goes hand in hand with a we-identity. This was one of the unusual aspects of Velazquez' self-portrait. As he presented himself in this group portrait his personal pride in what he had achieved as court painter and as the king's personal servant was unmistakable, but so too was his awareness that he was not the centre of his world.

Perhaps one can understand this feeling better if one remembers that few European painters of the seventeenth and eighteenth centuries succeeded in breaching the class barriers of their age. Painters worked with their hands for a living. In most cases that was enough to place them, in the eyes of the upper and upper middle classes, inescapably in the ranks of artisans. It was enough to exclude them from what was then called 'polite society'. Their extraordinary talent might be recognized, but neither Michelangelo nor Watteau were accepted as equals by the court societies of their age. Their position – high artistic rank, relatively low social rank – made for individual isolation. Rubens and Velazquez were two exceptions. The latter's self-portrait in *Las Meninas* appears to show that he was conscious of the fact. He represented himself as painter, with brush and palette in his hands, and at the same time as holder of a high court office. He is dressed elegantly in the court fashion of his age, and his moustache is groomed à la mode. To a modern viewer so much elegance could appear a little overwhelming if it were not redeemed by his posture and above all by the expression of his face. Velazquez was not unaware of his artistic achievements, but he did not present himself with a gesture of bravado or of showmanship. He stands there in full figure, but very quietly. The expression on his face is difficult to interpret; it can be regarded as open-ended. There is an intimation of absent-mindedness in his face, as if the inner vision he is just about to put on canvas has not entirely lost its hold over him, while the world outside is only just gaining access to his eyes. It is a quiet gesture, supplemented by a slight inclination of his head. One wonders how Velazquez did it. How did he know what he looked like when he was occupied with his inner vision? It is difficult to see him consciously posing before a mirror in order to catch exactly the right, slightly enigmatic expression on his face. Perhaps it was Velazquez' gift of pictorial imagination which allowed him to know exactly what he looked like when he was occupied with the picture at which he worked, particularly if it was a picture of himself.

Problems such as these, the painter's detachment from the objects he was painting, particularly if one of the subjects was the painter himself, and again his involvement, also most particularly if he himself was the object, were probably responsible for the fact that Picasso took Velazquez' *Las Meninas* as a model and, in 1957, repainted it in his own way. For two months Picasso was absorbed by the challenge of Velazquez' painting. All in all he made forty-four variations translating Velazquez' vision into his own pictorial language. That made it a very different picture, but the problem of the painter's relationship with his objects, and thus also with himself as object of his painting, was one of Picasso's lifelong concerns. There are quite a number of drawings in existence which show Picasso's preoccupation with the painter's – and not only the painter's – paradox: his task detached him from the world; he looked at it, as it were, from outside; and yet he desired to be, and in fact was, immersed and involved in it. A small drawing by Picasso shows symbolically the painter's paradox as Picasso experienced it. It shows the painter making love with the symbols of his trade, brush and palette, still in his hand. Picasso may have felt that Velazquez in his painting *Las Meninas* was, like himself, occupied with the problem of the painter's peculiarly divided self-consciousness, as someone who stood outside, who observed the world and formed pictures of it in his mind, and who, at the same time, was also very much part of this world – who was, in a word, detached and involved at the same time.

6   One further example may be of help. It is not unrewarding to turn from the level of self-restraint and the associated involvement-detachment balance which can be observed in societies with a strong and permanent external authority, to those to be observed in societies without such an authority, in the non-dictatorial societies of our own time. Compared with absolute monarchies or, for that matter, with totalitarian regimes of the contemporary type, external restraints in non-dictatorial, parliamentary societies, whose central authorities have strictly limited power-chances are less oppressive, and also less strong and more fluctuating. Accordingly, the demand which societies of this type make on the strength and stability of the self-restraint of their individual members and their various part-groups are very much greater. So are the demands on their members' capacity for detachment in the production and use of the knowledge guiding their actions. Differences in the regime, in particular differences in the power-chances and permanence of the central authorities of a state, have their counterpart in differences in the self-regulating pattern and thus in the involvement-detachment balance of the human beings who live under these different regimes.

Given the prevailing preference for a more involved approach to problems of human society, references to individual self-restraint and to detachment, in this wider context, can be easily misunderstood. They may appear as references to ethical or philosophical problems. Expressions such as 'individual self-restraint' may be read as references to 'individual responsibility'; statements about 'detachment' may be misunderstood as references to 'norms', to what people ought to do. However, the problems which are offered here for discussion, with the help of keywords such as 'detachment' and 'involvement', are not problems of norm, but problems of fact. They are not philosophical, but sociological problems. Societies without a permanently autocratic central authority can only function and indeed can only survive for long in that form if the relative weakness and instability of the central authority, of the leading external regulating agency, is matched by the relative strength and stability of the self-regulation of their members. That is a diagnostic statement; it is, as I have said, a statement of fact. It draws attention to the interdependence between the structure of society at large and the personality structure of individuals, between what are often distinguished as macro- and micro-structure. Refugees from Eastern autocratic societies to a Western country, for example, are sometimes disoriented because they are used to being told what to do in many cases where no-one in Western countries tells them; they may find the demands on their self-regulation disconcerting, perhaps unbearable. What conclusions people draw for their actions from factual knowledge of this kind is for them to decide. Sociologists are not lawgivers.

In the text that follows I am trying to prepare the way for a better understanding of the fact that, in terms of the prevailing social standards of knowledge, we live at present in a curiously divided world. As I have said before, in the field of knowledge of non-human nature, humanity, at least in its more developed sections, has reached a relatively high level of restraint and thus of detachment. A relatively high level of detachment and reality-congruence in their knowledge of non-human nature has enabled human beings to increase and to extend systematically the social fund of knowledge in this field. The movement in that direction is institutionalized and has become self-perpetuating. Reality-congruent knowledge of non-human nature grows at an increasing, perhaps exponential, rate. As a result the dangers threatening humanity from natural processes at that level, from non-human nature as such within the terrestrial orbit, have considerably decreased. This in turn has reinforced and helped to increase the relatively high standard of detachment represented by knowledge about non-human nature.

Restraint and detachment in the production and use of knowledge at the human level and thus in the handling of social processes is very much lower. Hence, this type of knowledge also shows a much lower level of reality-congruence. It is strongly imbued with fantasies, strongly fashioned by short-term wishes and fears. At this level of integration, the danger level thus remains very high, reinforcing the already high level of involvement of knowledge and the consequent actions which in turn tend to aggravate dangers. The circularity is easy enough to observe.

It is particularly evident at the highest level of integration, at that of humanity. The factual process of closer integration at that level, of the unintended drawing together of the tribes and states of humanity, is hard to overlook. So is the increase in tensions and conflicts which is a pronounced structural characteristic of this as of other strongly marked spurts towards closer interdependence and integration of human groups. Yet at the global level no effective authority exists which can regulate the process of integration and its consequences for the part-units concerned. Nor is it likely that humanity can ever be ruled for long, and ruled effectively, by one of its national subdivisions, by a hegemonial, a dictatorial central authority. All the greater are the demands – made by the ongoing process of increasing integration at the level of humanity – on the capacity for self-regulation, and in particular for self-restraint, of the states or tribes and their leaders that, willingly or not, are drawn into this net of closer interdependency. Clarification of the balance which exists on all levels between the standards of restraint imposed from without, from an external social agency, and the standard and pattern of self-restraint, can show the problem created by the process of closer integration at the level of humanity in fuller relief. However, one encounters at that level of humanity an unusual conjunction. No effective power or almost no power of this kind, imposing external restraint on part-units, exists at this level. At a guess one can say that most people would not wish to see humanity transformed into an absolute monarchy or, for that matter, into a dictatorship, open or disguised. If the rule of one nation or one group of nations over all others is not their wish, it may require a higher level of self-restraint and thus of detachment at all levels to maintain humanity permanently in a pluralistic condition. It is difficult to say whether the tribes and states of this world, both in terms of their populations and of their leaders, possess the self-restraint that is needed in order to steer humanity through the dangers which it has to surmount at this stage on its road, when the tensions and conflict of integration are growing.

To look at humanity from outside, as it were, that is in the manner in which it might be perceived by an external observer, requires a high level of detachment, a more than usual ability in self-distancing. This is a further and indeed the last of a series of examples in this introduction which illustrate the concepts of detachment and involvement. The exercise may be rewarding. Tradition has trained our sense of reality in such a manner that the term 'humanity' seems to refer to a distant ideal, not to an existing social formation, to the highest level of social integration. It requires a very considerable effort of detachment to recognize that this idealizing picture of humanity is no longer correct. A strong self-distancing spurt is needed in order to recognize that the conflict-ridden social unit to which the term 'humanity' refers is a stage in an ongoing process of advancing or, as the case may be, retreating integration. In the present phase, the term 'humanity', increasingly, refers to a clearly structured internally coherent social unit in flux – to a more and more closely woven network of a relatively small number (about 150) of warring and competing states. It requires indeed a considerable effort of detachment to perceive it as such.

That the fate of humanity is in the balance may well be known to a great number of human beings. But the leaders of the participant states, particularly of the most powerful states, at present, are still unable to act on that knowledge. Their actions are informed with knowledge that is wholly state-centred or in other words self-centred. Their involvement in the affairs of their own state, and thus in out-of-date knowledge upon which they act, is too strong and their capacity for detachment evidently too weak. Not only the governments but also the great majority of the population of states are as yet not able to ascend to a level of detachment from which they can perceive the human world as such, as a more and more integrated though highly vulnerable unit, as humanity, and can act upon this more detached knowledge. I have spoken before of the cirularity, often in the form of a spiral movement upwards or downwards, which binds to each other the safety-danger balance characteristic of a society and the involvement-detachment balance of its standard of knowledge. The present situation of humanity offers a good illustration of this circularity. High danger breeds high involvement of the knowledge guiding action, and this breeds high danger. Needless to say, the process of integration at the highest level as at others can easily go into reverse.

Sociologists can draw attention to, and perhaps help clarify the relationship between the standard of involvement and detachment that prevail among humans, and the danger to which they are exposed at the level of humanity. There is no external authority steering the fate of humanity. At the global level no external restraint can curb people's involvement. In a way not uncharacteristic of long-term social processes, the development of peoples social habitus lags behind the process of global integration. The demand made by an increasing interdependence of all sections of humanity on the self-restraint of human beings is all the greater because there is no external authority restraining them. As a sociologist, for the time being, one cannot and need not say more.

Part I

Problems of Involvement
and Detachment

Old Lady: Are you not prejudiced?
Author: Madame, rarely will you meet a more prejudiced man nor one who tell himself he keeps his mind more open. But cannot that be because one part of our mind, that which we act with, becomes prejudiced through experience, and still we keep another part completely open to observe and judge with?
Old Lady: Sir, I do not know.
Author: Madame, neither do I and it may well be that we are talking nonsense.
Old Lady: That is an odd term and one I did not encounter in my youth.
Author: Madame, we apply the term now to describe unsoundness in abstract conversation, or, indeed, any overmetaphysical tendency in speech.
Old Lady: I must learn to use these terms correctly.

E. Hemingway, *Death in the Afternoon*

I

One cannot say of a person's outlook in any absolute sense that it is detached or involved (or, if one prefers, "irrational", "objective" or "subjective"). Only small babies, and among adults perhaps only insane people, become involved in whatever they experience with complete abandon to their feelings here and now; and again only the insane can remain totally unmoved by what goes on around them. Normally adult behaviour lies on a scale somewhere between these two extremes. In some groups, and in some individuals of these groups, it may come nearer to one of them than in others; it may shift hither and thither as social and mental pressures rise and fall. But social life as we know it would come to an end if standards of adult behaviour went too far in either direction, As far as one can see, the very existence of ordered group life depends on the interplay in people's thoughts and actions of impulses in both directions, those that involve and those that detach keeping each other in check. They may clash and struggle for dominance, or compromise and form alloys of many different shades and kinds – however varied, it is the relation between the two which sets people's courses. In using these terms,[1] one refers in short to changing equilibria between sets of mental activities which in human relations other humans, with objects and with self (whatever their other functions may be) have the function to involve and to detach.

As tools of thinking, therefore, "involvement" and "detachment" would remain highly ineffectual if they were understood to adumbrate a sharp division between two independent sets of phenomena. They do not refer to two separate classes of objects; used as universals they are, at best, marginal concepts. In the main, what we observe are people and people's manifestations, such as patterns of speech or of thought, and of other activities, some of which bear the stamp of higher, other of lesser detachment or involvement. It is the continuum that lies between these marginal poles that presents the principal problem. Can one determine with greater accuracy the position of specific attitudes or products of people within this continuum? One might, impressionistically, say, for example, that in societies like ours people tend to be more detached in their approaches to natural than to social events. Can one trace, at least summarily, criteria for different degress of detachment and involvement? What in fact is meant, what does it imply, if one says that in societies such as ours, with a relatively high degree of industrialization and of control over non-human forces of nature, approaches to nature are on the whole more detached than those to society? The degree of detachment shown by different individuals in similar situations may differ greatly. Can one, nevertheless, speak, in this respect, of different degrees of detachment and involvement regardless of these individual variations?

II

The way in which individual members of a group experience whatever affects their senses, the meaning which it has for them, depends on the standard forms of dealing with, and of thinking and speaking about, these phenomena which have gradually evolved in their society. Thus, although the degree of detachment shown in one's encounter with natural forces may vary from individual to individual and from situation to situation, the concepts themselves which, in societies like ours, all individuals use in thinking, speaking and acting – concepts like "lightning", "tree" or "wolf" no less than "electricity", "organism", "cause" and effect" or "nature" – in the sense in which they are used today, represent a relatively high degree of detachment; so does the socially induced experience of nature as a "landscape" or as "beautiful". The range of individual variations in detachment, in other words, is limited by the public standards of detachment embodied in modes of thinking and speaking about nature and in the widely institutionalized use of natural forces for human ends. Compared with previous ages, control of emotions in experiencing nature, as that of nature itself, has grown. Involvement has lessened, but it has not disappeared. Even scientific approaches to nature do not require the extinction of other more involved and emotive forms of approach. What distinguishes these from other less detached approaches is the manner in which tendencies towards detachment and towards involvement balance each other and blend.

Like other people, scientists engaged in the study of nature are, to some extent, prompted in the pursuit of their task by personal wishes and wants; they are often enough influenced by specific needs of the community to which they belong. They may wish to foster their own career. They may hope that the results of their inquiries will be in line with theories they have enunciated before or with the requirements and ideals of groups with which they identify themselves. But these involvements, in the natural sciences, determine as a rule nothing more than the general direction of inquiries; they are, in most cases, counterbalanced and checked by institutionalized procedures which compel scientists, more or less, to detach themselves, for the time being, from the urgent issues at hand. The immediate problems, personal or communal, induce problems of a different kind, scientific problems which are no longer directly related to specific persons or groups. The former, more narrowly time-bound, often serve merely as a motive force; the latter, the scientific problems which they may have induced, owe their form and their meaning to the wider and less time-bound continuum of theories and observations evolved in this or that problem area by generations of specialists.

Like other human activities, scientific inquiries into nature embody sets of values. To say that natural sciences are "non-evaluating" or "value-free" is a misuse of terms. But the sets of values, the types of evaluations which play a part in scientific inquiries of this type differ from those which have as their frame of reference the interests, the well-being or suffering of oneself or of social units to which one belongs. The aim of these inquiries is to find the inherent order of events as it is, independently not of any, but of any particular, observer, and the importance, the relevance, the value of what one observes is assessed in accordance with the place and function it appears to have within this order itself.

In the exploration of nature, in short, scientists have learned that any direct encroachment upon their work by short-term interests or needs of specific persons or groups is liable to jeopardize the usefulness which their work may have in the end for themselves or for their own group. The problems which they formulate and, by means of their theories, try to solve, have in relation to personal or social problems of the day a high degree of autonomy; so have the sets of values which they use; their work is not "value-free", but it is, in contrast to that of many social scientists, protected by firmly established professional standards and other institutional safeguards against the intrusion of heteronomous evaluations.[2] Here, the human primary tendency to take the short route from a strongly felt need to a precept for its satisfaction has become more or less subordinate to precepts and procedures which require a longer route. Natural scientists seek to find ways of satisfying human needs by means of a detour – the detour via detachment. They set out to find solutions for problems potentially relevant for all human beings and all human groups. The question characteristic of involvement – "What does it mean for me or for us?" – has become subordinate to questions like "What is it?" or "How are these events connected with others?" In this form, the level of detachment represented by the scientist's work has become more or less institutionalized as part of a scientific tradition reproduced by means of a highly specialized training, maintained by various forms of social control and socially induced emotional restraints; it has become embodied in the conceptual tools, the basic assumptions, the methods of speaking and thinking which scientists use.

Moreover, concepts and methods of this type have spread, and are spreading again and again, from the workshops of the specialists to the general public. In most industrial societies, impersonal types of explanations of natural events and other concepts based on the idea of a relatively autonomous order, of a course of events independent of any specific group of human observers, are used by people almost as a matter of course, though most of them are probably unaware of the long struggle involved in the elaboration and diffusion of these forms of thinking.

Yet, here too, in society at large, these more detached terms of thinking represent only one layer in people's approaches to nature. Other more involved and emotive forms of thinking about nature have by no means disappeared.

Thus in falling ill one may find one's thoughts stray again and again to the question, "Who is to blame for this?" The childhood experience of pain as the outcome of an attack, and perhaps a certain urge to retaliate, may assert themselves even though under the pressure of an overgrown conscience the attack may appear as deserved, so that one may come to feel, rightly or wrongly, that one has only oneself to blame for it. And yet one may accept at the same time the doctor's more detached dictum that this illness followed primarily from a completely blind biological course of events and not from anybody's intentions, not from conscious or unconscious motives of any kind.

More involved forms of thinking, in short, continue to form an integral part of our experience of nature. But in this area of our experience they have become increasingly overlaid and counterbalanced by others which make higher demands on people's faculty of looking at themselves, as it were, from outside and of viewing what they call "mine" or "ours" as part systems of a larger system. In experiencing nature humans have been able, in the course of time, to form and to face a picture of the physical universe which is emotionally far from satisfactory, which, in fact, seems to become less and less so as science advances, but which at the same time agrees better with the cumulative results of systematic observations. They have learned to impose upon themselves greater restraint in their approaches to natural events, and in exchange for the short-term satisfactions which they had to give up they have gained greater power to control and to manipulate natural forces for their own ends, and with it, in this sphere, greater security and other new long-term satisfactions.

III

Thus in public approaches to nature, people have travelled a long way (and have to travel it again and again as they grow up) from the primary, the childhood patterns of thinking. The road they have travelled is still far from clear. But one can see in broad outline some of its characteristic patterns and mechanisms.

When humans, instead of using stones as they found them against enemies or beasts, with greater restraint of their momentary impulses, gradually changed towards fashioning stones in advance for their use as weapons or tools (as we may assume they did at some time), and when, increasing their foresight, they gradually changed from gathering fruits and roots towards growing plants deliberately for their own use, it implied that they themselves as well as their social life and their natural surroundings, that their outlook as well as their actions, changed. The same can be said of those later stages in which changes in human thinking about nature became more and more the task of scientific specialists. Throughout these developments the mastery of people over themselves, as expressed in their mental attitudes towards nature, and their mastery over natural forces by handling them, have grown together. The level and patterns of detachment represented by public standards of thinking about natural events were in the past and still are dependent on the level and the manner of control represented by public standards of manipulating them, and vice versa.

For a very long time, therefore, in their struggle with the non-human forces of nature, humans must have moved in what appears in retrospect as a vicious circle. They had little control over natural forces on which they were dependent for their survival. Wholly dependent on phenomena whose course they could neither foresee nor influence to any considerable extent, they lived in extreme insecurity, and, being most vulnerable and insecure, they could not help feeling strongly about every occurrence they thought might affect their lives; they were too deeply involved to look at natural phenomena, like distant observers, calmly. Thus, on the one hand, they had little chance of controlling their own strong feelings in relation to nature and of forming more detached concepts of natural events, as long as they had little control over them; and they had, on the other hand, little chance of extending their control over their non-human surroundings as long as they could not gain greater mastery over their own strong feelings in relation to them and increase their control over themselves.

The change towards greater control over natural phenomena appears to have followed what in our traditional language might be called "the principle of increasing facilitation". It must have been extremely difficult for people to gain greater control over nature as long as they had little control over it; and the more control they gained, the easier it was for them to extend it.

Nothing in our experience suggests that part-processes of this kind must always work in the same direction. Some of the phases in which they went into reverse gear are known from the past. Increasing social tensions and strife may go hand in hand with both a decrease of people's ability to control, and an increase in the fantasy-content of their ideas about, natural as well as social phenomena. Whether feedback mechanisms of this kind work in one or in the other direction depends, in short, on the total situation of the social units concerned.

IV

Paradoxically enough, the steady increase in the capacity of humans, both for a more detached approach to natural forces and for controlling them, and the gradual acceleration of this process, have helped to increase the difficulties which they have in extending their control over processes of social change and over their own feelings in thinking about them.

Dangers threatening people from non-human forces have been slowly decreasing. Not the least important effect of a more detached approach in this field has been that of limiting fears, of preventing them, that is, from irradiating widely beyond what can be realistically assessed as a threat. The former helplessness in the face of incomprehensible and unmanageable natural forces has slowly given way to a feeling of confidence, the concomitant, one might say, of increasing facilitation, of people's power to raise, in this sphere, the general level of well-being and to enlarge the area of security through the application of patient and systematic research.

But the growth of people's comprehension of natural forces and of the use made of them for human ends is associated with specific changes in human relationships; it goes hand in hand with the growing interdependence of growing numbers of people. The gradual acceleration in the increment of knowledge and use of non-human forces, bound up, as it is, with specific changes in human relations, has helped, in turn, to accelerate the process of change in the latter. The network of human activities tends to become increasingly complex, far-flung and closely knit. More and more groups, and with them more and more individuals, tend to become dependent on each other for their security and the satisfaction of their needs in ways which, for the greater part, surpass the comprehension of those involved. It is as if first thousands, then millions, then more and more millions walked through this world with their hands and feet chained together by invisible ties. No one is in charge. No one stands outside. Some want to go this way, others that. They fall upon each other and, vanquishing or defeated, still remain chained to each other. No one can regulate the movements of the whole unless a great part of them are able to understand, to see, as it were, from outside, the whole patterns they form together. And they are not able to visualize themselves as part of these larger patterns because, being hemmed in and moved uncomprehendingly hither and thither in ways which none of them intended, they cannot help being preoccupied with the urgent, narrow and parochial problems which each of them has to face. They can only look at whatever happens to them from their narrow location within the system. They are too deeply involved to look at themselves from without. Thus what is formed of nothing but human beings acts upon each of them, and is experienced by many as an alien external force not unlike the forces of nature.

The same process which has made people less dependent on the vagaries of nature has made them more dependent on each other. The changes which, with regard to non-human forces, have given people greater power and security, have increasingly brought upon them different forms of insecurity. In their relations with each other people are again and again confronted, as they were in the past in their dealings with non-human forces, with phenomena, with problems which, given their present approaches, are still beyond their control. They are incessantly faced with the task of adjusting themselves to changes which, though perhaps of their own making, were not intended by them. And as these changes frequently bring in their wake unforeseen gains for some and losses for others, they tend to go hand in hand with tensions and frictions between groups which, at the same time, are inescapably chained to each other. Tests of strength and the use of organized force serve often as costly means of adjustment to changes within this tangle of interdependencies; on many of its levels no other means of adjustment exist.

Thus, vulnerable and insecure as people are under these conditions, they cannot stand back and look at the course of events calmly like more detached observers. Again, it is, on the one hand, difficult for men in that situation to control more fully their own strong feelings with regard to events which, they feel, may deeply affect their lives, and to approach them with greater detachment, as long as their ability to control the course of events is small; and it is, on the other hand, difficult for them to extend their understanding and control of these events as long as they cannot approach them with greater detachment and gain greater control over themselves. Thus a circular movement between inner and outer controls, a feedback mechanism of a kind, is at work not only in people's relations with the non-human forces of nature, but also in their relations with each other. But it operates at present in these two spheres on very different levels. While in people's relations with non-human forces the standard of both the control of self and that of external events is relatively high, in relations of people with people the socially required and socially bred standard of both is considerably lower.

The similarities between this situation and that which humans had to face in past ages in their relations with the forces of nature, are often obscured by the more obvious differences. We do already know that people can attain a considerable degree of control over natural phenomena impinging upon their lives and a fairly high degree of detachment in manipulating and in thinking of them. We do not know, and we can hardly imagine, how a comparable degree of detachment and control may be attained with regard to social phenomena. Yet, for thousands of years it was equally impossible for those who struggled before us to imagine that one could approach and manipulate natural forces as we do. The comparison throws some light on their situation as well as on ours.

V

It also throws some light on the differences that exist today between the standards of certainty and achievement of the natural and the social sciences. It is often implied, if not stated explicitly, that the "objects" of the former, by their very nature, lend themselves better than those of the latter to an exploration by means of scientific methods ensuring a high degree of certainty. However, there is no reason to assume that social data, that the relations of persons, are less accessible to human comprehension than the relations of non-human phenomena, or that people's intellectual powers as such are incommensurate to the task of evolving theories and methods for the study of social data to a level of fitness, comparable to that reached in the study of physical data. What is significantly different in these two fields is the situation of the investigators and, as part of it, their attitudes with regard to their "objects"; it is, to put it in a nutshell, the *relationship between "subjects" and "objects"*. In this relationship, if situation and attitudes are taken into account, the problems and the difficulties of an equal advance in the social sciences stand out more clearly.

The general aim of scientific pursuits is the same in both fields; stripped of a good many philosophical encrustations it is to find out in what way perceived data are connected with each other. But social as distinct from natural sciences are concerned with conjunctions of persons. Here, in one form or the other, people face themselves;[3] the "objects" are also "subjects". The task of social scientists is to explore, and to make people understand, the patterns they form together, the nature and the changing configuration of all that binds them to each other. The investigators themselves form part of these patterns. They cannot help experiencing them, directly or by identification, as immediate participants from within; and the greater the strains and stresses to which they or their groups are exposed, the more difficult is it for them to perform the mental operation, underlying all scientific pursuits, of detaching themselves from their role as immediate participants and from the limited vista it offers.

There is no lack of attempts in the social sciences at detaching oneself from one's position as an involved exponent of social events, and at working out a wider conceptual framework within which the problems of the day can find their place and their meaning. Perhaps the most persistent effort in that direction has been made by the great pioneering sociologists of the nineteenth and early twentieth centuries. But their work also shows most conspicuously the difficulties which, under present conditions, stand in the way of such an attempt. On the one hand, they all attempted to discover, from one angle or the other, the inherent order of the social development of mankind, its "laws", as some of them called it. They tried to work out a comprehensive and universally valid theoretical framework, within which the problems of their own age appeared as specific problems of detail and no longer as the central problem from which those of other ages received their relevance and their meaning. And yet, on the other hand, they were so deeply involved in the problems of their own society that they often viewed, in fact, the whole development of people's relations with each other in the light of the hopes and fears, the enmities and beliefs resulting from their role as immediate participants in the struggles and conflicts of their own time. These two forms of approach – one, more involved, which made them see the development of human society as a whole in the light of the pressing problems of their own time, and the other, more detached, which enabled them to visualize the short-term problems of their own time in the light of the long-term development of society – were so inextricably interwoven in their work that, in retrospect, it is difficult to sift one from the other, and to sort out their contribution to the development of a more universally valid system of theories about people in society from ideas relevant only as an expression of their own ideals and idiosyncrasies in the struggles of a particular historical period.

Since then, a good deal more factual material about social phenomena has been brought to light. The elaboration of a more impersonal body of theories, and their adjustment to a widening range of observed facts brought to light under their guidance, have considerably advanced in some social sciences, and advanced in some more than in others.[4] To a greater or lesser extent, research in all human sciences still tends to oscillate between two levels of consciousness and two forms of approach, the one more akin, one might say, to a simple geocentric, the other more to a heliocentric, approach. And the constant upsurge of the former in connection with acute social and political tensions effectively bars in most social sciences the steady continuity of research which has become so marked a characteristic of many natural sciences. The pressure of short-term problems which can no longer be solved in traditional ways, of social problems which appear to require for their solution procedures evolved and employed by scientific specialists, has increased together with the complexity of human relations itself. Fragmentation of social research has grown apace. Even as an aim of research, the idea of a wider theoretical framework connecting and unifying the problems and results of more limited inquiries has become more remote; to many it appears unattainable, to others, in addition, undesirable. For the immediate difficulties of people springing up in their own midst from the unmanageable forces of social change, from conflicts and frictions among themselves, have remained exceedingly great. The strength of involvements, within the social context of men's lives, if it has not actually increased, has hardly lessened.

Hence, whatever else may have changed since the days of pioneering sociologists, certain basic characteristics of the social sciences have not. For the time being, social scientists are liable to be caught in a dilemma. They work and live in a world in which almost everywhere groups, small and great, including their own groups, are engaged in a struggle for position and often enough for survival, some trying to rise and to better themselves in the teeth of strong opposition, some who have risen before trying to hold on to what they have, and some going down.

Under these conditions, the members of such groups can hardly help being deeply affected in their thinking about social events by the constant threats arising from these tensions to their way of life or to their standards of life and perhaps to their life. As members of such groups, scientific specialists engaged in the study of society share with others these vicissitudes. Their experience of themselves as upholders of a particular social and political creed which is threatened, as representatives of a specific way of life in need of defence, like the experience of their fellows, can hardly fail to have a strong emotional undertone. Group images, those, for instance, of classes or of nations, self-justifications, the cases which groups make out for themselves, represent, as a rule, an amalgam of realistic observations and collective fantasies (which, like the myths of simpler people, are real enough as motive forces of action). To sift out the former from the latter, to hold up before these groups a mirror in which they can see themselves as they might be seen, not by an involved critic from another contemporary group, but by an inquirer trying to see in perspective the structure and functioning of their relationship with each other, is not only difficult in itself for anyone whose group is involved in such a struggle; expressed in public, it may also weaken the cohesion and solidarity feeling of the group and, with it, its capacity to survive. There is, in fact, in all these groups a point beyond which none of its members can go in his or her detachment without appearing and, so far as their group is concerned, without becoming, a dangerous heretic, however consistent their ideas or their theories may be in themselves and with observed facts, however much they may approximate to what we call the "truth."

And yet, if social scientists, although using more specialized procedures and a more technical language, are in the last resort not much less affected in their approach to the problems of society by preconceived ideas and ideals, by passions and partisan views, than the man in the street, are they really justified in calling themselves "scientists"? Does any statement, any hypothesis or theory, deserve the epithet "scientific", if it is ultimately based on dogmatic beliefs, on *a priori* assumptions, on ideas and evaluations which are impervious to arguments based on a more systematic and dispassionate examination of the available evidence? Can social scientists make any specific contribution to the solution of major problems, even of their own groups, of their own country, class, profession or whatever it is, if they accept as the self-evident foundation of their theories some of the religiously held creeds and norms of one or the other of these groups, so that the results of their studies are destined from the start to agree, or at least not to disagree, with the basic tenets of these communal beliefs? Without greater detachment and autonomy of thinking, can they hope to put in the hands of their fellow-humans more fitting tools of thinking and more adequate blueprints for the handling of social and political problems – more adequate blueprints than those handed on unreflectingly from generation to generation or evolved haphazardly in the heat of the battle? And even if they do not accept such beliefs unquestioningly, are they not often impelled to use them as the general frame of reference for their studies simply by sentiments of solidarity, of loyalty or perhaps of fear? Are they not sometimes only too justified in thinking that it might weaken a cause which they regard as their own if they were to subject systematically the religiously held social creeds and ideals of one of their own groups to a more dispassionate scientific examination, that it might put weapons in the hands of opponents or that, as a result, they themselves might be exposed to ostracism, if to nothing worse?

The dilemma underlying many of the present uncertainties of the sciences of humans is, as one can see, not simply a dilemma of this or that historian, economist, political scientist or sociologist (to name only some of the present divisions); it is not the perplexity of individual social scientists, but that of social scientists as a professional group. As things stand, their social task as scientists and the requirements of their position as members of other groups often disagree; and the latter are apt to prevail as long as the pressure of group tensions and passions remains as high as it is.

The problem confronting them is not simply to discard the latter role in favour of the former. They cannot cease to take part in, and to be affected by, the social and political affairs of their groups and their time. Their own participation and involvement, moreover, is itself one of the conditions for comprehending the problems they try to solve as scientists. For while one need not know, in order to understand the structure of molecules, what it feels like to be one of its atoms – in order to understand the functioning of human groups one needs to know, as it were, from inside how human beings experience their own and other groups, and one cannot know without active participation and involvement.

The problem confronting those who study one or the other aspects of human groups is how to keep their two roles as participant and as inquirer clearly and consistently apart and, as a professional group, to establish in their work the undisputed dominance of the latter.

This is so difficult a task that many representatives of social sciences, at present, appear to regard the determination of their inquiries by preconceived and religiously held social and political ideals as inevitable. They often seem to consider these heteronomous foundations of their pronouncements as characteristic, not of a specific situation and, within it, of a specific dilemma, but of their subject-matter as such. The latitude they allow each other in their use of dogmatic ideals and evaluations as a basis for the setting of problems, the selection of material and the construction of theories is very wide – and is apt to become wider still whenever the pressure of tensions and passions mounts in society at large.

VI

The chance which social scientists have to face and to cope with this dilemma might be greater if it were not for another characteristic of their situation which tends to obscure the nature of these difficulties. This is the ascendancy gained, over the centuries, by a manner or style of thinking which has proved highly adequate and successful in men's dealings with physical events, but which is not always equally appropriate if used in their dealings with others. One of the major reasons for the difficulties with which people have to contend in their endeavour to gain more reliable knowledge about themselves is the uncritical and often dogmatic application of categories and concepts, highly adequate in relation to problems on the level of matter and energy, to other levels of experience and, among them, to that of social phenomena. Not only specific concepts of causation or of explanation formed in this manner, are generalized and used almost as a matter of course in inquiries about human relations; this mechanical diffusion of models expresses itself, too, for example, in the widespread identification of "rationality" with the use of categories developed mainly in connection with experiences of physical events, and in the assumption that the use of other forms of thinking must necessarily indicate a leaning towards metaphysics and irrationality.

The same tendency towards over-generalizing shows itself in many current ideas of what is and what is not scientific. By and large, theories of science still use as their principal model the physical sciences – often not in their contemporary, but in their classical form. Aspects of their procedures are widely regarded as the most potent and decisive factor responsible for their achievements and as the essential characteristic of sciences generally. By abstracting such aspects from the actual procedures and techniques of the physical sciences, one arrives at a general model of scientific procedure which is known as "the scientific method". In name, it represents the distinguishing characteristics common to all scientific, as distinct from non-scientific, forms of solving problems. In fact, it often constitutes a curious compound of features which may be universal with others characteristic of the physical sciences only and bound up with the specific nature of their problems. It resembles a general concept, "animal", formed without reference to the evolutionary diversity and connections of animal species from a rather restricted observational field, so that structures and functions common perhaps to all animals, as distinct from non-living things and from plants, mingle in it with others characteristic only of certain types of animals – of, say, mammals or of vertebrates.

The assumption is that in this generalized form "the scientific method" can be transferred from the field where it originated, from the physical sciences, to all other fields, to biological as well as to social sciences, regardless of the different nature of their problems; and that wherever it is applied it will work its magic. Among social scientists in particular it is not uncommon to attribute difficulties and inadequacies of their work to the fact that they do not go far enough in copying the method of physical sciences. It is this strong concentration of their attention on problems of "method" which tends to obscure from their view the difficulties that spring from their situation and from their own approaches to the problems they study.

The superior achievement and status of the physical sciences itself constitutes a highly significant factor in the situation of those who work in the field of social sciences. If, as participants in the life of a turbulent society, they are constantly in danger of using in their inquiries preconceived and immovable social convictions as the basis for their problems and theories, as scientists they are in danger of being dominated by models derived from inquiries into physical events and stamped with the authority of the physical sciences.

The fact that people confronted with the task of formulating and exploring new sets of problems model their concepts and procedures on those which have proved their worth in other fields is in no way surprising or unique. It is a recurrent feature in human history that new crafts and skills, and among them new scientific specialisms, in the early stages of their development, continue to rely on older models. Some time is needed before a new group of specialists can emancipate itself from the ruling style of thinking and of acting; and in the course of this process their attitude towards the older groups, as in other processes of emancipation, is apt to oscillate. They may go too far for a while and may go on too long in their uncritical submission to the authority and prestige of the dominant standards; and then again, they may go too far in their repudiation and in their denial of the functions which the older models had or have in the development of their own. In most of these respects the emergence of the younger social sciences from under the wings of the older natural sciences follows the usual pattern.

But there can have been rarely a situation in which the gradient between the comparatively high level of detachment manifest in the older branches of knowledge and the much lower represented by the younger branches was equally steep. In the physical sciences, it is not only the development and use of a specific method for the solution of problems and the testing of theories, but the framing of problems and theories itself, which presupposes a high standard of detachment. The same method transferred to social sciences is not infrequently used for the exploration of problems and theories conceived and studied under the impact of strong involvements. Hence the use, in social sciences, of a method akin to that evolved in the physical sciences often gives to the former the appearance of a high level of detachment or of "objectivity" which those who use this method are in fact lacking. It often serves as a means of circumventing difficulties which spring from their dilemma, without facing it; in many cases, it creates a façade of detachment masking a highly involved approach.

As a result, a crucial question is often regarded as sealed and solved which in fact is still in abeyance: the question of which of the procedures and techniques of the physical sciences are commensurate to the task of social sciences and which are not. The abstraction from these specific procedures of a general model of the scientific method, and the claim often made for it as the supreme characteristic of research that is scientific, have led to the neglect, or even to the exclusion from the field of systematic research, of wide problem areas which do not lend themselves easily to an exploration by means of a method for which the physical sciences have provided the prototype. In order to be able to use methods of this kind and to prove themselves scientific in the eyes of the world, investigators are frequently induced to ask and to answer relatively insignificant questions and to leave unanswered others perhaps of greater significance. They are induced to cut their problems so as to suit their method. The exclusive and seemingly final character of many current statements about the scientific method finds expression in the strange idea that problems which do not lend themselves to investigations by means of a method modelled on that of the physical sciences are no concern of people engaged in scientific research.

On closer investigation, one will probably find that the tendency to consider a highly formalized picture of this one set of sciences and their method as the norm and ideal of scientific inquiries generally is connected with a specific idea about the aim of sciences. It is, one might think, bound up with the assumption that among propositions of empirical sciences, as among those of pure mathematics and related forms of logic, the only relevant distinction to be made is that between propositions which are true and others which are false; and that the aim of scientific research and of its procedures is simply and solely that of finding the "truth", of sifting true from false statements. However, the goal towards which positive sciences are striving is not, and by their very nature cannot be, wholly identical with that of fields like logic and mathematics, which are concerned with the inherent order of certain tools of thinking alone. It certainly happens in empirical investigations that people make statements which are simply found to be false. But often enough rough dichotomies like "true" and "false" are highly inadequate in their case. People engaged in empirical research often put forward propositions or theories whose merit is that they are truer than others or, to use a less hallowed term, that they are *more* adequate, *more* consistent, both with observations and in themselves. In general terms, one might say it is characteristic of these scientific as distinct from non-scientific forms of solving problems that, in the acquisition of knowledge, questions emerge and are solved as a result of an uninterrupted two-way traffic between two layers of knowledge: that of general ideas, theories or models and that of observations and perceptions of specific events. The latter, if not sufficiently informed by the former, remains unorganized and diffuse; the former, if not sufficiently informed by the latter, remains dominated by feelings and imaginings. It is the objective of scientists, one might say, to develop a steadily expanding body of theories or models and an equally expanding body of obser- vations about specific events by means of a continuous, critical confrontation leading to greater and greater congruity with each other. The methods actually used in empirical investigations, inevitably, vary a good deal from discipline to discipline in accord- ance with the different types of problems that present themselves for solution. What they have in common, what identifies them as scientific methods, is simply that they enable scientists to test whether their findings and pronouncements constitute a reliable advance in the direction of their common objective.

VII

Is it possible to determine with greater precision and cogency the limitations of methods of scientific research modelled on those of the physical sciences? Can one, in particular, throw more light on the limits to the usefulness of mathematical or – as this term is perhaps too wide in this context – of quantifying models and techniques in empirical researches?

At the present state of development, the weight and relevance of quantifying procedures clearly differ in different problem areas. In some, above all in the physical sciences, one can see today no limit to the usefulness of procedures which make relations of quantities stand for the non-quantitative aspects of the relations of data; the scope for reducing other properties to quantities and for working out, on the basis of such a reduction, highly adequate theoretical constructs appears to be without bounds.

In other fields of research the scope for similar reductions is clearly very much narrower; and theoretical constructs based on such reductions alone often prove far less adequate. Have problem areas which do not lend themselves as well as the physical sciences to the application of quantifying methods of research, certain general properties which can account for such differences in the scope and relevance of quantifying procedures as instruments of research?

It is possible to think that this problem itself can be readily solved in terms of quantities alone. As one passes from studies of matter and energy and its various transformations to those of organisms and their development as species and individuals, and again to studies of people as societies and individuals (in not quite the same sense of the word), according to a not uncommon view, the problems which one encounters become more complex; the greater complexity is often thought to follow from the fact that the number of interacting parts, factors, variables or suchlike increases as one moves from the study of inorganic matter to those of organisms and of people; and as a result of this increase in numbers, so the argument seems to run, measurements and mathematical operations, generally, become more and more complicated and difficult. If one accepts the idea that it is the aim of scientific investigations everywhere to explain the behaviour of composite units of observation by means of measurements from that of their simpler constituent parts, each of the variables affecting the behaviour of such a unit would have to be measured by itself so as to determine the quantitative aspects of its relations with others. The greater the number of variables, the greater would be the number of measurements and the more complicated would be the mathematical operations necessary to determine their interplay. In the light of this hypothesis, the demands made on the resources in manpower, in computing machines, in mathematical techniques and in money and time would progressively increase from one set of sciences to the other with the increase in the number of factors that has to be taken into account. More and more, these demands would become prohibitive, and research on quantitative lines alone would no longer be possible. According to this view, it is for that reason that one has to resign oneself to the use of less precise and less satisfactory methods of investigation in many fields of study.

In a way, this approach to the observable limitations of quantifying methods in research is itself not uncharacteristic of the manner in which forms of thinking most serviceable in the exploration of physical data become distended into what almost represents a general style of thinking. The choice of a heap of more and more factors or variables as a model for increasing complexity is determined by a general expectation which is evidently based on experiences in physical research, but which tends to assume the character of an *a priori* belief: by the expectation that problems of all kinds can be satisfactorily solved in terms of quantities alone.

However, the area within which this expectation can be safely used as a guide to the formulation of problems and theories has very definite limits. The properties of different units of observation characteristic of different disciplines are not only affected by the number of interacting parts, variables, factors or conditions, but also by the manner in which constituents of such units are connected with each other. Perhaps the best way to indicate briefly this aspect of differences is the hypothetical construction of a model or models which represent different frames of reference of scientific problems in a highly generalized form, as composite units arranged according to the extent of interdependence of their constituents or, more generally, according to the degree of organization which they possess.

Arranged in this manner, this continuum of models would have one pole formed by general models of units, such as congeries, agglomerations, heaps or multitudes, whose constituents are associated with each other temporarily in the loosest possible manner and may exist independently of each other without changing their characteristic properties. The other pole would be framed by general models of units such as open systems and processes which are highly self-regulating and autonomous, which consist of a hierarchy of interlocking part-systems and part-processes, and whose constituents are interdependent to such an extent that they cannot be isolated from their unit without radical changes in their properties as well as in those of the unit itself.

Between these two poles would be spaced out intermediary models[5] graded according to the degree of differentiation and integration of their constituents.

As one moves along this continuum of models from paradigms of loosely composed to others of highly organized units, as models of congeries step by step give way to those of self-regulating open systems and processes with more and more levels, many of the devices developed for scientific research into units of the first type change, or even lose, their function. In many cases, from being the principal instruments and techniques of research, they become, at the most, auxiliaries.

Less adequate, in that sense, becomes the concept of an independent variable of a unit of observation which is otherwise kept invariant and, with it, the type of observation and experimentation based on the supposition that what one studies is a heap of potentially independent variables and their effects.

Less adequate, too, becomes the concept of a scientific law as the general theoretical mould for particular connections of constituents of a larger unit. For it is one of the tacit assumptions underlying both the conception and the establishment of a scientific law, that the phenomena of which one wishes to state in the form of a law that the pattern of their connection is necessary and unchanging, do not change their properties irreversibly if they are cut off from other connections or from each other. The type of relationship whose regularity can be fairly satisfactorily expressed in the form of a law is a relationship which is impermanent, though it has a permanent pattern: it can start and cease innumerable times without affecting the behaviour of other constituents of the larger nexus within which it occurs, or the properties of the larger nexus itself. General laws for particular cases, in short, are instruments for the solution of problems whose referential frame is conceived as a congeries.[6]

The more the framework of problems resembles in its characteristics a highly self-regulating system and process, the greater in other words the chance that constituents are permanently connected with each other so that they are bound to change their properties irrevocably if these connections are severed, the more likely is it that laws assume a subsidiary role as tools of research; and the more does one require as the paramount vehicle for exploring and presenting regularities of part-connections, system- and process-models clearly representative of the fact that part-events are linked to each other as constituents of a functioning unit without which they would not occur or would not occur in this manner.

Nor do those time-honoured intellectual operations known as induction and deduction retain quite the same character throughout this continuum of models. In their classical form they are closely linked with intellectual movements up and down between discrete and isolated universals, which may be general concepts, laws, propositions or hypotheses, and an infinite multitude of particular cases which are also conceived as capable of preserving their significant characteristics if they are studied in isolation independently of all other connections.

When models of multitudes become subordinate to models of highly organized systems, another type of research operation gains greater prominence, modifying to some extent those of induction and deduction, namely movements up and down between models of the whole and those of its parts.

It is difficult to think of any well established terms expressing clearly the differential qualities and the complementary character of these two operations. Perhaps one might call "analytical" those steps of research in which the theoretical representation of a system is treated more or less as a background from which problems of constituent parts stand out as the prime object of research and as a potential testing-ground for theoretical representations of the whole; and one might call "synoptic" (not to say "synthetic") those steps which are aimed at forming a more coherent theoretical representation of a system as a whole as a unifying framework and as a potential testing-ground for relatively uncoordinated theoretical representations of constituent parts. But whatever the technical terms, one can say that the solution of problems whose framework represents a highly integrated unit depends in the long run on the coordination and balance between steps in both directions.

In the short run, synopsis may be in advance of analysis. Its theoretical results have in that case, at the worst, the character of speculations; at the best, if they are conformable to a larger body of observational and theoretical fragments, that of working hypothesis. Many of the ideas put forward by the pioneering sociologists of the nineteenth century, preoccupied as they were with the process of mankind as a whole, illustrate this stage. Or else analysis may be in advance of synopsis. In that case, knowledge consists of a plethora of observational and theoretical fragments for which a more unified theoretical framework is not yet in sight. A good deal of the work done by sociologists during part of the twentieth century can serve as an illustration of that stage. Many of them, in reaction from the more speculative aspects of the work done by the system-builders which preceded them, became distrustful of any overall view and of the very idea of "systems" itself; they confined themselves more and more to the exploration of isolated clusters of problems which could be explored as nearly as possible by methods used by representatives of other sciences, though they themselves lacked what these others already possessed: a more unified, more highly integrated system of theoretical constructs as a common frame of reference for isolated studies of part-connections.

In the case of units of observation such as multitudes and populations, it is an appropriate aim of research to develop theoretical models of a composite unit as a whole by treating it as the sum total of its components and by tracing back its properties to those of its parts. But this reduction of the whole to its parts becomes increasingly less appropriate if one moves within the continuum of models towards more highly organized units. As the constituents of such units lose their identity if their connection with others is broken off, as they become and remain what they are only as functioning parts of a functioning system of a specific type, or even of an individual system, the study of temporary isolates is useful only if its results are again and again referred back to a model of their system; the properties of parts cannot be adequately ascertained without the guidance provided by a theoretical model of the whole. At an early stage in the development of a particular field of problems, such models, like maps of largely unexplored regions, may be full of blanks and perhaps full of errors which can be corrected only by further investigations of parts. But however much one or the other may lag behind, studies on the level of the whole system and studies on the level of part-units are greatly impeded if they cannot rely on a measure of correspondence and coordination which allows scientists to move the focus of their observations and reflections freely from one level to the other.

VIII

The difficulty is that there are often more than two levels to be considered. Highly structured systems and processes often have parts which are also systems and processes; and these in turn may have parts which again are developing systems, though with a smaller measure of autonomy. In fact, such systems within systems, such processes within processes, may consist of many levels of varying relative strength and controlling power interlaced and interlocked with each other; so that those who are digging up knowledge on one of them stand in need of free channels of communication with others who are working in the many galleries above and below and, at the same time, of a clear conception of the position and functions of their own problem area, and of their own situation, within the whole system.

In practice, such lines of communication are often deficient or non-existent. Problems on different levels are frequently investigated by different groups of specialists who look hardly beyond their particular pitch. Many of them draw from limited experiences with problems characteristic of one level, or merely of one of its aspects, inferences for the solution of problems whose frame of reference comprises many levels or perhaps the whole system. And if one of these groups, if, as it has in fact happened, specialists for the study of units which represent a relatively low level of organization, such as physicists, are greatly in advance of others in the exploration of their level and the development of corresponding techniques, the unselect imitation of their models and methods in studies of more highly organized units is likely to give rise to a welter of misconceived problems.

For not only the whole system, but also each of its constituent systems, may display patterns of connections and regularities which are different and which cannot be deduced from those of their constituent systems. Theoretical models and methods of research designed for the study of units which are less differentiated and integrated, can be, therefore, at best, only partially appropriate as means of research into more highly organized units, even if the latter contain the former, or homologues of the former, as constituent parts.

There are many instances of the difficulties that can ensue from the application of models designed for the study of part-systems at one level of organization to that of systems at another level or of the paramount system as a whole.

Take, for example, the old controversy about the usefulness of physical systems such as machines as explanatory models for biological systems such as animals and humans. If one adheres to the traditional way of thinking, one can usually perceive only two possible solutions to the focal problem of this controversy. One can either accept physical systems of one kind or the other as complete models for organisms and assume, explicitly or not, that an organism as a whole is a set of physical events on exactly the same level as physical events outside organisms. Or one can adopt vitalistic models and assume that special non-physical forces are at work in organisms, which account for the observable differences between living and non-living systems.

In order to accept either of these two alternatives, one has to stretch a good many points. As in other cases in which it is difficult, not simply to find a solution for a problem, but to think of any possible model for a solution which would fit the available evidence reasonably well, it is the type of available models rather than the evidence which requires re-examination. The difficulties with which people have met, at least since the days of Descartes, in tackling the question of whether or not living systems can be adequately explained by analogies with non-living systems, are closely bound up with the tradition of thinking which decrees that the behaviour of whole units has to be explained from that of their parts. It becomes less difficult to conceive of a more fitting model for the solution of this question if it is accepted that there are types of problems which require a different approach – problems which can be brought nearer solution only if one is aware that the units under observation have properties which cannot be inferred from those of their parts.

Human-made machines, as we know them, are homologues not of all, but only of some levels in the hierarchic order of open systems represented even by animals of a simpler type. As each system of a higher order may have properties different from those lower-order systems which form its parts, and as animals rising in the evolutionary scale represent systems within systems on a steadily rising number of levels, one would expect the behaviour and characteristics of organisms to correspond only partially to those of machines or of chains of chemical reactions; one would expect organisms to display characteristics which are only in some regards similar to, but in others different from, physical systems, and yet to reveal themselves as nothing but heaps of physical particles if their many-levelled organization is destroyed or if component parts are studied in isolation.

But one could no longer expect, in that case, that all problems of organisms will be solved in the end by analogies with machines or with other physical systems, and that biological sciences will gradually transform themselves into physical sciences. In living systems physical processes are patterned and organized in a way which induces further patterning and organizing of these processes. Even if people should succeed in constructing artefacts with very much more and much higher levels of organization and control than those of any known machine, artefacts which could build and rebuild their own structure from less highly organized materials, which could grow and develop, feel and reproduce themselves, one would have to apply to their construction and to their study biological as well as physical categories and models.

In controversies between vitalists and mechanists, both sides take it more or less for granted that the model of explanation according to which studies in the properties of parts are expected to provide the key for the problems presented by those of the whole, is a universal model. In fact, it is a specific and partial model appropriate only to the study of units on a relatively low level of organization.[7]

Or take the much discussed question of the relationship between the behaviour of higher animals and that of humans. Attempts to explain the latter in terms of the former are not uncommon. Yet, again, one cannot comprehend the functioning and structure of systems which embody a higher level of organization and control alone in terms of others which are less highly organized, even if the former are the descendants of the latter. While people function partly as other animals do, as a whole they function and behave in a way no other animal does.

The change towards greater cortical dominance (to mention

only one aspect of these differences) provides a useful illustration of the way in which an increase in the controlling and coordinating power of a part-system on a very high level in the hierarchy of interlocking systems, goes hand in hand with changes in the equilibrium and the functioning of systems on all levels, and with a transmogrification of the overall system itself. It is to differences such as these that one will have to turn in order to establish more clearly and more firmly that, and why, the sciences of humans cannot be expected to transform themselves, sooner or later, into a branch of the biological sciences, even though results of studies into aspects of humans within the competency of the latter form an integral element of the former.

Finally, similar problems and similar difficulties can be found, again on a different level and in a different form, in the long-drawn-out dispute about the relationship of "individual" and "society". Again, one seems to be left with the choice between two equally unsatisfactory alternatives. However much one may try one's hand at some kind of compromise, on the whole, opinions are so far arrayed in two more or less irreconcilable camps. One can place oneself nearer those who think of societies as heaps or masses of individual people and of their properties and their development, simply as the outcome of individual intentions and activities; and one can place oneself nearer those who think of societies, of social processes in all their various aspects, more or less as if they existed in some sense outside and apart from the individual people by whom they are formed.

Common to both sides, again, is a style of thinking, an idea as to how phenomena ought to be explained, which has been found most serviceable in men's attempts to explain, and to gain control over, physical events. But in this case the impasse is not only due to the uncritical transfer of models of thinking from one field to another. Attempts to work out better theoretical models for the relationship of individual and society suffer even more from the fact that this relationship has become, in our age, one of the focal points, if not *the* focal point, in the clash of value systems, of social beliefs and ideals which divide some of the most powerful groupings of men. In society at large, the question of what the rights and duties of individuals in society *ought* to be, or whether the well-being of society *ought* to be considered as more important than that of individuals, and other questions of this kind, are evocative of a wide range of practical issues which are highly controversial. Answers to such questions form in many cases the shibboleth by which followers of different social and political creeds recognize friend and foe. As a result, reinforced as it constantly is by tensions and passions of rivalling groups, the question as to what the relationship of individual and society ought to be tends to mask and to muffle in discussions and studies the question as to what kind of relationship it actually is – so much so that the simple question of fact often appears to be almost incomprehensible. And as it happens that this factual question is representative of one of the basic problems of the social sciences, the difficulties which stand in the way of any attempt to distinguish and to detach it clearly from the topical social and political questions which are often expressed in similar terms, constitute one of the major barriers to the further development of the social sciences, and particularly to that of sociology.

What has been said, so far, about other types of part-whole relationships can be of some help, if not in solving, at least in clarifying this problem. In many respects the relationship between people as individuals and people as societies differs from these other types. It is quite unique, and not all its features fit entirely in the schema of a part-whole relationship. At the same time, it shows many of its characteristics and presents many of the problems generally associated with it.

All societies, as far as one can see, have the general characteristics of systems with sub-systems on several levels of which individuals, as individuals, form only one. Organized as groups, individuals form many others. They form families; and then again on a higher level, as groups of groups, villages or towns, classes or industrial systems and many similar structures which are interlocked and which may form with each other an overall system, such as tribes, city–states, feudal kingdoms or nation–states, with a dynamic power equilibrium of its own. This, in turn, may form part of another less highly organized, less well integrated system; tribes may form with each other a federation of tribes; nation–states a balance-of-power system. In this hierarchy of interlocking social units the largest unit need not be the most highly integrated and organized unit; so far in the history of Humanity it never has been. But whatever form it may take, that system in the hierarchy of systems which constitutes the highest level of integration and organized power is also the system which has the highest capacity to regulate its own course. Like other open systems, it can disintegrate if the pressure of tensions from within or without becomes too strong. As long as its organization remains more or less intact, it has a higher degree of autonomy than any of its constituents.

And it is the structure and development of this system which in the last resort determines those of its part-systems, including those of its individual members. Different levels in this hierarchy of systems, such as individuals as such or as families or classes, have a greater or smaller measure of autonomy; they may, for example, cooperate or they may fight with each other. But the scope for autonomous actions varies with the properties of the paramount system as well as with the location of part-units within it; and so does the basic personality structure of its individual members. For on the properties and the development of this system depend those of the institutionalized set of relationships which we call "family"; this, in turn, induces the organization and integration of functions in individual children who as adults will be called upon to carry on, to develop and perhaps to change the institutions of the paramount system which, by means of this and of other homeostatic devices, is enabled to perpetuate at least some of its distinguishing characteristics.

Thus unique as the relationship of "individual" and "society" is, it has this in common with other part-whole relationships characteristic of highly organized, self-regulating systems, that the regularities, the attributes and the behaviour of systems on different levels, and above all those of the paramount system itself, cannot be described simply in terms appropriate to those of their parts; nor can they be explained as effects of which their constituents are the cause. And yet they are nothing outside and apart from these constituents.

Those who approach social phenomena, wittingly or unwittingly, as if societies were nothing but heaps of individual people, and who try to explain the former in terms of the latter, cannot conceive of the fact that groups formed by individuals, like other organizations of part-units, have properties of their own which remain unintelligible for an observer if his attention is focused on individual people as such and not, at the same time, on the structures and patterns which individuals form with each other.

Those who approach social phenomena, wittingly or not, as if these phenomena existed independently of the individuals by whom they are formed, are usually aware of the fact that phenomena of this kind have their irreducible regularities. But expecting, as they have been trained to expect, that the regularities of composite units can be deduced from those of their parts, and perhaps puzzled by the fact that they cannot deduce the social regularities which they observe simply and clearly from individual regularities, they tend to fall into a manner of speaking and thinking which suggests that social phenomena exist in some sense independently of individual people. They tend to confuse "having regularities of their own" with "having an existence of their own", in the same way in which the fact that organisms have regularities which cannot be deduced from those of unorganized physical events is often interpreted as a sign that something in organisms has an existence independently of physical events. Here as elsewhere, the inability to think in terms of systems leaves people with the choice between two equally unpalatable alternatives – that between atomistic and hypostatic conceptions.

Some problems cannot be brought nearer solution mainly because one has not sufficient facts to go on, others mainly because, as problems, they are misconceived: general ideas, types of classes, the whole manner of thinking, may be malformed or simply inadequate as a result of an uncritical transfer of intellectual models from one context to another. Some of the difficulties encountered in social sciences are of this type. They are due to insufficiencies, not so much in the knowledge of facts, as in the basic ideas, categories and attitudes used in making observations of, and in handling, facts. Since people conceived the idea that one might explore not only physical but also social phenomena, as it were, scientifically, those who tried to do so have always been, more or less, under the influence of two types of models developed, in different contexts, by two more powerful groups: models of setting and solving problems about social phenomena current in society at large, and those of dealing with problems about "nature" developed by natural scientists. It is a question of how far either of these two types of model is suited to scientific inquiries into social phenomena. By raising it, one adumbrates the need for re-examination of a wider problem: that of the nature and acquisition of human knowledge generally.

Models of the first type are often used unintentionally by social scientists. They are concerned with phenomena from a sphere of life in which the contingency of unmanageable dangers is continuously high; it is difficult for them to disengage the ideas and concepts they use in their specialized work as scientists from those used day by day in their social life. The hypothetical model used for the study of problems of this kind is a continuum of which one marginal pole is formed by properties of persons and their situation characteristic of complete involvement and complete lack of detachment (such as one might find in the case of young babies), and the other of properties characteristic of complete detachment and a zero-point of involvement.

Models of the second type, those of natural sciences, are often, though not always, copied deliberately by social scientists; but they do not always examine, at the same time, in what respect these models are consonant with their specific task. Pressed by uncertainties not unconnected with the strength of their involvements, they are apt to seize upon these models as on ready-made and authoritative means for gaining certainty, often enough without distinguishing clearly whether it is certainty about something worth knowing or something rather insignificant which they have gained in this way. As one has seen, it is this mechanical transfer of models from one scientific field to another which often results in a kind of pseudo-detachment, in a malformation of problems and in severe limitations of topics for research. The hypothetical model used for the study of problems of this kind is a continuum of models of composite units arranged according to the degree of interdependence of part-units. By and large, problems of the physical sciences have as their frame of reference concepts of units with a relatively low degree of organization. Problems referring to units of an equally low degree of organization – for example, to populations in the statistical sense of the word, are not lacking in the social sciences. But in their case units of this type are always parts of other far more highly organized units. Types of concepts, of explanations and procedures used for inquiries into the former are, at best, only of limited use in scientific studies of the latter; for in their case, in contrast to that of units of low organization, the knowledge one has gained about properties of isolated parts can only be assessed and interpreted in the light of the knowledge one has gained of properties of the whole unit.

If it is difficult for social scientists to attain greater autonomy of their scientific theories and concepts in relation to public creeds and ideals which they may share, it is no less difficult for them to gain greater autonomy in the development of their scientific models in relation to those of the older, more firmly established and successful physical sciences. The crucial question is whether it is possible to make much headway towards a more detached, more adequate and autonomous manner of thinking about social events in a situation where people in groups, on many levels, constitute grave dangers for each other. Perhaps the most significant insight to be gained from such reflections is the awareness of what has been named here, inadequately enough, the "principle of increasing facilitation": the lower the social standards of control in manipulating objects and of detachment and adequacy in thinking about them, the more difficult is it to raise these standards. How far it is possible under present conditions for groups of scientific specialists to raise the standards of autonomy and adequacy in thinking about social events and to impose upon themselves the discipline of greater detachment, only experience can show. Nor can one know in advance whether or not the menace which human groups on many levels constitute for each other is still too great for them to be able to bear, and to act upon, an overall picture of themselves which is less coloured by wishes and fears and more consistently formed in cross-fertilization with dispassionate observation of details. And yet how else can one break the hold of the vicious circle in which high affectivity of ideas and low ability to control dangers coming from people to people reinforce our work?

Addenda 1977/78

Page 14: Scientific investigations are very far from "value-free", but the type of valuations prevalent in the works of natural sciences is not determined by extra-scientific factors. This distinguishes the natural sciences from the social sciences at the present stage. In the latter, the influence of valuations entering scientific work from outside, from positions taken up within the conflicts of society at large, that is, the influence of heteronomous valuations, is very great. In the former, the natural sciences, the influence of this type of valuations, has been virtually eliminated. In them, a different type of valuations has come to the fore. The cognitive value of the result of a piece of research is determined primarily by its function in relation to a still unsolved scientific problem, e.g. by its contribution to the discovery of the immanent connections between physical or biological events; to this function the relation of research results to the person of the scientist, or to his or her extra-scientific ideals are wholly subordinated. This is what is meant by the term "autonomous valuations" referred to here. They prevail in the natural sciences.

In contrast, extra-scientific, heteronomous valuations prevail in the social sciences, particularly in sociological theories.

The distinction between heteronomous and autonomous, extra-scientific and intra-scientific valuations supersedes the misleading one between "evaluative" and "value-free" . . disciplines.

However, the distinction in absolute terms is useful only as long as one works with a short-term perspective, such as that which is used if one compares natural and social sciences here and now. In terms of a process-sociological, a long-term perspective, it is preferable to use, as a conceptual tool, the model of a balance. In that sense one can speak of the scale between the imaginary poles of absolute autonomy and absolute heteronomy of valuation. It coincides with that between the imaginary poles of total involvement and total detachment. The greater the involvement the greater the tendency towards heteronomous valuations: the greater the detachment the greater the tendency towards autonomous valuations. In this form the sliding scale of a balance-relationship between involvement and detachment, between the heteronomy and autonomy of valuations, can be applied to observable structural changes in people as societies and as individuals. It can be tested by studies of changes in human speech and thinking from their magical–mythical to their scientific forms, of changes from infantile to adult behaviour and experience, or by systematic comparisons between the human and natural sciences at the present stage of development. In all these cases the first term of the pair, as compared to the second, represents more involved behaviour and experience, more I– or We–centred communication, a greater heteronomy of valuations. In all these cases and many others, the theoretical model under discussion here can serve as a verifiable and modifiable means of orientation.

Page 14: Through magical practices one could – as one saw it – secure direct help in danger or the fulfilment of wishes. Magicians can say: I shall deliver you here and now from your sufferings. Scientists who for instance were called upon to fight a yellow-fever epidemic or who today combat cancer, may be very deeply affected by the suffering of the sick and dying; but until they have discovered, through impersonal and often very protracted research, the explanation for the illness, they cannot presume to help the sufferers. That is, they can only contribute to remedying human problems by the detour of research, the detour *via* detachment.

Page 19: Only by being aware of the compelling nature of this vicious circle can one understand the extraordinary slowness of the development of mankind in its early stages. Only thereby can one divest oneself of the naive egocentrism which today – now that the jaws of the trap posed by non-human natural events have opened somewhat, now that one has learned as the result of a blind process how to control oneself in order to control extra-human nature – presents this relatively late phase in human development as the natural and eternal state of mankind. This idea is embodied in concepts such as "reason" or "nature", which suggest that one's own way of mentally coming to terms with natural events has been inbuilt by nature in people for all eternity. One encounters here a central problem of the whole development of humanity, which has been concealed up to now by the naive egocentrism embodied in our whole conceptual world: how was it possible at all for people to prise open the jaws of the trap and escape the vicious circle?

Page 36: The idea that the method of research is the decisive criterion of its scientific status, and the closely related idea that the goal of research is the discovery of ultimate "truth", lead among other things to a blurring of the distinction between empirical–theoretical sciences and areas of research such as pure mathematics and formal logic. In the case of the latter one cay say with some justice that they aim at discovering definitively true knowledge and at distinguishing this from absolutely wrong judgements. But as applied to the positive sciences, the concept of absolute, ultimate truth as a description of the goal of their research is ambiguous and inadequate.

To touch briefly on the difference between pure mathematics and logic on the one hand and the theoretical–empirical sciences on the other: the former are concerned exclusively with investigating the immanent order, unplanned by humans, of human-made symbols of relationships. In this case one does not need to be concerned whether and how far human symbols are suited to expressing connections between observable events not created by human beings. To reach the pure mathematician's goal of cognition, no experiments are needed. To the purely mathematical and logical sciences the conceptual distinction between theoretical and empirical aspects cannot be applied. They are, if one may put it like this, single-track sciences. To be sure, one can distinguish various levels of abstraction within them – for example, symbols for relationships between symbols and then symbols for the relationships between these symbols – but what is at issue is always the validity of the mental operations through which the immanent order of the symbols is unfolded; and just because one is here concerned solely with the internal consistency of the symbolic operations, one can call the results of the investigation, if one will, "true" or "false" in the traditional manner.

But in the theoretical–empirical, the positive sciences, the situation is different. They are attuned to the exploration of relationships between events which, while being representable by human symbols, are not created by human beings and are consequently non-symbolic in nature. Unlike the purely mathematical–logical sciences, the empirical–theoretical sciences are double-track. The common feature of their procedure is not what is today called, physicalistically, "the scientific method", but a specific form of interdependence between theoretical and empirical research. They demand a constant guiding of detailed empirical investigations by comprehensive, integrating theories and a constant testing of these theories by detailed empirical investigations. The fundamental interdependence and inter-change between empirical and theoretical studies are the struc-tural property which all the empirical–theoretical sciences share, and which distinguishes them from non-scientific attempts to attain knowledge. The isolating excision of a single research operation from the advancing dialectic of this scientific process, which is a pre-condition for labelling its results ultimately true, has at best instrumental significance. The advance of research shows how experience has taught us that what may first seem the absolutely definitive result of research, while not necessarily wrong, is at all events only a partial result. It is consequently a misleading simplification to present the discovery of absolute truth or falsehood as the goal of these double-track sciences.

To do justice to their goals, considerably more complex concepts than "true" or "false" are needed. What distinguishes the results of research from each other in this sphere is often enough no such absolute dichotomy, but a greater or lesser measure of "truth", of reality–congruence of symbols.

By this use of comparative instead of polar concepts one can convey that all research in the case of two-track sciences is relatively open-ended. Even in choosing one's terms one does well to leave room for the possibility that today's results of research which represent an advance compared with those of yesterday, will be followed by others tomorrow which will represent an advance in relation to today's results. The philosophical notion of absolute truth or absolute validity, as the goal of the natural sciences or of any other empirical–theoretical science is as deficient as conceptualization of this goal as its counterpart, as absolute relativism. Both lack understanding of the fact that terms such as the development of science or the growth of knowledge refer to a specific type of order. It can be figuratively represented by the ascent in multi-storey buildings. One cannot ascend to the fifth floor without having passed the first, the second and the other preceding floors. But there is no predetermined necessity which makes it predictable that people will or must ascend from the fourth to the fifth floor. The goal of science is best described in terms of progression or regression. At any given moment in time, their representatives try to solve unsolved problems of their generation of problems; they attempt to progress beyond the given state of knowledge of their generations or inadvertantly regress.

Notes

1. It is still the prevalent practice to speak of psychological characteristics and of social characteristics of people not only as different, but as separable and, in the last resort, independent sets of properties. And if this is the assumption underlying one's form of discourse, terms like "involved" and "detached", as they are used here, must appear as equivocal and vague. They have been chosen in preference to other perhaps more familiar terms precisely because they do not fall in line with linguistic usages which are based on the tacit assumption of the ultimate independence of psychological and social properties of humans. They do not suggest, as some current scientific concepts do, that there are two separate sets of human functions or attributes, one psychological and one social in character, which communicate with each other only occasionally during a limited span of time with a definite beginning and a definite end by means of those one-way connections which we call "causes-and-effects", and then withdraw from each other until a new causal connection is established again with a definite beginning and a definite end.

   Both these terms express quite clearly that changes in a person's relation with others and psychological changes are distinct but inseparable phenomena. The same holds good of their use as expressions referring to people's relation to "objects" in general. They seem preferable to others which, like "subjective" and "objective", suggest a static and unbridgeable divide between two entities, "subject" and "object". To give a brief and all too simple example of their meaning in this context: a philosopher once said, "If Paul speaks of Peter he tells us more about Paul than about Peter." One can say, by way of comment, that in speaking of Peter he is always telling us something about himself as well as about Peter. One would call his approach "involved" as long as his own characteristics, the characteristics of the perceiver, overshadow those of the perceived. If Paul's propositions begin to tell more about Peter than about himself the balance begins to turn in favour of detachment.

2. This concept has been introduced here in preference to the distinction between scientific procedures which are "value-free" and others which are not. It rather confuses the issue if the term "value", in its application to sciences, is reserved to those "values" which intrude upon scientific theories and procedures, as it were, from outside. Not only has this narrow use of the word led to the odd conclusion that it is possible to sever the connection between the activity of "evaluating" and the "values" which serve as its guide; it has also tended to limit the use of terms like "value" or "evaluation" in such a way that they seem applicable only in cases of what is otherwise known as "bias" or "prejudice". Yet, even the aim of finding out the relatedness of data, their inherent order or, as it is sometimes expressed, at approximating to the "truth", implies that one regards the discovery of this relatedness or of the "truth" as a "value". In that sense, every scientific endeavour has moral implications. Instead of distinguishing between two types of sciences, one of which is "value-free" while the other is not, one may find it both simpler and more apposite to distinguish in scientific pronouncements between two types of evaluations, one autonomous, the other heteronomous, of which one or the other may be dominant.

3. The problem of "facing oneself" is no doubt far more complex than can be shown here. It plays its part in explorations of nature as well as in those of society. For humans form part of both. Every major change in people's conception of nature, therefore, goes hand in hand with a change of the picture they have of themselves. So does any change in their conception of the social universe. Success and failure of any attempt to change from a more involved to a more detached view of social phenomena are bound up with the capacity of people to revise the picture they have of themselves in accordance with the results of more methodical studies, and often enough in a way which runs counter to deeply felt beliefs and ideals. In that respect the problem of increasing detachment in the social sciences is hardly different from that which plays its part in the development of the natural sciences.

However, it must still be regarded as an open problem how far people are capable of "facing themselves", of seeing themselves as they are without the shining armour of fantasies shielding them from suffering past, present and future. It is fairly safe to say that their capacity to do so grows and declines with the degree of security which they enjoyed and enjoy. But it probably has its limits.

However that may be, at present such problems can be discussed only in societies which demand and produce a high degree of individualization and in which people are being brought up to experience themselves, more perhaps than ever before, as beings set apart from each other by very strong walls. There can be little doubt that the picture of self which is thus built up in the growing person makes it rather difficult to envisage oneself in a more detached manner as forming patterns with others, and to study the nature and structure of these patterns as such.

4. The evident differences in the levels of development of different social sciences have perhaps not attracted quite the attention they deserve as a subject of research. Like the differences in the development of natural and social sciences generally, they are relevant to any theory of knowledge and of sciences.

To set out here more comprehensively the problems raised by such differences would require an exposition of the wider theory of knowledge implied in these observations on detachment and involvement; it would require fuller elaboration of the general conceptual framework that has been used here and within which, as one has seen, the development of scientific thinking, as of thinking in general, and that of changes in the situation of those who think, instead of being allotted to largely independent fields of studies, are linked to each other as different, but inseparable and interdependent, facets of the same process. Only with the help of such an integrating framework is it possible to determine with greater precision different stages and levels of thinking and knowing, whether or not one adopts concepts like "level of detachment", "level of fitness", "level of control" and others which have been used here.

On these lines, one might say, for example, that, under present conditions, anthropologists have a better chance of developing theories on human relations to a higher level of fitness than, say, those engaged in the study of highly differentiated societies to which they themselves belong or which are antagonists or partners of societies to which they belong; they have a better chance, not only because it is easier to survey, and to form relatively fitting theories about, social units which are small and not too complex in structure, but also because the investigators themselves are, as a rule, less directly involved in the problems they study. Anthropologists, in most cases, study societies to which they do not belong, other sociologists mostly societies of which they are members.

But in saying this, one refers only to one facet of the relationship between the mode of thinking and the situation of those who think. To complete the nexus one would have to add that the more detached theoretical tools of thinking which anthropologists have a chance to build up in accordance with their specific situation, can themselves act, within certain limits, as a shield against the encroachment upon their scientific work, and perhaps even on their personal outlook, of more involved, more emotive forms of thinking, even if tensions mount between social units to which they belong as participant members and others in relation to which they play mainly the part of investigators.

Here, too, in comparative studies on the development of social sciences, it may be more appropriate and more profitable to focus on the relations of observers and observed than on either of them or on "methods" alone.

5. Even in the elementary form in which it is presented here, such a serial model may help to clarify the confusion that often arises from an all too clear-cut dichotomy between congeries and systems. Not all frames of

reference of physical problems cluster narrowly around the congeries pole of the model. Not all frames of reference of biological or sociological problems have their equivalent close to the other pole. They are, in each of these areas of inquiry, more widely scattered than it is often assumed. And although, in each of these areas, their bulk can probably be assigned to a specific region of the serial model, frames of reference of the problems of different disciplines, projected on this model, frequently overlap.

6. In the case of the second law of thermodynamics, an experimental and statistical law has been interpreted as a statement about qualities possessed by the referential system as a whole, that is, by the physical universe. However, if one may use experiences in other fields as a model, it is not always safe to assume that properties observed as those of constituent parts of a system are also properties of the system as a whole. Whether or not one is justified, in this case, to assume that regularities observed in a part-region of a system, in a part-region of both time and space, can be interpreted as regularities of the whole system, only physicists are entitled to judge.

However, these general considerations about laws are hardly affected by this case. In physics as in other scientific disciplines the referential framework of problems is far from uniform. Although, in the majority of cases, the units of observation are simply conceived as heaps, there are others in which they are envisaged as units endowed with properties approaching to those of systems. But compared with the models of systems and processes developed in some of the biological and some of the social sciences, those which have been produced in physical sciences show, on the whole, a relatively high independence of parts and a relatively low degree of organization.

This may or may not account for the fact that although the status of laws, in the classical sense of the word, has to some extent declined in the physical sciences with the ascendance of models which have some of the characteristics of systems, the change does not appear to be very pronounced. What apparently has become more pronounced is the implied expectation that the diverse laws discovered in studies of isolated connections will eventually coalesce and form with each other a comprehensive theoretical scaffolding for the behaviour of the overall system as a whole. Perhaps it is not yet quite clear why one should expect that the unconnected clusters of connections whose regularities one has more or less reliably determined will subsequently link up and fall into pattern. To expect that they will do so, at any rate, means assuming that in the end all congeries including that of energy-matter will turn out to be systems of a kind, or aspects and parts of systems.

7. One need hardly say that the same argument holds good with regard to the old dispute about the relationship of what is traditionally called "body" and "mind". In this case too proposals for the solution of the problem on purely physical and on metaphysical lines are usually representative of the same style of thinking, and equally inept. They may be monistic or dualistic; they may credit the "mind" with qualities of "matter" or "matter" with qualities of the "mind", all these propositions trying to account for the whole in terms of its parts.

Part II

The Fishermen in the Maelstrom

IX

Perhaps one can clarify what has been said so far about this circularity by using as an illustration an episode from Poe's story about the descent into "the Maelstrom".

One may remember that the fishermen, while they were slowly being drawn into the abyss of the whirlpool, for a while still floated, together with other pieces of wreckage, around the walls of its narrowing funnel. At first, both brothers – the youngest had been lost in the storm already – were too overcome by fear to think clearly and to observe accurately what was going on around them. After a time, however, one of the brothers, so Poe tells us, was able to shrug off his fears. While the elder brother cowered helplessly in the boat, paralysed by the approaching disaster, the younger man collected himself and began looking around with a certain curiosity. It was then, while taking it all in almost as if he were not involved, that he became aware of certain regularities in the movements of the pieces that were being driven around in circles together with the boat. In short, while observing and reflecting, he had an "idea"; a connecting picture of the process in which he was involved, a "theory," began forming in his mind. Looking around and thinking with sharpened attention, he came to the conclusion that cylindrical objects went down more slowly than objects of any other shape, and that smaller objects sank more slowly than larger ones. On the basis of this synoptic picture of the regularities in the process in which he was involved, and recognizing their relevance to his own situation, he made the appropriate move. While his brother remained immobilized by fear, he lashed himself to a cask. Vainly encouraging the older man to do the same, he leapt overboard. While the boat, with his brother still in it, descended more rapidly and was, in the end, swallowed by the abyss, the cask to which he had tied himself sank very slowly, so that gradually, as the slope of the funnel's sides became less steep and the water's gyrations less violent, he found himself again at the surface of the ocean and eventually returned to the living.

The fisherman, in short, found himself involved in a critical process which at first appeared wholly beyond his control. For a time, he may have clutched at some imaginary hopes. Fantasies of a miracle, of help from some unseen persons, may have crossed his mind. After a while, however, he calmed down. He began to think more coolly; and by standing back, by controlling his fear, by seeing himself, as it were, from a distance like a figure on a chess–board forming a pattern with others, he managed to turn his thoughts away from himself to the situation in which he was caught up. It was then that he recognized the elements in the uncontrollable process which he could use in order to control its condition sufficiently for his own survival. Symbolically representing in his mind the structure and direction of the flow of events, he discovered a way of escape. In that situation, the level of self-control and the level of process-control were, as one can see, interdependent and complementary.

X

However, what one encounters here is a critical process of a specific type. People,[8] in this case, still have a chance of controlling both their own strong affects and some aspects of the critical situation itself. They still have a chance to observe the relations of relevant elements in the process with a measure of detachment, to find a possible solution to the problem of their own survival unimpeded by emotional fantasies, that is, in a relatively object-adequate or "realistic" manner, by forming an integrating symbolic representation (a "model", a "theory"), and to change their situation in accordance with their requirements by means of an action based on this symbolic representation.[9]

Not all forms and stages of critical processes offer those involved in them such chances. There are processes where the experience of an imminent danger is so overwhelmingly strong that relative detachment and the control of fear become, for most people, unattainable, even though the process itself, as they might see if they could collect themselves and reflect with a measure of detachment, still offers them chances of control and thus of remaining whole.

There are, however, also critical processes which have gone so far that, for those involved in them, no chance remains of keeping their physical and mental integrity intact or even of securing their survival. Great though their detachment, their capacity for realistic reflection, might be, the process has reached, for them, the point of no return. They cannot save themselves, whatever they might think or do. It is less likely that, if his boat had already drifted deeper down towards the bottom of the funnel, the fisherman would have been able to think realistically and, without being deflected by fear or despair, to form as a guide to action a fairly well fitting symbolic model of the process that involved him. And even had he been able to form such a model, at that stage it would no longer have been of any use. His position within the process would no longer have given him a chance to change by means of any action what were, for him, its relevant aspects.

Nor is a cool head in a dangerous situation always best suited to a person's salvation or survival. A warrior, for instance, may have no choice but to enter the fray fighting furiously and valiantly. In such a situation, taking a risk may be more realistic than a high measure of caution and affect-control, or long pauses of anticipatory reflection. Force, skill, courage and a hot temper may be here of greater value for a person's survival than a high capacity for sustained self-control – even though a bit of reflection may still help.

There are also cases where people hit upon a way of getting out of a critical situation more by accident than design. But even that is only possible if the structure of the process in question offers the humans involved in it loopholes for escape. If huge meteors rain from the sky on men at a stage of social development where they have neither the knowledge nor the means for coping with such an emergency, or where, having the knowledge and the means, they are not prepared for it, the chances of escaping destruction are, for people in the territory concerned, rather dim. Some may nevertheless survive by accident or good luck. However, if the attack is sustained and covers the whole of the earth, neither foresight nor luck will be of much help.

XI

The parable of the fisherman underlines the functional interdependence of a person's emotional balance and the wider process to which it is geared. It brings into fuller relief the possible circularity of this relationship. The attitude of the older brother points to this circularity. High exposure to the dangers of a process tends to heighten the emotivity of human responses. High emotivity of response lessens the chance of a realistic assessment of the critical process and, hence, of a realistic practice in relation to it; relatively unrealistic practice under the pressure of strong affects lessens the chance of bringing the critical process under control. In short, inability to control tends to go hand in hand with high emotivity of response, which keeps the chance of controlling the dangers of the process at a low level, which keeps at a high level the emotivity of response, and so forth.

This kind of circularity – a physio-psychological and socio-psychological double-bind – is by no means rare in the development of human societies. If it has not been readily perceived and has hardly been conceptualized so far, it is because the categorical apparatus characteristic of the presently dominant code of thinking militates against its discovery. People brought up in a physicalist tradition are used to looking only for explanations in terms of mechanical cause-and-effect connections. In these terms, the whole world is made to appear as a heap of ontologically independent bits and pieces – what interdependence there is, appears to be additional to independently existing entities or events. The understanding of existential interdependencies is still retarded. Again and again, people argue as if a "subject" of knowledge, a "man without world" or "reason without anything to reason about", existed on their own as independent entities, and as if the world, too, under names such as "objects" or "environment", existed as an independent entity on the other side of a divide.

Yet it is obvious that the whole existence of human beings is geared to a world – their lungs to the air, their eyes to the sunlight, their legs to the firm earth, and their hearts to other humans. The interdependence is basic: it determines the way "objects" act upon "subjects", "subjects" upon "objects", non-human nature upon humans, humans upon non-human nature. Whatever one likes to call it, it is an ontological, an existential interdependence. Ontological dualism, the notion of a world split into "subjects" and "objects", is misleading. It gives the impression that "subjects" can exist without "objects". It induces people to ask which of the two functions is cause and which is effect. Where units stand ontologically in a relationship of functional interdependence, as in the case of stomach and brain, economic and political institutions, or, for that matter, human beings and non-human nature, one encounters connections of a type no longer adequately covered by a mechanical cause-and-effect model. Circular processes, and double-binds as one of their subdivisions, are, in that case, the rule.

Even the classification as a feedback mechanism cannot reconcile the circularity of such processes with the cause-and-effect model. The former is a stationary and harmonious device, the latter an aspect, or, as the case may be, a phase in a natural or social process. If it has the character of a double-bind, moreover, it is, unlike a feedback, fuelled by pent-up structural tensions and conflicts; that is, it has a potential for change even though the change may be blocked or take the form of a very slow and gradual process, ending perhaps in a break through the double-bind, as in the case of the take-off into science.

As part of an interdependence theory, the sociological concept of a double-bind figuration covers a wide variety of cases. Some examples may help to clarify this type of circularity and the related problems of involvment and detachment. Inevitably, the examples are more complex than the parable; nothing more than a brief outline is possible here – just enough to put a bit more meat on the empirical bones. The examples chosen are perhaps a bit unexpected. They are, firstly, the relationship between pre-scientific, magical–mythical forms of thinking and the level of danger and insecurity that impinges upon the lives of people who experience the world and themselves in this manner; and, secondly, the present drift towards atomic war. Under the dominant code of our age, one may not recognize these episodes of what are, respectively, the physio-social and the social process, as examples of a double-bind. That is just the point.

XII

The people of pre-scientific societies are, to a much greater extent than those of scientific societies, exposed to the blind vagaries of nature, including their own. Their capacity for protecting themselves against unwelcome natural processes and of bending them to their needs is comparatively limited. The members of more developed societies enjoy the benefit of a vast social fund of knowledge. Thanks to a perhaps unusual continuity of inter-generational transmission of knowledge over several thousand years, they have become the heirs of great riches in the form of knowledge and the practices connected with it. The stupendous knowledge growth of the last four or five hundred years is the greatly accelerated later phase of a long, antecedent social process where advances in knowledge were far more haphazard and intermittent and the tempo of advance very much slower. Helped by the spade-work of these earlier ages, the fund of knowledge available in scientific societies has become more comprehensive and, at least with regard to the non-human levels, more realistic – that is, more congruent with the factual course of events than with the promptings of people's wishes, fears and the fantasies connected with them. In conjunction with the growth of knowledge, the safety area which men build for themselves, the area amenable to their control, has become very much larger than it used to be.

All planned social practices take place within a stream of unplanned and aimless, though structured, processes at a variety of interdependent levels. They are known by a variety of names, such as "nature", "society" and "self". The extent of control which people can exercise over these processes and the manner of their control differ from society to society in accordance with their stage of development. Over the millenia, human groups, with the help of the growing social fund of their knowledge, have been busily building into the undiscovered and uncontrollable universe a widening safety area for themselves – an area of known connections which they can more or less control. As a result, people are now able in certain areas to steer their way through the flow of blind and unmanageable processes better than their forebears – at least at the physical levels, if less so at the human levels, just as people aboard ships steer their way through the unmanageable waters of the ocean or, in spaceships, through the uncontrollable processes of the sun-system. In that way, by expanding their control within the uncontrollable flow of events, humans, in the more advanced societies, have managed to provide themselves with a larger protective shell designed, as far as possible, to keep out the dangers that emanate from the non-human levels of the overall process. They have not yet managed to develop an equally comprehensive and realistic fund of knowledge at the human or social levels. Hence, they are not yet able to bring under control the dangers that human beings constitute for each other and themselves. In that respect, the double-bind situation in which low ability to control dangers and high fantasy-content of knowledge maintain and perhaps escalate each other – the situation at work all round in simpler societies – still prevails in those societies which at present count as the most advanced.

Like other heirs of great riches, the members of scientific societies are not, as a rule, particularly interested in knowing how their ancestors in earlier days managed, with many ups and downs and although this growth was not planned by them, to make the fund of human knowledge grow, in that way contributing to the wealth which they, the living, have inherited. The heirs appear to have some hesitation in picturing for themselves what it was like to cope with the necessities of life and to struggle for survival equipped with a social fund of knowledge which was very much smaller and in many respects more uncertain than their own. Perhaps they feel that a more realistic knowledge of the long knowledge process would conflict with their image of themselves as independent and self-contained individuals who owe their knowledge and self-control entirely to their own learning and reasoning – in short, to themselves; or else that it might impair the wisps of superiority-feeling that they have in relation to people from societies with a smaller social fund of knowledge and a lesser capacity for sustained self-control and detachment? Members of more advanced societies sometimes appear to believe that the wider compass, the lower fantasy-content and greater realism of their knowledge are due, not to their position in the sequential order of social development, but to some superior personal qualities – of "rationality", "civilization" or "self-control" – which they possess by virtue of their own nature and which people at earlier stages of this development, including their own ancestors, did not or do not possess or possess only in smaller doses. They might say of these people, "They are just superstitious and irrational", which may seem like an explanation but, in fact, explains nothing. It simply means: "We are better."

These ancestral groups, or comparable contemporary groups not in the line of succession of a knowledge heritage akin to that of scientific societies, could not know all that is now available to members of the latter. But some of them contributed to that knowledge. The advances of knowledge, like those of other developing fields, follow a strict sequential order. To put it in a nutshell: advance C could not be made before advances A and B, D not before C and so forth. Thus, metal-smelting was not possible before fire-making, carriages not before wheels, the heliocentric view of the universe not before the geocentric, and the relativistic not before either of them. A firmly structured sequential order, widely known from the planned development of technical prototypes – that is, the development leading from "mark 1" to "mark 2", to "mark 3", to "mark 4" and so on – also rules the sequential order of the unplanned long-term development of knowledge. The much more limited, much more fantasy- and emotion-filled fund of knowledge of earlier generations necessarily preceded, though was not necessarily followed by, the very much wider and, by comparison, more realistic and detached fund of knowledge that helps to pattern life and experience in more developed societies.

It is not too difficult to understand that the knowledge of any particular human individual is dependent on the fund of knowledge available in his or her society. Nor is it too difficult to understand that the structural characteristics of this fund of knowledge, for their part, are a function of its position in a diachronic sequential order. They bear, in other words, the stamp of a specific stage in a long intergenerational knowledge process. There is a wealth of evidence to support this statement. Yet people brought up with the rich and, in some parts, comparatively realistic knowledge of scientific societies do not, as a rule, find it easy to understand that their own code of thinking and their own experience of nature as an impersonal, aimless, but structured process, are late products of a long development. They find it difficult to accept that human groups whose fund of knowledge and whose protective shell of controls represent an earlier stage and are, accordingly, much smaller, experience and think about the world according to a different code. This code, however, is an ancestral form and thus a condition and, at the same time, a layer of their own. Being rich in knowledge, they cannot imagine what it is like for human groups to be poor in knowledge and thus, correspondingly, poor in goods. They suffer, in other words, from a peculiar blockage of their power of imagination: they cannot imagine how much of all they know it is possible for human beings not to know.

XIII

To determine the structure of people's "not-knowing" in the words of people who already know is not a simple matter. All these words represent a social level of synthesis or, if one likes, of abstraction, representative of a later stage in a knowledge process. Thus one may ask, for instance, how people of earlier societies experienced nature. Yet, not knowing all that we know, they did not perceive birds and elephants, trees, mountains, clouds and all the rest as a unitary nexus of events connected as mechanical causes and effects and following impersonal laws, or, in other words, as "nature". They did not have conceptual symbols at the very high level of synthesis and abstraction that is characteristic of concepts like "cause", "time" or "nature". If one asks, therefore, how they experienced "nature", one is already prejudicing one's case. They did not orientate themselves or communicate with each other about the world around them in these terms. They did not perceive the world as split into the world of humans and the world of nature, into "subjects" and "objects". They experienced it as a world of living things, centred on their own groups and divided by great differences in power and status. Only the most powerless were treated and thought about by them in a manner akin to that in which we treat and think about "objects" – although, of course, at these early stages one could never be entirely certain whether they really were powerless. The Maya had a tale that, at the end of time, the pots, pans and all other domestic utensils would avenge the beating, pushing and shuffling they had suffered from the hands of people and that then they would, for their part, beat people and push them around.

If one wants to find out what people knew and what they could not possibly know of all that is known in our society, one has to be well aware that the knowledge process is not simply additive, one bit of knowledge being added here and another bit there. In the course of this process, the whole structure of human knowledge, and thus of experience, changes as well as the whole manner of thinking. For the operation we call thinking forms part and parcel of people's social fund of knowledge. Like any other knowledge, thinking, the silent manipulation of social symbols, has to be learned; and when one has learned it, one knows it.

At one time or another, humans could not say and, therefore, could not know that two times two is four, because in the process of their development they had not experienced a need for developing conceptual symbols at the relatively high level of synthesis and abstraction represented by our numerals. But that did not mean they could not distinguish between two sticks and four sticks, or even between herds of fifty animals and two hundred animals. If it was of vital interest to them, humans certainly developed at an early stage word- or gesture-symbols that enabled them to orientate themselves and to communicate with each other about such matters as the size of a group of animals. But they did not necessarily proceed as we do by means of a piecemeal operation; they did not mentally dissect the herd into single animals and correlate these "atoms" of the herd to a system of abstract numerals. What they perceived and were able to distinguish at a flash as a result of their training were different configurations. They noticed with a very great power of discrimination different *gestalten* of herds, of groups of enemies or of other matters of relevance to them. Where, at a later stage, people count and measure, at an earlier stage they often performed what one might call an unreflected or primary synthesis. In that way, they were able, within the small range of their vital interests, to distinguish different *gestalten* with great accuracy and with many more details than people from more advanced societies would be able to notice in a similar situation. However, the *gestalten* they perceived and could represent through social symbols were usually conceptualized not as diachronic patterns but as momentary point-like patterns. They indicated what could be seen here and now. To develop symbols of continuous processes in the sequence of time was even more difficult then than it is now.

In the same way, it is possible for humans not to know

distances between localities in terms of our very precise and impersonal concepts such as "miles" and "kilometres" that represent a high level of generalization. Yet if distances were of importance to them, they were well able to develop communicable gestures indicating sleep, which they could use in order to convey to others the distances between localities: they showed how often one would have to go to sleep, how often light would turn into darkness, before one could get there from one's present place. Instead of representing distances as so many kilometres, they represented them clearly, if less precisely, by making, for example, four times, a gesture denoting sleep. The difference is significant. The relative vagueness of certain parts of their knowledge compared with ours is characteristic of their way of life: if translated into our precision, it can easily be falsified.

There are many other examples of such differences. It is very likely that at an earlier stage, human beings did not, and indeed could not, know that the thin sickle of the new moon and the fat round face of the full moon were different appearances of the same thing. They may have had different words for them without necessarily having a unitary word akin to our term "moon", which, after all, represents a synthesis at a higher level compared with the concepts for the different shapes of the moon which one is able to see here and now.

Again, human beings who did not have the integrating concept of an impersonal, mechanical and purposeless course of natural events that follows general laws could not be sure that the sun, after setting, would reappear in the sky. Thus the Aztecs believed that there were special periods during which the danger of the sun, which they saw as a god, not returning from his journey and thus abandoning people was particularly great. In such cases, his continued reappearance could only be assured, they believed, by specific rites and sacrifices, especially human sacrifices.

Members of scientific societies appear to have great difficulties in understanding that members of societies at an earlier stage of development were often unable to distinguish what they themselves distinguish easily and as a matter of course. Thus, they themselves possess, as part of their knowledge heritage, a very precise and highly reality-adequate conceptual distinction between living and non-living things. This distinction is so clear and so easily confirmed by reality-tests that they tend to believe it has sprung up in their own heads. In fact, this distinction took a very long time to develop to its present level of reality-adequacy.

It did so as a result of the combined conceptual labour of a long line of generations in conjunction with the recurrent reality-testing of their concepts in the crucible of their experiences. It is, after all, not particularly difficult to understand that human beings, at some stage in the past, could not yet have known that a volcano or the wild sea, though threatening to destroy them, were not alive and that, if they did destroy human lives, did so unintentionally.

Nor is it imaginable that people always had the very wide knowledge of themselves, of human beings, that is necessary in order to be quite sure that a person could not transform himself or herself into a leopard or a tree. To be certain of it was all the more difficult for them since human beings saw such things happening in their dreams. There, they could easily find themselves or other people changing into whatever it was, a serpent or a baobab tree. How could humans know, *ab ovo*, that many things which happen in dreams cannot happen in reality? How could they know that there is a difference between dream and reality, and what this difference is? For small children everywhere the difference between fantasy and reality is blurred. They learn the distinction between fantasy and reality, along with other items of knowledge, in accordance with the standard reached by their society.

The fact that many human groups at an earlier stage of development regard as living objects those that we know to be inanimate, finds expression in the classificatory label which we attach to them: they are often called "animists". Labels such as this, however, do not help to explain why earlier-stage societies experience as animate, objects that we know to be wholly lifeless. Nor do they explain why, in all known cases, animistic preceded scientific knowledge. Classifying earlier-stage societies in a Linnaean manner, that is, by establishing differences without establishing relationships, is of little help towards a better understanding of the men and women who experience the world in this manner.[10]

The relationship between the development of human knowledge and civilizing processes is of some relevance here. I have already said that earlier-stage people whose fund of knowledge, and especially the knowledge of what we call "nature", was very much smaller than ours, who had not inherited the results of a continuous knowledge growth over thousands of years, could not possibly have related events to each other, could not possibly have thought, in quite the same way that we do. Their standard modes of thinking were, to a much higher extent, permeated by their own affects, by their own wishes and fears. They were to a higher extent geared to fantasies, collective and individual. Having a smaller and less consistently reality-orientated fund of knowledge, their capacity for controlling the dangers to which they were exposed and for evenly and temperately controlling themselves, was also smaller. Greater, therefore, was the insecurity in which they permanently lived; greater, too, their concern with questions like "What does it mean for me or for us?" "Is it good or bad for me or for us?" Greater, in other words, was the innocent self-centredness, higher the level of affectivity of all experiences, all concepts and operations of thinking. The strength and depth of people's involvement in all events which, in their view, could affect their lives, left little room for the preoccupation with problems characteristic of a higher level of detachment and emotional restraint – with questions such as "What is it and why is it so?" "What is it *per se*, independently of what it means for us or for me?"

Once more a brief story may facilitate the understanding of this difference. It is the story of a French general, probably in the nineteenth century, who had command over a force of local troops in one of the warmer parts of Africa. He received the order to march with his troops as quickly as possible to the Mediterranean coast. Accordingly, he started northwards with his warriors, marching hurriedly and, for a while, making very good progress. One night, however, there happened to occur an eclipse of the moon. Next day, his troops refused to continue the march. On inviting their leaders to his tent, he learned that, according to their belief, the darkening of the moon meant that one should stop whatever enterprise one was engaged in for two or three days. The darkening of the moon was an omen. The prophet John, so the leaders told the general, put his cloth in front of the moon as a sign to his people on earth that they should immediately interrupt what they were doing. To disobey such an order, they said, was extremely dangerous. The general, not quite understanding their deep concern, said to them that, if the eclipse of the moon they saw last night was what was bothering them, they really need not worry. If they liked, he would explain to them what had happened on that occasion.

When they consented and said they were very glad to hear what the general had to tell them, he asked them to sit around his table. He took two match-boxes and a stone, put them on the table and indicated with their help the positions of the earth, the sun and the moon in relation to each other. Then, by making the appropriate circular movements with these three objects, he explained to them in a simple way the mechanism of an eclipse. He noticed that they were following him attentively with their eyes. Then, when he had finished, he looked round expectantly at their faces, saying that it was, as they could see, not at all complicated. The leaders nodded their heads in agreement. They were polite men and thanked the general for having taken the trouble to tell them all those interesting things. "All right," said the general. "You can see there is really nothing to worry about. An eclipse of the moon is a perfectly natural thing. So please tell your troops they should be ready to move on in an hour. We must really continue the march as quickly as possible, because I have my orders." "No," said the leaders, "that we cannot do because, as the general has seen, the moon darkened last night and that, as everybody knows, means that the prophet John has given us a sign that we should interrupt any enterprise we were engaged in at the time." The general, in some despair, once more tried to explain to them the nature of an eclipse and they, patiently and politely, again pointed out that, although the general was certainly right, the darkening of the moon was the doing of the prophet and it would be quite impossible to disregard his warning.

Here one has, in a nutshell, the key to the difference of which I have spoken. The tribesmen, as a matter of course, are concerned with the problem: "What does this unusual event signify for us?" It is for them self-evident that what they had seen the night before was a signal for them from the spirit world that some unspecified danger lay ahead. The self-centredness of their mode of experience was spontaneous and unreflected. Their question was not: "What are the inherent mechanics of this event?" The question to which they needed an answer was: "What is the meaning of this event for us?" The general's explanation of the eclipse in purely mechanical terms was without relevance for his troops. It was simply meaningless for them. It did not correspond to the emotional needs of people who normally live at a danger level which was very much higher than the normal danger level of scientific societies.

The difficulty is that the blockage of communication, in this case as in others, is reciprocal. The general, the innocent representative of a scientific society, considers his own code of experience and thinking simply as rational, as something which every human being to whom it is explained is able to understand. Hence he cannot understand the total incomprehension of his troops. They, in turn, cannot understand his total incomprehension of their reasoning. Yet it is not difficult to understand that people who live with a smaller fund of knowledge and, therefore, with a smaller capacity for controlling events that are relevant to their welfare and survival, experience all events to a higher extent in personal terms.

This is another clue to the so-called animistic character of their experience. A causal explanation is, for them, meaningless: it cannot satisfy their emotional needs. Something extraordinary has happened. Their agitated feelings induce a question regarding its significance in personal terms. That question demands an answer in terms of a communication from one living being to another. The traditional knowledge of their tribe provides an answer in these terms. In this case, too, a social fund of knowledge has been handed on from generation to generation, forming the basis for the orientation of the living generations. But this fund of knowledge is attuned to, and represents, a personality structure of a kind that can make communication rather difficult with people of a personality structure whose key word is "rationality".

The clue to what we call "animism" lies both in the higher level of involvement and emotionality characteristic of thought and experience, and in the more limited scope of knowledge which is equivalent to a more limited scope for controlling dangers. The latter, in its turn, helps to maintain a high level of involvement and emotionality. This finds expression in the fact that anything perceived as strongly affecting one's life is also, at that stage, perceived as intended or planned by someone. Members of scientific societies are not as a rule conscious of the high degree of detachment, of self-restraint, of emotional neutrality, that is required in order to realize that events that give one pleasure or pain – especially pain – may be totally unintended results of lifeless causes, of the aimless mechanics of nature, or of what we call accidents.

In the perception of earlier-stage people, accidents happen, if at all, only in matters which are experienced as unimportant and which can thus be treated with emotional indifference – matters which one can dismiss without asking for an explanation. But whatever is perceived as important for oneself, individually or collectively – and unusual events, possible harbingers of unknown dangers, are always experienced as important at this stage – is perceived as intended and, like a human action, raises questions as to its purpose. It is along this line that one has to proceed if one wants not merely to describe, but also to understand and to explain the type of experience and belief which is labelled "animism". The sun is burning relentlessly, no rain is coming, the fields are dry, the crops are withering, the harvest is in danger – we shall starve. For people helplessly exposed to dangers of this kind, to be told in their distress what conflux of impersonal causes has brought these weather conditions about, is meaningless. A comparatively realistic knowledge may offer the only chance of gradually improving the conditions which make them suffer. But they want an immediate answer in personal terms to such questions as "Who is angry with us? Who is punishing us? And why?" If lightning strikes a man's house, burning it down together with two of his children, the bereaved man, who knows nothing about electricity, thunderstorms and the accidents of nature, in his distress more likely than not will ask, "Who has done this to me?" If he has an enemy or a rival, his feelings may fasten onto this other person and he may find relief from the pressure of his emotions by the knowledge that he can act, that he can do something about it, that he can avenge the nefarious deed on that person. Later-stage people in an analogous situation have no one to hate and blame. One cannot hate electricity. But, of course, they have lightning conductors and fire insurance. Possessing a wider and more realistic knowledge, they can protect themselves better against dangers. But theirs, inevitably, is a later stage in the development of knowledge.

The man who accuses an enemy of having, by bad magic, made lightning destroy his house, like the men who experience an eclipse of the moon as a signal given to them by an unseen power, is an exponent of an earlier people, of the primary code of experience of all human beings. Such people perceive the world in terms not of subjects and objects, but of interpersonal relationships between living agents who, though they may not be human, act more or less like the people of their own society. They, one's own group, and other, interdependent groups, serve as the primary model for the perception of the whole world. To be exact, what serves as a model are known groups of people as they are experienced by those who form them, which is, at that stage, in some respects rather different from the way in which later-stage people experience themselves and each other. The latter possess a much wider and comparatively more secure knowledge of the natural processes of humans. At an earlier stage, people are far less certain as to what others are – they may have secret powers, be good or bad spirits – or as to what they may do – they may practise black or white magic, transform themselves into wolves. One is less certain even as to who one is oneself.

The crucial point is that people of scientific societies are brought up with a code of knowledge and thus have a personality structure which enables them normally in their adult life to distinguish relatively clearly between dream and fantasy on the one hand and reality on the other, although, of course, for the children of these societies, as for children everywhere, dream and fantasy merge more easily into reality; for them, dream, fantasy and reality often flow into one another so that the distinction is blurred. Again, to adults of more developed societies it may seem obvious that a grown-up person can distinguish between what is dream and what is real. But it is far from obvious. They had to learn that distinction. The public standard of knowledge makes it possible; the public standard of norms makes it imperative for people in scientific societies to distinguish clearly between dream and reality, as far as these standards demand it, and to act accordingly. This distinction, too, in other words, forms part of the knowledge that people acquire in these societies. In their case, if they act out their dreams in a manner not in agreement with the public standard, they are liable to be declared insane.

However, it took humanity a very long time before they reached that measure of certainty with regard to the distinction between dream and reality that has now been reached in the more developed societies. Even there, however, the blurring of the distinction between fantasy and reality in certain areas of their lives, for instance in politics, is more or less the rule, is publicly permitted and required. There, according to the wider process, the process of disentangling the two may or may not continue. To remember that members of more developed societies learn the distinction between dream and reality while they are growing up, that it forms part of the knowledge they acquire, makes it easier to understand that people at an earlier stage did not have and could not have the same level of knowledge, the same certainty about that distinction. In these earlier societies, the knowledge of the difference between dream and reality, inevitably, was smaller; socially and personally, the boundary line between the two was less firmly drawn and the share of fantasies, public and private, as determinants of action was correspondingly greater.

One needs to know that people's capacity for distinguishing clearly between fantasy and reality has changed, in order to understand fully that people in earlier-stage societies experienced the world as a unitary society of living agents distinguished by their power and status. This primary mode of experience of the world as a society of living beings resembling humans, and of all relevant happenings as deeds with an aim intended by someone, structures the public fund of knowledge in these societies. Hence with the help of this fund, for instance, in the form of traditional communal myths, members of these societies canalize the strong individual need for explanations in terms of human-like living agents in a direction which makes it understandable for, and communicable to, the whole group concerned. In later-stage societies, on the other hand, the public fund of knowledge represents – at least so far as it concerns non-human nature, less so far as human societies are concerned – a comparatively high level of emotional detachment, of reality-orientation as distinct from fantasy-orientation. In these societies, the latter, even in private life, becomes more controlled.

Receiving less support from the public fund of knowledge and its powerful guardians, the primary code of human experience, without losing its force, becomes, while people grow up, a more or less submerged layer of the personality structure. Freud discovered it there and called it – with a not wholly appropriate term – the "unconscious"; not wholly appropriate, for it refers to experience which, although stored in memory, as a result of some blockage cannot normally be remembered at will, even though it continues indirectly to participate in the steering of people's conduct. Thus, although submerged, the primary mode of experience, in magical–mythical terms, remains alive in the adult members of scientific societies. In small children, there as everywhere, it is always very much at the surface – the child runs away from its mother, falls down, hurts itself a little and runs crying back to the mother, perhaps because it feels pain, but also probably because it experiences the falling and the pain as something the mother has magically brought about as a punishment for disobedience or "sin". In fact, one might compare the growth of knowledge to that of a tree: in the wood of the older tree, its surface shape as a young tree still remains visible as an inner layer or ring within the larger shape. Even in scientific societies, almost everyone may experience wisps of paranoiac thought crossing their minds when they have an accident or when something else goes wrong that arouses strong feeling, and their emotion-charged thoughts wander around seeking someone on whom they can fasten, some person or another whom they can blame for the mishap.

It is part of the elementary make-up of people that their emotions, their affects and drives, are primarily attuned to other persons on whom they can fasten, rather than on lifeless things. What we call animism is a stage in the development of societies at which this mode of thought and experience is still both a public and a private mode. It combines with the smaller scope of human knowledge to make people experience everything about which they feel strongly as denoting the intentions of someone and, thus, as being alive.

With that, another aspect of what earlier-stage societies did not and could not know becomes clearer. Later-stage people are apt to ask with regard to them, "Why can't they rely more on what can be seen and observed rather than on their fanciful stories, their mythological fantasies? If they did that they would soon find out that many of the myths they believe in are just fairy-tales and that their magical practices have no effect whatsoever, except by means of a kind of autosuggestion on themselves." Arguing in this manner, one treats it as obvious that systematic observation in the scientific manner, combined with individual reflection, is the gateway to reliable knowledge of the world.

But that means missing the problem. The suitability of a combination of systematic observation and reflection as a method of acquiring worthwhile knowledge depends on what kind of knowledge one regards as worthwhile. Where people experience the world as a society of spirits – and most data about which it is worth asking questions, as the wilful acts of living agents – the essential aim of discovery is the acquisition of knowledge about the hidden aims and intentions behind events, the hidden meaning, for oneself, of signs. These, however, cannot be discovered with the help of the methods we call scientific; they can only be discovered, directly and indirectly, through communication with the spirit world in which its intentions and plans, its character and its aims, reveal themselves. Such a revelation may be contained in the body of tales, of proverbs and prescriptions, oral or written, that is handed down in a group from one generation to another. It may be contained in messages received by a priest, a diviner, an oracle, and handed to those who come to them with a problem. It may be contained in a dream at night or in a sudden illumination in broad daylight – whichever it may be, it is not that people living at an earlier stage of the knowledge process were less able than those at the scientific stage to observe facts. On the contrary, earlier-stage people are, as a rule, extremely observant – within the boundaries of their interests. Nor is their capacity for reasoning in any way less great. If they reason differently, it is because their substantive picture of the world, and of the connections of events within it, is different at this stage. That is the crucial point. The method which people use in acquiring knowledge is functionally interdependent with, and thus inseparable from, the substance of the knowledge they possess, and especially from their basic image of the world. If this image is different, the method they devise for acquiring relevant knowledge is, as a matter of course, different too.

It is not very usual to compare scientific with pre-scientific knowledge in a manner which shows comprehension of both as successive stages in a sequential and directional order. The method used by physicists in acquiring knowledge, often regarded as *the* scientific method *per se* and prescribed normatively for the exploration of processes at all levels of the universe, regardless of the different character of their integration, is thus widely treated as a form of inquiry usable with equal success, whatever the content of the inquiry may be. It is easy to observe, however, that what we now regard as the scientific method came into its own when, and insofar as, people conceived the world as a purely mechanical causal nexus and regarded it as the primary aim of the quest for knowledge to discover causal connections devoid of any purposes or aims. There was no separation of form and content when the substance of the mechanical world-image began to form itself; a method of inquiry appropriate to this kind of nexus began to emerge simultaneously.

One can see it more clearly if one reconstitutes in one's mind the factual sequence in the development of human knowledge that led from the world perceived as a world of human-like agents, spirits who act, who are friendly or hostile as the case may be, to a world of blind, mechanical cause-and-effect connections that obey universal laws. To be sure, in the long process during which the scientific conception gained the ascendancy, one encounters many periods in which these two world models were treated as equivalent, with many attempts at transitional forms. Plutarch wrote an essay discussing the problem of how it can be that people can have two explanations of natural events – explanations in terms of acts of gods and causal explanations. Ptolemy wrote an astrological as well as an astronomical treatise and, as far as we know, considered the knowledge they contained as equal in value.

Thus the changeover from the dominance of a magical– mythical conception to the dominance of a causal conception was anything but abrupt. But the problem of how and why the mechanical conception and the concomitant method of acquiring knowledge, after many ups and downs, gained the ascendancy, still remains largely unanswered. It is not difficult to see the reason why that is the case. Most inquirers, historians of science no less than philosophers of science, treat the pre-scientific conception, the anthropocentric conception, of the world as a society of living agents full of omens, signals and other communications to men, simply as an erroneous conception, as a wrong theory about which one need not bother or about which one needs to bother only insofar as one can discover there anticipations and intimations of the right view. However, this way of perceiving the problem is beside the point. It conceals the human problem of why humans everywhere experience the world, in the first instance, as an animated world, connected by acts of will and interlocking purposes, by signs, omens and other forms of communication, and only rather late as a purely mechanical causal nexus. If, in this way, the order of succession is restored, the difficulties which men had to overcome in order to arrive at the difficulties which people had to overcome in order to arrive at the aim of bringing these difficulties into the open that this and the following discussion are concerned.

XIV

It may be useful once more to cast one's mind back to those early days of mankind when the scope of people's realistic knowledge of the world in which they lived was comparatively small and when correspondingly small, therefore, was the protective shell, the area within which they were able effectively to control dangers. At that stage, the double-bind processes of which I have spoken were probably at work in their most drastic and unrelenting form – a higher danger level perpetuating a high affect – and fantasy-level of knowledge and beliefs, a low level of danger-control thus maintaining exposure to dangers at a high level. The very slow tempo of the advances made by stone-age people, even by those who were biologically our equals, probably had one of its roots here. Today, men and women are very much aware of the fact that they can improve their lot. In those early days, that was not part of their knowledge. Humans at that stage lived like the wild animals they hunted, always on the alert. They lacked the protection of a specific inborn reaction pattern to dangers. Instead, they had a generalized inborn alarm reaction, putting them into a different gear, ready for strenuous action such as fight or flight. But the actual decision as to what to do, what skeletal muscles to move, had to be taken at the non-automatic cerebral levels, patterned by collective and individual experiences of past dangers stored in the memory.

Like anything unusual, innovations probably aroused fears (as they still do to some extent today). One could not know what spirits they might offend, what unknown forces they might set free. Fear of change, noticeable even today, must have been much stronger in those early days. That made the double-bind processes in the life of our ancestors particularly inescapable. They were short of knowledge and short of the triad of basic controls – control over natural processes, over social processes and, individually, over the processes of their own selves. Even at later stages double-bind processes can be observed at all three levels.

Earlier-stage societies did not and could not experience these three levels as specialized and different compartments; they were, for them, not yet "nature" as distinct from "society", nor "society" as distinct from "individual". Their world had the character of a unified society divided into those who were friends and those who were enemies, those who had high status and a high power ratio and, through a whole hierarchy of intermediaries, those who had little power and were nothing. In their lives the danger rate was high and thus reproduced, again and again, a high affectivity and a high fantasy-content in a group's knowledge and beliefs, which kept people's capacity for control at a very low level and danger at a high level.

Moreover, the compelling force of this double-bind was reinforced by the fact that a high fantasy-content can make knowledge emotionally much more attractive for people than knowledge which is more reality-orientated. In our age, learned approaches to the problem of knowledge – philosophical, sociological or historical – tend to neglect this aspect. Knowledge tends to be treated purely as an intellectual problem. The knowing person often appears as "pure reason", or perhaps as *res cogitans*. The problems of knowledge are thus discussed as if knowledge existed in a human vacuum, that is, without reference to human beings, their condition and their personality.

Yet it is easy to see that it is not only the "intellect" but human beings all round who are involved in the pursuit of knowledge. Its emotional significance plays no less a part than its cognitive value in its production and development – it plays a part, for instance, in the struggles that surround innovations in thought. Nor is this aspect of knowledge a matter of guesswork and speculation. The changes which knowledge undergoes, from the earlier, more emotive and naïvely self-centred forms to the later, emotionally more controlled and more object-orientated forms, are as firmly structured as changes in what one may call the purely intellectual aspects of knowledge – in fact, they are hardly separable.

That the transition to the "scientific" form of knowledge entailed a major spurt towards greater emotional control, towards greater detachment, has already been said. But that is not all. Many major scientific discoveries run counter to antecedent wishes and beliefs which people cherish and about which they feel strongly. Hence the struggle for recognition of such discoveries is misrepresented if it appears simply as a contest between unemotional intellectual arguments, and if its emotional relevance is disregarded. Promoters of a scientific innovation have to fight for it, not only because it has to stand up to reasoned counter-argument, but also because the picture of the world that emerges from the discovery may entail, for many people, a profound emotional disenchantment and sometimes an almost traumatic shock.

In fact, spurts of emotional disenchantment are almost a standing feature of great advances in scientific knowledge. Take the transition from the geocentric world-image, represented in the late Middle Ages by the Aristotelian scholastics, to the

Copernican world-image which proclaims – quite contrary to the unreflective evidence of the senses – that the earth moves around the sun. If this change in human knowledge is understood only in narrow scientific terms as a theory which agreed better than the antecedent theory with measurements and calculations, one misses the emotional significance of this change: one overlooks its impact on people's image of themselves and their place in the universe. The geocentric world-image was an expression of unreflected self-centredness, an aspect of people's primary form of experience. For thousands of years, human beings had experienced the heavenly bodies as moving around themselves and thus around the earth as the centre of the universe. They perceived, as a matter of course, the whole world as made for them. Even the gods did not have much else to do apart from being gods for humans. The severe jolt to people's elementary self-love entailed in the assertion of learned people that the earth was moving around the sun is often forgotten today. Yet it is only if one is aware of the emotional significance of the geocentric world-experience that one can give full weight to the question: how was it possible for people to give up an emotionally highly satisfactory picture of the world and to accept, instead, a picture which, although more realistic, relegated humans from a central to a peripheral position in the world and which was thus emotionally rather unsatisfactory? Moreover, this is only one of a whole series of emotional disappointments which people had to suffer with the advance of the sciences.

In this context, this aspect of the developing sciences can only be spoken of in passing. But it helps to put into fuller relief the double-bind processes that were at work in the earlier stages of the development of knowledge. The refutation of the geocentric world-image and the acceptance of the Copernican view as propogated by Galileo raises the question of the changes in the structure of society and the structure of people's personality which made it possible for such a strange idea to be accepted, not merely by a few learned people, but by public opinion in society at large. At least once before, in Greek antiquity, the idea of a sun-centred world, of an earth moving around the sun, had been put forward. Aristarchus of Samos propounded and gave reasons for that view. It was suggested that he should be condemned for impiety, and for a long time the view remained a philosophical oddity without resonance in society at large. One does not in the least belittle the achievement of Copernicus in working out a theoretical model of the world that showed it moving around the sun if one says that a new view of the universe, now recognized as a major scientific advance, as more reality-orientated than the antecedent model, need not necessarily be recognized as an advance and accepted as such in society at large. All too often, the take-off into science is seen only as a change represented by the brilliant ideas of a few great men.

The question of how and why these innovations, among which Galileo's advocacy of the Copernican world-system was one of the most significant, came to be accepted in society at large is, by comparison, rather neglected. The problem of the antecedent double-bind operating at the level of nature stands out more clearly if one asks: what changes in society and in people's personality made possible the acceptance of a world-view which was not only emotionally disappointing but also ran counter to the immediate evidence of the senses? Nor were other innovatory ideas propounded by the pioneers of a scientific method more pleasing. The idea put forward with great emphasis by Descartes, and taken up by many other learned people, that animals were just automata and that even man was an automaton, albeit with a soul, also jolted the traditional dream picture of humans. So, much later, did Darwin's evolutionary theory of people's descent and Freud's recognition of the part played by animalistic drives in people's lives, even in the life of children. The bleak picture of the real moon compared with the beauty of the lovers' moon and the recognition of the sun as a big chain-reaction fuelled mainly by helium and hydrogen point in the same direction.

In fact, the overall picture of the physical universe with its millions of purposeless galaxies and its black holes is rather dismal compared with the beauty of the starlit night-sky as people have learned to see it. The emotional disenchantment in the wake of major scientific advances is not accidental. It is a structural characteristic of that advance. The reason why, again and again, the picture of the natural world unravelled by science proves emotionally disappointing for people, is easy to see: in many respects the natural universe is not the world people would wish it to be. In fact, as it is emerging, through the continued effort of scientists, from the more affective fantasies of human beings, the universe reveals itself as a rather unattractive place. No doubt it has its possibilities. The emergence of humans from unicellular organisms by what appears to be an extraordinary, perhaps unique and certainly aimless conjunction of natural processes, points to these possibilities. The concept of "nature" that has formed itself under the impact of scientific exploration at its simplest, at the physical levels, is incomplete – humans no less than atoms form part of "nature". In fact, it shows the range of nature's possibilities that such complex organisms as human beings, endowed with such extraordinary propensities as consciousness, infinite linguistic varieties and a prodigious memory, have emerged, unplanned, from it. By and large one can say that the rather unfriendly world, nature in the raw, has been made liveable for humans, and probably can be made much more enjoyable for them than it is, but only through their continued and concerted intergenerational effort.

This is, as one can see, the basic paradox of a scientific approach: not only does this approach itself demand considerable emotional restraint, but the picture of the world it presents offers little joy to the feelings of men. However, the removal of dreams – which offer emotional rewards, whether pleasant or unpleasant – the transition to a more reality-orientated approach to the physical world, undoubtedly had its rewards. The more realistic approach which we now call "scientific" or "rational" showed its greater object-adequacy, its higher cognitive value, among other things by the greater power of manipulating physical events and especially of controlling dangers with which it endowed people. It equipped people with much more secure and reliable means of orientation than they had ever possessed before. But, despite the delight which people in the sixteenth and seventeenth centuries took in subjecting traditional views to reality-tests – Descartes, for example, spent a good deal of his life conducting laboratory experiments of various sorts – they could not know at the time the full measure of the rewards which lay ahead for people in the form of health improvement, technical advances, domestic comfort, travel, and in many other fields, if they were willing to give up cherished dream-pictures and accept means of orientation which, although perhaps emotionally unattractive, fitted the realities of their situation, the observable connections of physical events, more closely.

The release from the double-bind that kept people for so long at the magical–mythical level of the experience of "nature" could hardly have taken the form of a short-term event. One touches, at best, the surface of the take-off into science if one treats this transformation only as a change concerning "reason" and as a change represented solely by the great scientific discoveries of a few remarkable people. Both the making of these discoveries and their increasing resonance in society at large suggest that human beings, after a very long preparatory process, had arrived at a stage where their certainty of the new rewards, including new emotional rewards, that awaited them in the form of a more adequate orientation and greater power over "nature" – if they were ready to lessen the hold of magical–mythical beliefs which answered to deeply felt emotional needs – must have been very great indeed. Such certainty, however, could not possibly have been acquired in a generation or two. It could only have been the slowly growing result of a very long process.

If one were to develop a theoretical model of such a process as a provisional guide for future research into the long-term conditions of the take-off into science, one would have to start from the remarkable continuity in the transmission of knowledge from the Middle East via Greco-Roman antiquity and a number of transmitting agencies – Byzantium, the Arabs, the Roman Church among them – to medieval and modern Europe. One would have to say that, in this social-knowledge continuum, proto-scientific forms of knowledge emerged relatively early, and quite often within a framework of magical–mythical forms of knowledge. One would have to say that this proto-scientific knowledge in a magical–mythical framework – for example, in the form of astrology – led to a first take-off into science in antiquity which was relatively short-lived and which failed. It failed, among other reasons, because it was confined to small circles of learned men and found relatively little resonance in society at large. But it did not fail entirely. It left a heritage of both scientific discoveries and scientific concepts. It is doubtful whether the take-off into science during the European Renaissance would have been possible or would have gone as far as it did without these antecedents. In Greek and Roman antiquity purely causal types of explanation and magical–mythical types very often existed side by side. As we have seen, Plutarch wrote an essay in which he raised the question of how it was possible for there to be explanations in terms of gods as well as explanations in causal terms. We have also seen how, in the same manner, Ptolemy wrote not only a treatise on astronomy but also one on astrology. In fact, one can follow, with many great fluctuations, the coexistence of purely mechanical–causal and magical–mythical models of explanation and their struggle for precedence or reconciliation until late in the European seventeenth century.

This reminder of the possibility of taking a long-term approach to the take-off into science may help to round off what was said before about the double-bind processes that have been at work for a very long time in people's relationships with "nature", as well as in their relationships with each other. Many accounts of the rise of science give the impression that human beings, after having for no particular reason believed in all kinds of fantasies, pleasant or hair-raising as the case may be, at one time or another in Athens and Florence – also for no particular reason – came to their senses and from then on, in their steady scientific and technological advance, never looked back again to the old errors. Perhaps I have said enough in order to indicate that this self-image of members of scientific societies – a self-image which underlies most philosophical and many historical and sociological approaches to the rise of science – flatters the self-love of those who believe in it. Pleasing fantasies play a part in it, but it does not stand up to closer examination. In fact, it is quite character-istic of the prevailing approach to the human world of which science forms part. It indicates that, at the level of their social existence, people are still much more deeply involved in double-bind processes than they are at the physical level. Again and again, one comes across symptoms of the contradictory character and the unevenness of what many contemporaries like to envis-age as a uniform "rationality" operating in the same way in people's dealings with "nature" and in their dealings with each other. However, in their dealings with "nature", people have reached a steadily advancing standard of detachment and danger-control. In their dealings with each other, standards of detach-ment and danger-control are lower, and in some spheres, for example, in inter-state relations, not much above the level of early people.

The question of how humans succeeded in loosening the constraints of the double-bind trap in their dealings with "nature" thus gains added weight from the fact that at the social level, in their dealings with each other, they have not yet succeeded in loosening the double-bind constraints to the same extent. With regard to this level, too, the question is raised: how can human beings escape from the circularity of the movement which, from knowledge and beliefs with a strongly emotional fantasy-content, leads to a low ability to control the dangers that humans constitute for each other, and back again from a high level of danger to a high affectivity of knowledge and beliefs?

Among the structural features of the present age, one of the most significant is the discrepancy between the level of object-adequacy and control attained in people's dealings with non-human nature and that attained in the practice and theory of societies. In the former, a definite breakthrough has been achieved; the knot of the double-bind has been undone. This breakthrough, the ultimate take-off into science after an age-long ascent in that direction, was followed by an almost exclusive advance in both scientific knowledge and practical canalization and control. At the level of people's knowledge and control of each other, in spite of a good many proto-scientific advances, no comparable breakthrough has yet been achieved. At this level, people still drive rather helplessly around in circles like the panic-stricken elder fisherman in the maelstrom. Here, high emotionality of thinking and high exposure to the dangers that emanate from humans themselves, reinforce and often enough escalate each other. Moreover, the danger is greatly increased by the fact that people caught in this double-bind, but unaware of it, often consider the wishful thinking and emotive knowledge it engenders as entirely "rational", as reality-orientated.

In earlier days, the danger for humans that came from non-human natural processes probably surpassed, for a time, the danger which humans constituted for each other. At present, in the more developed parts of the world, the reverse is the case. The dangers from non-human forces, although they have in no way disappeared, have receded somewhat, while some of the gravest dangers that menace people emanate from people themselves. At the level of people's life with each other, at the social level, the measure of detachment in thought and action lags far behind that which we have reached at the physical and biological levels. At the social level, the circular movement of relatively high affectivity of thought and action that perpetuates itself in response to the uncontrollable dangers that emanate from human groups and vice versa, continues at a level comparable to people's pre-scientific relationships with non-human nature in former days. Here, groups are still widely chained to each other in the form of inescapable double-bind relationships. Some of these have a potential for destruction resembling that of a natural catastrophe of global dimensions.

XV

An obvious example is the drift towards atomic war. As a case study in social dynamics, the example is illuminating. Nothing shows the compelling force of a double-bind figuration, seen as an unplanned social process, more clearly than this drift.

It is not unreasonable to assume that no person or group of persons on earth that has the means, seriously wants an atomic war or, in cold blood, plans to bring it about. Its likely boomerang effect is fairly obvious. Nevertheless, the drift in that direction is unmistakable. Like the proverbial sword, the threat of an atomic war hangs over us, even though no one wants that war. It is a paradigmatic case of figurational dynamics – of the dynamics that result from the manner in which human groups are bound to each other. The groups in question are, in this case, the states into which humanity is divided, particularly the most powerful among them.

The states of this world are at present bound together in the form of a complex hierarchical order, bipolar at the top, multi-polar at the lower levels. They are arranged in this manner on the basis of differences in their power ratio.[11] This – a state's power ratio – is a combination of a number of basic determinants. Among them are manpower, social capital, raw-material resources, strategic position relative to military techniques, level of productivity, of education, of integration, and some others. As a calibrated combination, they account for the power ratio of a state in relation to other states, and thus for its position in the status and power hierarchy of states which, under competitive pressure, is continually changing and moving.

Within this combination, one determinant plays a key role in the ranking of states – their violence potential, the capacity of a state for using physical violence in its relationship with other states as a means of maintaining or improving its position in the hierarchy. Nothing is more characteristic of the structure of inter-state relations than this fact. It indicates that human beings, at the level of inter-state relations, are still bound to each other at the primeval level. Like animals in the wilderness of the jungle, like tribal groups in humanity's early days, like states throughout history, so the states of today are bound to each other in such a way that sheer physical force and cunning are, in the last resort, the decisive factors in their relationships. No one can prevent a physically stronger state from lording it over weaker states, except another state which is its match in terms of physical force. If another such state exists, the two experience one another, with great regularity, as rivals, each trying to prevent the other from attaining hegemonial power within the whole field. Thus, unless a state is checked by another state that is militarily its equal, there is nothing to prevent its leaders and the people who form it from threatening, exploiting, invading and enslaving, driving out or killing the inhabitants of another state, if they are so minded.

Within states, conditions are different. There, physically stronger persons or groups are normally no longer in a position to exploit, to rob, to injure or to kill weaker persons. That this is normally not possible is a condition of what one usually calls today a "civilized" way of life. That it can be maintained for any length of time is not due simply to the insight, the good will, the morality or the rationality of individual people – not all people can be relied upon to be of good will and to act reasonably. That, within states, the physical superiority of individuals or groups is no longer a decisive determinant of people's relationships with each other – in contrast to the situation in inter-state relationships – is entirely due to the way in which people organize themselves in the form of states or, in other words, to their figuration as states. It is one of the principal characteristics of the type of human grouping which today is called a "state" that, within its web of relationships, people are more or less effectively protected from each other's physical violence. One might say that this is due to the state's legal system, to "the rule of law". Anyone who uses superior capacity for physical violence, whether it is based on muscles or on weapons, in order to exploit, oppress or kill another person, is taken to court. If a verdict of guilty is returned by the jury, the judge will sentence him or her and determine the penalty. However, the effectiveness of legal institutions in the long run depends entirely on the ability of the executive organs of the judiciary to get hold physically of those who have broken the law, to take them to court and, eventually, to prison or the gallows, as the case may be. Thus, legal institutions, up until now, have only functioned effectively if their representatives have been able to rely, actually or potentially, on the use of physical violence to enforce their decisions. Within a state, in other words, there exists as a principal structural characteristic, a special organization whose members are authorized to use physical violence if that is necessary to enforce the law.

One could imagine a condition of human coexistence where people do not need external restraint in order to refrain from the use of violence in their relationships with others. One could imagine a society whose members are able to rely entirely on self-restraint without any extraneous restraint in observing the common rules they have worked out in the course of generations as regulators of their lives together. In that case, individual self-restraint would be strong and reliable enough to make any external restraining force unnecessary. The burden of self-restraint would, in that case, one could assume, balance better and more evenly throughout society against the fulfilment of individual needs for personal satisfaction, meaningfulness and the wish for a pleasant life. In such a society, people who, in conflict with others – there will always be conflicts – or from a lapse of self-control under the pressure of strong affects, have broken the common rules, might be expected to pay whatever compensation or penalty such a society might wish to exact from an individual member for a breach of the common rules. They might submit voluntarily and without the threat or the use of physical force on the part of society's agents, because they could be expected to have insight enough into the workings of human societies to know that no decent and enjoyable coexistence of human beings is possible without everybody's submission to rules, and because, if any person does not keep the rules voluntarily and does not willingly submit to the penalties for breaches of the rules, no one else can be expected to do so either.

That would be a very advanced form of human civilization. It would require, as one can see, a measure and a pattern of individual self-constraint all round which, at the present stage of the social, and within it, of the civilizing process, are not yet attainable. Nor is it certain that they will ever be attainable, though it is worth trying. As long as this condition has not been reached, the individual self-restraint of men and women requires reinforcement through external restraints by means of agencies which are specially licensed to threaten or to use physical violence if that is necessary, in order to ensure a peaceful coexistence of people within their society. All kinds of problems are connected with the existence of such agencies, which I must leave to one side here. Control of these agencies can be misused by the controllers themselves as a means of increasing their own power ratio. It can be used in support of one section of a society in its conflicts with another. But such possibilities do not impair the simple factual diagnosis I have given. Unless the level of individual self-control is very much higher than is normal today and is equally high in all individual members of a society, and unless, in addition, the pattern and balance of restraints differ considerably from those at present known, no peaceful life within a society is possible for any length of time without specialized external restraining agencies that reinforce and supplement individual self-restraint.

At present, these external restraints in a state have, as Max Weber recognized, the character of the state's monopoly of physical violence. The representatives of states in our age have, in most cases, inherited an institutional tradition that makes it a punishable offence for any member of the state to use violence against another, unless he or she has received a special licence to use it from the state authorities. This licence is at present normally given to some specialized armed forces, such as police forces, whose overall function is that of protecting the members of the state in their dealings with each other and of calling to account anyone who acts against the law. The civilizing of these monopolists of physical violence within a state is an unsolved problem. Nevertheless, the existence of such an institutional monopoly, even at the present stage, has far-reaching consequences for the whole tenor of human relationships within a state.

For example: the production and distribution of goods and services, especially distribution and exchange over long distances, take on the characteristics of economic relationships only where state organizations with a fairly effective monopoly of physical force exist, where, in other words, internal pacification has gone fairly far. Without it, contractual obligations cannot be enforced and the acquisition of goods by violent means, whatever its name – war, pillage, piracy or robbery – will be fairly normal. In fact, the specific regularities of economic transactions which form the subject-matter and the *raison d'être* of the science of economics, become operative only in connection with the formation of internally pacified states with a fairly effective monopoly of power that provides a measure of physical security for economic exchanges, including those between states. The formation of state monopolies of physical force, in turn, is functionally interdependent with economic developments such as the formation of social capital and the increasing division of labour. State formation processes and economic processes, or, in other words, processes of social integration and social differentiation, are functionally interdependent, but not reducible one to another.

XVI

In a number of states, particularly the older ones, the efficiency of the monopolization of physical force, and thus the control over violence, has steadily increased during the last three or four hundred years. There, the pacification of human relationships – with frequent relapses – has progressed, and the level of individual revulsion against the use of physical force has risen correspondingly. Yet the relationships between states have hardly changed. Basically they have retained their primal character. Every state can freely use physical violence in its relationships with other states, unless its leaders and citizens are discouraged from using it by another, stronger state. At this level, no monopoly of physical power, no superior force, exists, which can compel even the strongest and most powerful states to keep the peace and to refrain from threatening or using violence in their dealings with other states. There are legal institutions at the inter-state level, too. However, since their rulings cannot be backed by military or police forces which are stronger than those of any possible law-breaker, their effect on inter-state relationships is, at present, rather small.

It would be interesting to explain how this striking structural difference between human relationships within states, where an often quite efficient monopoly of physical force normally exists, and human relationships between states, where no such relationship exists, has come about. I have gone some way towards explaining this difference in *The Civilizing Process* (vol. 2), which contains, among other things, a detailed account of the process whereby the central monopolies of a state, those of violence and taxation, form themselves. To discuss them in detail in this context would lead the analysis too far astray. But it is perhaps of some relevance to say that the existence of such monopolies within states, and their non-existence at the inter-state level, is a good example of the high degree of precision with which sociologists are able to determine differences in social structure.

Many historians and not a few sociologists find it difficult to understand that societies, which are, after all, nothing but networks of functionally interdependent human beings, can have a structure of their own or – what is saying much the same – that human beings as individuals or as groups are bound to each other in specific figurations whose dynamics have a constraining and compelling influence on those who form them. The existence of a monopoly of physical force within states and its non-existence in the relationships between states is an example of the firmness of the structure which interdependent human beings form with one another. It also shows the far-reaching effects which these structures have on those who form them.

At the inter-state level, as I have already mentioned, only one way exists in which a state with a stronger violence potential can be prevented from exploiting to the full its power ratio in relation to other states. It can only be checked by another state with a roughly equal power ratio, or by a group of states if they are able to control the rivalries between them sufficiently to optimalize their combined power potential. Yet in either case, the most powerful state units at the top of the hierarchy of interdependent states are almost invariably driven into a competitive struggle with each other. So strong is the pull of this polarization between the two hegemonial states at the top of the hierarchy that the other states tend to be drawn – sometimes against their better judgement and their wishes – into the orbit of one or the other of the two, just as iron filings are drawn to one or the other pole of a powerful magnet. Thus, the elimination struggle for hegemony between the power units at the top determines, to a considerable extent, the grouping of states throughout the whole hierarchy of states, though not without reciprocity, since the groupings of the less powerful states in turn affect the tension balance between the states at the top.

In a social field where no effective monopoly of physical violence exists, each power unit, in this case each state and particularly each of the hegemonial states, finds itself drawn into an unplanned process, which, to a considerable extent, determines the decisions and actions of their members and leaders in relation to other states. As I have already said, at this level, human groups still live in relation to each other under conditions that prevailed long before groups with the characteristics of states developed. In our age, human groups in the form of states – as was the case before with bands or tribes – are still bound to each other in such a way that the stronger can exploit, subdue or annihilate the weaker groups without any prospect of effective help or redress for the latter. The stronger group need not fear any punishment. No one has a power ratio higher than that of the strongest states.

One may ask why a stronger state should wish to attack a weaker one. But that is not quite the point. The decisive fact is that, at the inter-state level, the stronger power unit *can* attack weaker groups. As there is no one who can prevent such attacks, human groups bound to each other without a central monopoly of physical violence inevitably live in a continuous state of insecurity. If there are some who are, or who believe they are, stronger than their neighbours in terms of violence potential, there is always the possibility that they may try to turn their superior force to their own advantage. They can do that in a variety of ways – by harassing them, by making demands on them, by influencing their internal affairs, or by invading and annexing them. They may not do it today; they may not do it tomorrow; but the fact they can do it at all, that the use of violence is an ever-present threat and the normal instrument of last resort in inter-state relations, while it has been almost totally eliminated from normal relations within states, is not only indicative of the fundamental difference between the structure of human relationships within states and that of the relationships between states. It also means that human beings, particularly in the more effectively controlled and pacified industrial nation–states, live, as it were, simultaneously at two levels whose structure is not only different, but in some respects contradictory. Correspondingly, they live with two different and contradictory codes of conduct.[12] At one level it is strictly forbidden to assail violently and to kill people; at another, it is demanded as a duty to prepare for, and to use, violence in relations with other humans.

Differences between the code of conduct valid within a group and that which rules conduct between groups can be observed almost everywhere. But in the case of societies with a less well controlled and less effectual monopoly of physical violence, the gradient between the violence level within a group and that of relationships between groups is less steep. In ancient Athens, for instance, and in many medieval towns, the need to defend oneself and the readiness to attack others bodily in the event of conflict were very much greater, and physical fighting within one's own society very much more common than it is today. The growing effectiveness of violence-control within states and the growing subjection of state authorities to public control went hand in hand with corresponding changes in the personality structure of people. It helped to develop stronger individual self-constraint in conflicts and to raise the threshold of revulsion against the use of physical force in people's dealings with each other. That is why the majority of people brought up in internally fairly well pacified state-societies, and thus with perhaps a strong feeling of repugnance against the use of physical violence in human relations, often find it extremely difficult to understand that and why, in inter-state relations, the use of physical violence is still a normal means of tackling rivalries and of settling conflicts. They themselves may be in conflict if they are called upon to do to the members of other human groups what they have learned to hate doing within their own group – to use violence and to kill.

Moreover, the monopolization of physical violence under the control of the central authorities of a state-society does not mean that the use of violence within such a society is universally prohibited. It only means that the use of violence is reserved for the members of specific social formations, such as police forces, who have a licence to use violence according to set rules for specific ends, and above all, for the prevention of violence by anybody else within their society. Thus there is not only a contradiction between the code of non-violence within states and the code of permitted violence in inter-state affairs: there is also a permanent tension within societies between the code of total non-violence valid for the majority of citizens and the code of licensed violence, more or less under public control, valid for the police and other armed forces.

No doubt the monopoly of physical violence, the use of organized physical force according to set rules, is open to abuses. As I said earlier, the problem of how to control its controllers and their agents is one of the practical social problems which have not yet been solved. Yet at the level of inter-state relations where no monopoly of physical force exists, not even an effective police force has come into existence. Hence, at that level, the rule of the strongest still prevails in its primal form.

The standard of civilized conduct reached by humanity so far is not all of a piece; it is not a unified standard. Recognizable contradictions which account for a good many of the personal tensions and conflicts of our age, are built into its structure.

Perhaps we have gone too far in separating the study of persons as I from the study of persons as We or in other words, the study of persons as individuals from that of persons as groups. Thus there is a type of psychology devoted almost exclusively to the study of individuals and another called social psychology supposed to be concerned only with people as groups. There is also relatively little regard for the fact that groups have different levels of integration. The intra-state and inter-state level, for instance, though inseparable, have a relative autonomy in relation to each other. Each of these two levels has structural characteristics of its own, but they are also closely interdependent. In fact, the relative autonomy and the distinctness of the personality structure of each individual have increased markedly in the more developed societies, compared with earlier stages. Formerly, the mass of individuals identified themselves with relatively small units, with regions of comparatively restricted boundaries; today, they identify with nations that often consist of many millions of people. Highly individualized though they are, their personality structure is linked by an invisible cord to the structure of their state-society as "we", and as "they" to the structure of inter-state relationships, which – together – also determine a person's relationships with the objects of "nature". Each of these levels has structural characteristics of its own, as well as relative autonomy of varying degrees in relation to the other levels. At the same time, they all developed in close interdependence, and the most comprehensive level, that of inter-state relationships, is the most powerful. Within this four-level structure, it is ultimately the dynamics of inter-state relationships which give the lead.

XVII

As a social field without effective violence-control, the structure and dynamics of the inter-state level have special characteristics. Every power unit, every state within it, is drawn into a competitive struggle, often a survival struggle, with others, whether its representatives want it or not. If other states get stronger, if their power ratio increases, any state which does not get stronger, gets weaker. It automatically moves to a lower position within the status and power hierarchy of states. Hence, in a social field with immanent dynamics of this type, every unit is forced to compete, or else its representatives, lacking the resources or the will to compete, have to resign themselves to a lower position within the hierarchy and to the possibility of pressure or invasion from others. A state, as constituent of such a field, which cannot expand while others are expanding, loses power and status.

However, for the people of a country to accept themselves as a country of lesser power and status than before, as what may appear to many of them to be *déclassé* country, is a painful and difficult process. This is an example of the invisible cord that links the inter-state level to the individual level. The lowering of status and the loss of caste of a nation–state within the hierarchy of states is widely felt, among the individuals who form this state, as a personal loss of caste. Not infrequently, they revolt against their collective fate and try to turn the clock back – even violently. Unable to adjust their we-image to the realities, they may engage others in power probes and tests of strength and build up fantasy images of their country, trying to prove to themselves and the world at large that nothing has changed. They may even admit the changed position of their country "nationally" as a reality, and yet deny it emotionally and in their fantasy. Self-acceptance as a country of lower status – and power ratio – than before can be a very long and painful process that may last many generations.

A field of states without a central monopoly of physical violence is inherently unstable. There are a hundred and one reasons why tensions and conflicts between states may arise. But whatever the particular reason, the primary driving force is provided by the intrinsic competitive pressure of the figuration, by the elementary survival struggle between the constituent units and by their power- and status-conflicts.

At present, explanations in terms of the built-in dynamics of a figuration may appear strange. Other types of explanation predominate. An obvious explanation is the explanation of inter-state conflicts in terms of the aggressiveness of one or another of the states concerned. This appears to imply that a whole nation as a collectivity is biologically endowed with a higher propensity for violence than most others. Differential biological characteristics are thus held responsible for the instability and the recurrent violent encounters which are a standing feature of all inter-state relationships.

Perhaps the most obvious and also the most easily understandable reason why the dynamics of this survival struggle of states are not fully grasped, is the tendency to explain it in voluntaristic terms. Instead of considering the structure of the figuration of states which – without effective violence-control – engenders violent conflicts, one focuses attention exclusively on individual persons who wilfully started the conflict. Such persons may exist and yet, to content oneself with voluntaristic explanations of inter-state conflicts, emotionally satisfying though it may be to have someone to blame, is at most a partial explanation. It shows a certain affinity to the explanations that dominated the thoughts and practices of earlier-stage societies. They explained everything that was important to them voluntaristically. Whatever it was, as I indicated before, they perceived it in terms of the wilful acts and intentions of living forces. That human affairs, the events of this 'men'-made world, can and must be explained in this manner may seem obvious. In fact, the wilful acts and intentions of humans can play a part at all levels – in the ongoing development of a person, of people's relationships with non-human nature, with each other at the tribal or state level and at the inter-tribal or inter-state level. However, since people act wilfully within a framework of functional interdependencies which they have not wilfully produced, voluntaristic explanations of such processes are insufficient. There is no denying that the plans and intentions of humans can play a vital part in the struggle of states. What needs correction is the belief that they are the primary reason either of the struggle itself or of its course.

The primary reason is the figuration which binds two or more states to each other in such a way that each of them constitutes, actually or potentially, a danger for the others, and that none of them is capable of removing or controlling that danger. In our world of highly tradition- or culture-conscious nation–states, not even the total defeat of one side by another, as the case of Germany after 1918 has shown, guarantees the removal of the threat. Since the threat is reciprocal, it is very difficult, if not impossible, for any one of the countries concerned to lower the temperature, to ease the tensions of the power- and status-struggle on its own and, as it were, single-handed.

It is difficult to do that unless the contestants relax the tension of the frozen clinch simultaneously, each trusting the other sufficiently to be confident that the other will not hit out as soon as he himself relaxes his grip. A boxing match is supervised by a referee who sees to it that the rules are obeyed. No power exists on earth which can effectively supervise and control the struggles between powerful states and force both sides to submit to rules. They can only do that themselves, simultaneously and voluntarily. Unless and until that is done, each constitutes for the other an uncontrollable danger. In that situation, the people and the leaders on both sides may still believe that they are free and rational agents, able to do what they like. In fact, it is the double-bind situation itself, their indissoluble interdependence with the other side, which, in the last resort, dictates the actions and decisions of both. A more reality-adequate, a more "rational", way of acting would perhaps be possible if both sides bound to each other in this manner could perceive themselves and each other in terms of the double-bind figuration which they form together. At present, that is perhaps too much to expect. By and large, the peoples of the world and their leaders are still too strongly caught in the circularity of their double-bind processes to be able to control more permanently the dangers that they constitute for each other and for themselves.

In order to investigate and to communicate the compelling force which this form of interdependence – or any related type of bondage – exercises upon the groups that are bound to each other in this manner, sociologists, like other scientists, need some technical terms, some conceptual tools as a means of orientation. Here, the term "figuration" has been used as a generic concept for the pattern which interdependent human beings, as groups or as individuals, form with each other. With its help, one can say more clearly, for instance, that the drift towards atomic war is not simply a result of the plans or intentions of one side or the other. Instead, one can speak of the immanent dynamics of the figuration which two or more hegemonial states form with each other and which determine, to a large extent, the plans and actions of each side. By concentrating attention on the latter, on the plans and wilful acts of the other side, experts on each side get only a limited aspect of the situation into focus. Their perception is tied to a low-level synthesis. They see only individual plans and actions, not the unplanned process, the figuration that forms the frame of reference within which people take their decisions and act.

Basic for the structure of such a process, as I have said, is the primeval pattern of a figuration of human groups which are interdependent because each of them is without redress, without the chance to appeal for protection to any superior force or to a binding code of self-restraint and civilized conduct, and which are thus exposed to the possible use of violence by the other group or groups. Wherever human groups are arranged in the form of such a figuration, they are, with great regularity, drawn into a power struggle and, if they form the top of a hierarchy of states, they are regularly drawn into a hegemonial struggle with a strong self-perpetuating tendency. In scientific societies it is liable to become, in addition, self-escalating because research groups on each side try to outrun their colleagues and rivals on the other side, thus providing for their respective countries a higher defensive and offensive potential in military techniques compared with that of their opponents. In this way, each side, by increasing its own violence potential and, hopefully, its own security, automatically increases the insecurity and fear of the other side. The other side in turn tries to make up for the increased violence which, once more, increases the feeling of fear and insecurity of the other side, and so on *ad infinitum*, until one or the other side makes a false move or, feeling that it cannot keep up the pace, that it is in danger of losing the "cold war", in panic starts the "hot war" – starts shooting.

XVIII

Double-bind processes in the relationships between human groups can be observed throughout the development of humanity, especially since the emergence of human groupings in the form of centralized states. The oldest written documents of humanity, so far as is known, Sumerian records from the third millennium before our era, already provide a vivid picture of these elimination or hegemonial struggles. Even though their territory and the destructive power of their weapons were comparatively small, the dynamics of the survival struggle between the Sumerian city–states were unmanageable for them, and their power- and status-competition were as intense as those of our own age. Now one, now another, of these city–states gained for a time a hegemonial position, until all of them were defeated by the Akkadian kings and became, in spite of a strong cultural impact upon their conquerors and an occasional renaissance of their power, part of larger empires.

In the same way, Athens and Sparta, having for a time gained the highest power ratio among the competing Greek city–states, fought each other to a standstill. The former favoured a democratic, the latter an aristocratic, regime in their dominions, each city–state establishing one or the other wherever it gained power, just as the Russians establish one-party regimes and the Americans multi-party regimes wherever their influence is strong enough. In the end, the quarrelling Greek city–states came under the control of Philip and Alexander of Macedon, who had grown more powerful than any of the city–states in the old heartland of Greece. Alexander, in turn, tried to bring final peace and security to Hellas by removing once and for all the age-old threat to its independence that emanated from the Persian kings. However, when he had conquered Persia, he soon became aware that there were other independent kingdoms further east which would represent a threat to the security of his dominions. When he had conquered them, too, he became aware once more that absolute security was not yet within his grasp. Like Genghis Khan and Napoleon after him, he felt that he was more powerful – and probably *was* for a time more powerful – than any possible competitor, and so he tried to bring final peace to humanity and final security to his empire by marching to what he believed to be the end of the earth, bringing under his control all the people whom he encountered on the way. But the earth turned out to be very much larger, and humanity much more variegated, than he had imagined. As he was advancing, he became aware that there always remained other portions of humanity who remained unconquered. And so, while hoping to achieve absolute security for his dominions, he strained his lines of communication, his resources, his means of control and the patience of his soldiers to such an extent that he had to retreat.

There is, at any given stage of social development, a limit to the size of the territory and the population which can be effectively pacified and controlled from a single centre. Alexander had conquered a far greater area and a far greater variety of peoples than could be kept together in times of peace with the then existing technical and administrative means of control. His vast empire broke up as soon as he died.

One can observe in antiquity a steady advance in the size of the territories and the human populations that could be effectively held together for any length of time within the framework of a single state. The Sumerians, the Akkadians, the Babylonians, the Egyptians and the Persians were all stops along this road. Akkad was larger than Sumer, Babylon larger than Akkad, and Assyria larger than Babylon. The Persian empire was larger than the Assyrian and Alexander's empire larger than that of the Persians.

In antiquity, the culminating point of this sequence was the Roman Empire. The Romans were first drawn into a competitive struggle with other city–states in Italy. When they had gained hegemony in Italy, they were drawn into a survival struggle for hegemony over the Mediterranean and its coastal areas with Carthage and its network of Mediterranean colonies. It is not difficult to think of analogous multipolar and bipolar elimination processes in medieval and modern Asia, Africa or Europe. The struggle between the rulers of England and France for supremacy in the Anglo-French dominions that ended in the division of these dominions into what we now call England and France, is one example. Another is the long-drawn-out struggle between the Bourbon kings of France and the Hapsburg emperors.

XIX

In details, of course, such long-drawn-out elimination processes can vary greatly. Yet the basic structure of the processes which pluralities of interdependent states with a fairly even distribution of power chances but without a monopoly of physical power undergo, is always the same. Willy-nilly, they are drawn into a competitive struggle conducted with all suitable means, including the use of violence. It is a struggle for survival – as some contestants get stronger, others, merely retaining their existing power ratio, automatically get weaker. The immanent drift of such a figuration, starting with a fairly even distribution of power, is towards an increasing inequality of power chances.

As a rule, in the course of the elimination struggle, two or three power units emerge with a power ratio beyond the reach of all the others, who are, therefore, no longer able on their own to compete with them effectively. Increasing hierarchization forces the two or three units with the highest power ratio into a competitive hegemonial struggle with each other for, at this, the inter-state level, as I have already mentioned only one way exists of preventing a physically stronger power unit from exploiting to the full its high power ratio in relation to other states. It can only be checked by another state with a roughly equal power ratio or, as the case may be, by a group of states, if they can compose their rivalries sufficiently to optimalize their combined power potential. The most powerful state units at the top of a hierarchy of interdependent states are almost invariably drawn into a competitive struggle with each other, not because of a freely taken decision – although, of course, decisions play a part in it – and not because of any innate aggressiveness – although an aggressive temper in such a situation can be of some advantage – but because each has reason to be afraid that the other may get stronger, and then each would be at the mercy of the other. Thus both make the appropriate moves of which I have spoken. Both try to increase their security; and every move made by one of them in order to gain greater security is likely to heighten the insecurity of the other side. Each side tries to increase its potential for destruction. That, too, has a spiralling effect.

Nor is that all. As a rule, both sides manoeuvre for position in the territories outside their own frontiers. They fight a stubborn competitive struggle for allies and clients in the areas between their heartlands. Afraid of each other, they seek to make friends with countries which might become allies. They may seek to gain influence over others which are potential or actual producers of materials which are useful in the case of war. In the struggle for position, which is a fairly normal feature of the preparatory period on the road towards a war, each side is on the look-out for the most favourable strategic positions which can have an important, even a decisive function, in a war. They can facilitate communications and help to keep supply lines open, or hamper those of opponents. They can help to improve the range of destructive weapons and the effectiveness of intelligence sources. However, in former days, this preparatory manoeuvring for position between two hegemonial powers was usually localized. At the present stage, it affects the whole world. A major war, if it comes, is likely to be of global proportions. That is one of the points in which the figuration formed by the United States and the Soviet Union differs from similar bipolar figurations in the past. Previous figurations of this kind were *de facto* regional in character, even if those who formed them considered themselves as representing mankind. Hence the victor in an elimination struggle was usually confronted, sooner or later, by outsider groups with a roughly equivalent or an even higher power ratio. In the present phase of the millennial elimination struggle, all possible actors are already on the stage.

XX

One may assume that, in former days, survival units such as wandering tribes which were bound to each other in the form of a double-bind may sometimes have had a second option, besides the struggle dictated by their reciprocal need for protecting themselves against the other's possible attack. In an age in which wide-open spaces still existed on earth and territories were not yet everywhere considered to be the inalienable properties of particular groups of people, human groups tied to each other in the form of a double-bind could sometimes escape from the trap simply by moving away. One side may have felt itself weakening, or it may have got tired of the continuous struggle and the irremovable danger constituted by the violence potential of the other side. In that case, its members could simply decide to break up their camp and to try their luck elsewhere.

For some time now, this option has been less and less available to human groups. Above all, the two or three hegemonial powers which have emerged in our age, from the long elimination struggle between states, as the largest and most powerful state units on earth, constitute a deadly threat for each other simply by their existence as equally powerful states and by the absence of any superior power capable of checking them. Yet, although each of them is an enormous irritant for the others, they cannot move away from each other. Not even after the victory of one side does the defeated side disappear – as the case of Germany, which is still there after two defeats, indicates – unless the whole population is killed off. In our world, the antagonists are, as it were, saddled with each other for good. For the time being, each of the hegemonial powers constitutes a deadly threat for the others – but the danger is irremovable and almost wholly beyond the control of any side.

That they are also divided as the foremost representatives of two different, and in some respects antagonistic, social belief systems certainly plays a part in the hostility between the two main contenders. These divergent social beliefs have a real function in inflaming the inter-state struggle. They link the inter-state rivalries and dangers to the major intra-state issue of the industrial age: the conflict between industrial entrepeneurs and industrial workers. However, neither such intra-state struggles nor the divergent social beliefs generated in an intra-state context form the root-cause of the conflict between the two super-powers. If nothing else, the relationship between the two major communist powers, Russia and China, shows this quite clearly. Both countries profess to be communist. But the common creed counts for almost nothing compared with the traction of the double-bind they form with one another – compared with the fact that the two countries constitute a deadly danger for, and live in fear of, each other.

Thus, the linkage of an intra-state issue – communism or capitalism – to an inter-state conflict helps to rally the mass of the people within each state to its own side. Alternatively, it produces potential allies for either side. But the inter-state conflict itself does not, as is often believed, derive its whole dynamic force from intra-state conflicts between workers and managers, and from the social beliefs which identify and legitimize the two sides. The relationships between states and the conflicts they generate cannot be adequately explained in terms of relationships and conflicts within states. They have a dynamics of their own. Although – with the important exception that I have mentioned – both sides interpret the tensions and conflicts between them in terms derived from those of an intra-state class conflict, their antagonism and its dynamics in no way differ structurally from the hegemonial struggles into which, as far back in the past as one can see, the power units that have emerged as strongest from a long drawn-out elimination contest have almost invariably been drawn.

As I have shown elsewhere,[13] these elimination struggles form a normal part of a state-formation process. It can be blocked in the form of a stalemate, as was the case in ancient Greece; lead to the supremacy of one of the contestants, as was the case in the development of Rome and France; or lead to a lasting compromise between the principal contenders. As far as one can see, the latter has never happened, but it cannot be excluded as a possibility at the present level of self-restraint, reinforced by the external restraining power of the bomb.

Perhaps it is of some use to see that, in its primary structure, the power struggle between the Soviet Union, China and the United States does not differ very much from the many multi-polar hegemonial and elimination struggles of this kind which have taken place in the past wherever a social field of power units without a monopoly of physical violence has come into existence. As has often been the case, the two principal actors in the present power struggle may not have engaged in it with the intention of gaining hegemony. But that is the drift of the figuration which great powers form with each other. Only what is at stake this time is hegemony over the whole of humanity. In all likelihood, to gain supremacy of this kind is neither the declared nor the undeclared aim of either of the contestants. In fact, both set out on their way to the top of the hierarchy of states with fairly strong anti-imperialist beliefs. Yet, as time went on, both were driven towards a steady expansion of their spheres of influence, towards a direct or indirect control over other countries – in short, towards empire-building. They were driven in that direction simply by the pull of the figuration they formed with each other, by the dynamics of the process that involved them. As in comparable cases in the past, the two super-powers are driven towards continuous tests of strength. Every increase in the military potential of one side has to be countered by a corresponding increase on the other side. Every alliance which one side forms with another country anywhere in the world has to be countered by a compensating alliance by the other side. Previous imperial powers also started on their road, not because their representatives planned to build an empire, not by design, but because of the pressure of specific rivalries. Only at a later stage of the process do the leaders of such countries take up more consciously the role into which they have been driven, the role as centre of an empire.

Inherently, the drift towards empire-building of the two greatest hegemonial powers of the late twentieth century has little to do with the social ideals of either communism or capitalism. As I have already said, inter-state relations have a dynamics of their own. Sociological means of orientation derived from the intra-state level, from the conflict of interests between workers and management, can be of little help in the attempt to achieve a better orientation towards problems at the inter-state level, among which the most pressing is the drift towards war. Explanations in the usual terms, according to which this drift is either the fault of the capitalists or the fault of the communists, is not only a misorientation. It obscures the double-bind character of the figuration and also makes the struggle more intractable. On each side, it gives the hegemonial struggle between the two superpowers the character of a crusade. The simple fact that here are two great powers bound to each other in such a way that each constitutes a deadly danger for the other is obscured, and both constituents identify themselves, as Christians and Moslems did at the same time of the great crusades, as Protestants and Catholics did in the great wars of religion, through two different and antagonistic belief systems.

In former days, the belief systems were centred on supernatural powers. The present belief systems revolve around two different ways of ordering human affairs. One of them claims that, through favouring the interests of industrial workers, it will produce an ideal society for the whole of humanity. The other claims that it will produce an ideal society by giving a free reign to management. In both cases, the social practice which they have created is so far removed from an ideal state that it is impossible, by any stretch of the imagination, to see how, from that social reality, an ideal social condition can emerge. Yet that is what each of the two antagonistic states claims for its own side; that is what fires the emotions.

XXI

The often envisaged visitor from outer space who looked with a measure of detachment at the polarization of terrestial state-societies around the champions of communism and the champions of capitalism might easily detect the wide gap that separates reality and ideal on either side. In reality, both societies ruled in the capitalist manner and societies ruled in the communist manner have grave defects. Both generate a great deal of human suffering and misery. They are both beset with severe and persistent difficulties of which the misuse of power differentials, faulty planning, inflation, unemployment and deprivation are only a few examples.

In those countries on either side which are highly industrialized, the differences at the lower levels are not so very great. Among the main differences, the most obvious, and structurally the most significant, is that the societies of the one camp are one-party states, and those of the other, multi-party states. Equally significant, probably, is that the party and governmental establishments in the two camps are recruited from different social strata and represent different cultural, intellectual and moral party and class traditions. Representatives of the capitalist countries are easily suspected by those of the communist side of showing off their traditional middle- and upper-class superiority, while the former suspect the latter of the resentment and over-sensitivity of newly risen men.

Both sides tend to represent their own society as an ideal social order, as the best possible form of human society in the world. In both camps, the ruling social beliefs blur the differences between reality and ideal, between what is and what ought to be. They make it appear that they have already achieved a social order which, in essentials, need not and cannot be bettered. However, if one examines the ideal pictures of the two sides, one soon becomes aware of how closely they are geared to each other. In the nineteenth century, the traditional social ideals and beliefs of the age on the spectrum between, on the one hand, nationalism and conservatism, and on the other, socialism and communism, were primarily fuelled by intra-state tensions and conflicts. Power struggles between the traditional upper classes, the landed aristocracy and gentry, and the rising commercial–industrial middle classes, as well as those between the latter and the rising industrial working classes, played a part in fashioning these beliefs. In the course of the twentieth century, the centre of gravity shifted from the intra-state to the inter-state level. The various shades of upper- and middle-class beliefs and the various shades of working-class beliefs did not lose their functions as means of orientation and as ideological weapons in the power struggles of different social strata within states, but that function became increasingly overshadowed by their function as ideological weapons of defence and attack in the polarized struggles of hegemonial states and the other states that were drawn into their orbit.

Moreover, in the nineteenth century the two polar extremes on the spectrum of social beliefs, dictatorial nationalism and dicta-torial communism, still had the character of fairly remote ideals which might or might not be realized in the future. During the twentieth century both were realized in fact and, although the blight of realization did not efface their function as social ideals, as the centre-pieces of social creeds, or the emotional attraction they had for their followers, realization did cast a shadow over the dream. The social beliefs of our age have some of the functions and some of the characteristics which supernatural religions had in former days and which they still have today in many parts of the world. They are rich in emotional content and in fantasy-content, yet, by comparison, poor in their reality-orientation. They are usually expressed with the help of magical formulae which are often highly ritualized and have for their believers a strong emotional appeal. Like some supernatural religions, they have strong integrating functions, first for specific social groups within states, then for the members of the states themselves. With some margin for tolerance, the old social practice applied to supernatural forms of religion and summed up in the slogan, *cujus regio, ejus religio*, applies to the social religions of our age as it did to the supernatural religions in former times. Yet there is one significant difference: supernatural religions cannot be subjected to reality-tests, and social religions can. The latter can be examined with regard to their fantasy-content and the degree of their reality-orientation, both in the form of social experiments by being put into practice and in the form of systematic sociological inquiries in conjunction with the former.

Even a very preliminary inquiry can show that the antagonistic ideal images of human societies which today play such an important part in the grouping of countries at the inter-state level do not represent, as they may appear to do, an all-round image of an ideal society. They represent highly selective utopias. What their flag-bearers select as relevant are mainly aspects of societies which appear to be important in the context of group conflicts, where these images and the social beliefs they represent serve as ideological weapons of defence and attack. As a rule, these idealizing images of society in the spectrum of social beliefs stress as virtues those features of their own idealized social order, whose lack in the social order of their antagonists they can stigmatize as vices.

Thus, in the great hegemonial conflicts at the inter-state level, one side legitimizes itself by praising the freedom vouchsafed for its citizens by its own social order. Yet freedom is not understood here in any intrinsic sense but only in contrast and, thus, relative to a specific form of unfreedom seen as characteristic of the social order of the antagonists. The representatives of the latter, for their part, praise the social equality and justice of their own social order. Yet, again, they praise it not because social inequality, the hierarchization of social relationships has, in fact, disappeared or is about to disappear in their countries, but because, as they see it, a particular type of inequality and hierarchization character- istic of the social order of their antagonists has disappeared from their own social order. The social beliefs of the great antagonists are, in other words, functionally interdependent. Both highlight what appears to be ideologically relevant in their survival struggle with each other, and leave in the shadow many other aspects of their own societies which, however relevant they may be for their functioning intrinsically, do not appear to have any ideological significance in their inter-state conflict with the other side.

Seen from a distance, the picture that thus emerges is rather strange. Two powerful countries – militarily, perhaps the most powerful that have ever existed on earth – are bound to each other in the form of a double-bind, each being able to destroy the other, each through its agents, day and night and year by year, on the look-out for a sudden and wholesale attack mounted on its territories and its citizens by the other. The danger they constitute for each other is reciprocal: neither can control it on its own.

Compared with this primary – and primeval – structural characteristic of the great conflict, another, which is perhaps more clearly in the public eye, plays a secondary though by no means insignificant role in the sociogenesis of the conflict. Pitted against each other, here, are two types of social establishment which, mostly recruited from different social strata, legitimize themselves through different and antagonistic social beliefs. Both establishments, devoted to their social creeds, experience each other and are, in fact, bent on each other's destruction. Hence they live in fear of each other.

Structurally, they have a good deal in common – above all, the fact that they occupy commanding positions in party and state and are, understandably, opposed to any major changes in the power structures of their respective countries; yet ideologically, they are bitter and, apparently, irreconcilable enemies. In the sociogenesis of their conflict, the ideological antagonism between the two establishments presents, as it were, a second loop of the double-bind. The first loop is that of the reciprocal physical threat that the two powers constitute for each other, the fear of physical annihilation that follows from it and which, in turn, ensures the maintenance of and, often enough, escalates the physical threat. The second loop is the circularity of the movement which leads from the threat of the two establishments to each other's social existence to the fear engendered by it and back again to the threat.

In the public eye, the second loop of the double-bind, and particularly its ideological aspects, probably stands out more clearly than the first. No doubt, it contributes greatly to the intractability of the conflict. The idealization characteristic of the two social creeds, their fantasy character, makes it appear that what is at stake here are eternal human values. While the reality shows two ways of ordering human affairs which are both full of defects and in need of improvement, the ideologies present an ideal picture which is apt to disguise and to obscure that reality. It makes it appear that the struggle is freely and voluntarily entered into by the two sides for the sake of some absolute and eternal human values. In actual fact, one can only perceive two kinds of human societies with many flaws, neither of which is quite as bad as it is made out to be by the other side nor quite as good as it is made out to be by its own representatives. Yet, the belief in some eternal values represented by one's own society, and thus the locating of the social order of the other side which lacks these values, tends to be kept alive as a deeply felt belief irrespective of the so far irreparable defects of the two societies.

XXII

Although social creeds and ideals are not quite as inaccessible to reality-tests as supernatural beliefs, they can, in certain situations, become encysted so firmly, encapsulated so strongly, that they are beyond the reach of any reality-orientated argument or experience. The encystment of nation-centred social beliefs and ideals in that form has a clear social function; in a tense danger situation, it ensures the complete emotional identification of people with their own side. In a survival struggle such as this, the members on each side must be prepared to lay down their lives if the fighting starts in earnest. In former days, people were often prepared to do that for the sake of a supernatural religion. Nowadays, they may be motivated in the same way by social beliefs, by a belief in the high value of their country and its specific social order. The encystment of the belief ensures this motivation. Yet, at the same time, it is the complete inaccessibility of the antagonistic social beliefs to reality-orientated arguments and evidence – in other words, the hardening of the ideological antagonism – which immobilizes the antagonists in their frozen clinch, and which makes the double-bind process and thus the drift towards war almost uncontrollable.

Here, once more, one encounters an aspect of the double-bind situation which one encountered before in people's involvement with the uncontrollable processes of nature. In their relationships with the forces of nature, people have, to a considerable extent, succeeded in breaking the hold which the double-bind process had over them in that field. They have succeeded in tempering the fantasy-content of their knowledge of nature. The reality-orientation of this knowledge, as well as their control over nature, has increased. Increasing control over nature has helped people to contain the dangers of nature and thus their fears. The lessening of their fears has helped to lower the fantasy level of their fund of knowledge. What we call "science" is merely an expression of people's ability to break the hold of the double-bind process in their relationships with inanimate nature, to lower, at the same time, the fantasy level of their knowledge, the danger level of natural events, and thus to put the double-bind process into reverse gear.

But in people's relationships with each other, particularly at the inter-state level, the dangers to which people are exposed are still as great and almost as uncontrollable as they were in primeval times. Here, the circular movement, which can be observed in earlier-stage societies in their dealings both with non-human nature and with other human groups, still retains its full force. It may be useful to recall its structural characteristics. As I described them earlier:

High exposure to the dangers of a process tends to heighten the emotivity of human responses. High emotivity of responses lessens the chance of a realistic assessment of the critical process, hence of realistic practice in relation to it. Relatively unrealistic practice under the pressure of strong affects, lessens the chance of bringing the critical process under control.[14]

It is often believed that one may be able to prevent the escalating propensities of the double-bind process at the inter-state level by an agreement on material weapons alone. But ideological weapons, and more generally the emotional fantasies and beliefs of the antagonists in relation to each other, play as significant a part in keeping this process going as the circularity in the development of material weapons. Relaxation of the double-bind process – which may just be possible because fear of the bomb may outweigh the fear and hatred of the enemy – can only be very slow; for it requires, as one of its conditions, a change in the mentality of both sides, a higher level of detachment and self-control in their dealings with each other. But it also requires an understanding of the fact that changes in human attitudes do not and cannot occur in a social vacuum, solely as a result of a voluntary decision. If the danger which one group of humans represents for another is high, the emotivity of thinking, its fantasy-content, is also likely to remain high. If the fantasy-content of thinking and knowledge is high and thus its reality-orientation low, the ability of both sides to bring the situation under control will also remain low, the danger level and the level of fear will remain high, and so *ad infinitum*.

The crux of the matter is the unplanned circularity of such a process. To bring it into focus may thus be of some help, for the prevailing mode of thinking about such matters is wholly volun-taristic, making it appear that they can be setttled simply by an act of will. The sociological aspects of inter-state processes, as of other social processes, their character as blind and purposeless processes, is still, for most people, difficult to grasp. Thus one still tends to imagine that a war-like catastrophe, if it comes, can only come because someone plans it. The unplanned drift towards atomic war remains more or less incomprehensible because sociological theories of unplanned processes are lacking as a means of orientation. And if they are presented, they may not be received; they may fall on deaf ears. For, at present, almost all social beliefs, almost all programmes of social action – and not a few sociological theories themselves, as I have said – are geared to the notion that what happens in human societies can all be explained in terms of acts of will, of the deliberate actions and decisions of human beings as individuals and groups. Many social beliefs, a multitude of "isms", are cut according to this pattern. The emotional attraction or, alternatively, the emotional revulsion and hatred they arouse can be very strong indeed. Often enough, their fantasy-content outweighs by far their reality-orientation. At this level of our societies, where dangers are very great and almost uncontrollable, social standards not only allow, but demand, a high emotional involvement, a high affectivity of thinking, a lower control of personal feelings both in social practices and in the means of orientation connected with them. Correspondingly low is the ability to control the social processes that are kept going by the intertwining of these practices with their boomerang effect on the actors themselves.

In some respects, the prevailing tendency to interpret unplanned social processes as processes which will eventually lead to the fulfilment of the wishes of one side or the other – to what one or the other side desires and has planned, or, in short, the voluntaristic structure of social beliefs and sociological theories – has a marked affinity to the structure of thought and action of earlier-stage societies to which we refer as animistic or magical–mythical. Only, in their case, highly involved forms of cognition and social practice were all of a piece; for them, the danger level was equally high in their relationships with "nature" and in those with humans themselves. There, as I have tried to show, the elementary capacity of people to soothe, by wishful thinking and fantasy images, their fears of the uncontrollable dangers to which they were exposed, enabled them to believe that they themselves, by their own deliberate and voluntary action here and now – by magical operations – could influence natural and social processes alike.

Members of the more advanced state-societies, as heirs of a long development, have learned different forms of controlling natural events. They have learned that a high degree of detachment and self-control, an exploration of the immanent structure of natural processes themselves and thus a temporary abstention from wishful thinking, offer a greater chance of achieving their goals than magical operations, which may be emotionally much more satisfying, which appear to promise immediate help against the danger surrounding people, but which cannot keep their promise, except accidentally. As a rule, members of the more advanced industrial societies interpret their strategy for lowering the danger level of non-human nature as simply a result of their own intellectual propensities. They do not usually attribute it to their relatively late position in the development of human practices and means of orientation *vis-à-vis* nature, but to certain intrinsic qualities which they possess, to their own reasoning power and, above all, to their own rationality. Because of this manner of conceptualizing their relatively high level of reality-orientation and danger-control in relation to natural events, they are unable to come to grips with the fact that the reality-orientation of their concepts and their capacity for controlling dangers do not apply equally in all spheres of their lives. If these concepts are interpreted as manifestations of "rationality", one cannot help thinking that one's own mode of cognition and one's own practical strategies, since they are "rational" in human relations with "nature", must also be "rational" in their relationships with each other as groups and individuals. The conceptualization of contemporary attitudes towards "nature" in terms of their "rationality", suggests that earlier-stage societies with their animistic beliefs were "irrational", and that the people of more developed societies are "rational all round".

The conventional form of conceptualizing this problem, in other words, does not allow a clear statement of the fact that the vicious circle in which people initially moved on all levels of their existence, on those which we call "nature" as well as on those which we call "society", has been brought under control in the former case but not, or, at any rate, to a far lesser extent, in the latter case. In people's social life with each other, and particularly at the inter-state level, the force of the double-bind is still almost unbroken. Here, the reciprocal reinforcement and perpetuation of a relatively low capacity for controlling the dangerous processes on which the survival and well-being of humans depends – or, in other words, the capacity for a more reality-orientated practice, and a low capacity for a relatively detached mode of thinking, for curbing affects and fantasies, for restraining immediate wishes and fears and preventing them from dominating action and thought and thus the dangers which people constitute for each other – are still operative and still largely beyond human control. In fact, from a consideration of the double-bind at the inter-state level, which keeps people in our own time most visibly trapped, one may gain a better understanding of what kept humans trapped on all levels at an earlier stage. Here, on the inter-state level, the low ability of those involved in the dynamics of the inter-state process to control its course, and a high incidence of affective, involved, we- and I-centred forms of thinking, reinforce and often enough escalate each other. The situation is made more difficult by the fact that the subject-centred and strongly emotional fantasy character of the leading ideas in this field is not recognized as such. The notion that one is rational all through acts as a barrier.

XXIII

Nor, as a rule, does one perceive the affinity between the affective types of fantasy thinking and social practices that prevail on that level, and the mythical types of thinking and magical types of acting that prevail among simpler peoples. The latter, usually, because they are classified as "irrational", are experienced as wholly unconnected with the former. Yet a closer study of the types of reasoning that prevail in inter-state affairs could show, without undue difficulty, the affinities of their structure with that of the highly involved, magical–mythical types of reasoning that are characteristic of earlier-stage societies. An example is that characteristic of the mentality of the latter, once conceptualized by Lévy-Bruhl – for whom it was strange and incomprehensible – as "mystical participation".[15] It refers to the fact that, in many earlier-stage societies, one can encounter beliefs and practices which indicate that individual persons experience themselves as directly involved and participating in processes which, according to our mode of thinking, are extraneous to their persons, are classified as "nature" or "society" or as relating to other persons of their group.

To people brought up in the tradition of "rational" thinking, this can, indeed, appear incomprehensible, yet this "participation" is structurally not so very different from that which can be observed if one examines the sentiments and conduct of individual members of contemporary nation–states, parties and other groupings that are linked to each other through bonds of strong and strongly affective identification. In these cases, too, many individuals experience themselves as "mystically participating" in the fortunes of their groups. Their successes are felt, often very deeply, as one's own successes, their failures as one's own failures. The difference is that, in less differentiated societies, mechanisms of identification can probably permeate the feeling-structure of a person more deeply, and that identification can extend to animals and other manifestations of what we now classify as non-human "nature". But that is quite understandable, since, at that stage, men and women do not experience such neat boundaries between "nature" and "society" as we do. Hence, at an earlier stage, people may participate in the strength and agility of a totemic animal, in the well-being or decay of a holy tree, in the inviolability of a stone or mountain, just as they may participate in the vigour of a chief or in the health of a king.

In scientific societies, participation no longer extends to nature, which has become more or less depersonalized. It is confined to the human level. It can apply to leading personalities as well as to groups such as political parties, social classes, sects and, above all, to nation–states. In fact, a we-image, charged with positive or, as the case may be, ambivalent and negative feelings, forms part of the self-image of every person. The difference is that, in earlier-stage societies, this we-image or, in other words, participation, could include physical objects as well as human objects such as ancestors. For peoples at a more advanced stage of development, "nature" has become depersonalized. It is no longer included in the we-image or, at most, is included in an attenuated form – for instance, as attachment to the locality where one grew up and to its surroundings.

As in the earlier stages, this kind of emotional participation is, in the later stages, too, closely connected with specific social beliefs. The "American dream" is one example; Soviet Russia's "mission in the service of the proletarian revolution" is another. Almost every major nation–state has its own dream, an idealized fantasy picture of its own peculiar merit, of its mission and its superiority over other nations which is worth fighting and dying for. Every individual member of a nation can participate in this group charisma. It enhances the sense of a person's own worth as if it were his own merit.

Such affinities between the structure of magical–mythical thinking and that of the cognitive processes in certain spheres of later-stage societies are anything but accidental. With the extension of human control over "nature", the danger at that level of their existence, though it has not disappeared, has in some measure receded. At the level of people's relationships with each other, dangers remain comparatively high and less controllable. At the inter-state level, they are as high and as uncontrollable as they were at the inter-tribal level and in relations with "nature" in the life of earlier-stage societies. Regarding the basic human condition in social areas where no violence-control exists or where violence-control is subject to frequent breakdowns, the difference between simpler and more advanced societies is not so very great. Hence their cognitive processes, too, are less dissimilar. In that area of our lives, the emotional charge of their concepts, of their means of orientation and communication, is relatively high, the reality-orientation of their knowledge relatively low and so, therefore, is people's ability to bring the dangerous tensions and conflicts in that area under better control.

In short, while, in later-stage societies, the force of double-bind processes has, for the time being, been broken in human relationships with "nature", it has remained strong at the inter-human and particularly at the inter-state level. Within states, the operation of this double-bind has been tempered in some cases because social groups no longer threaten the physical existence, but only the social existence, of other groups. In that sense, the monopolization of violence has made itself felt. But even within states, violence-control can be weakened and break down. In many contemporary states, the awareness of that possibility is kept alive at the back of people's minds by a multitude of precedents. It helps to keep fears, the adherence to wish-fulfiling beliefs and thus also the dangers themselves at a high level.

At the inter-state level, these dangers are particularly great. Hence the affinity of modes of cognition, of knowledge and thought with those of earlier-stage societies is in that sphere most noticeable. There, as I have indicated, in the area without violence-control, the physically – or militarily – strongest group can impose their will on those who are weaker. In that respect not much has changed since humanity's earlier days. It is not surprising that, in this sphere, modes of cognition and modes of acting show structural affinities with those of simpler societies.

XXIV

The voluntaristic character of many beliefs and theories in this field, the tendency to perceive social processes, among them the unplanned drift towards war, solely as planned and wilful acts – usually of the antagonist – can serve as an example. At an earlier stage, human beings explained everything of relevance to them voluntaristically, namely as the deliberate and planned actions of someone. The "logic" of the "emotions" makes it easy to understand this mode of cognition. Strong human drives, strong affects and emotions, exert upon people strong pressure to act. The recognition of the impersonal character of natural processes thwarts this elementary tendency to act when one feels strongly about something. One cannot act out one's pleasure on a rain-cloud nor one's anger on a stone. Nor can one sit still if illness afflicts one's child and one does not know what brought it about. Magical practices that are believed to restrain the evil intentions which have brought about the illness, relieve the pressure. One must do *something*; and if factual knowledge of the nexus of events is lacking, fantasy knowledge merrily takes its place. It conjures up the picture of some living agent who, by an act of will, has brought about that which gives us pleasure or inflicts upon us pain. In relation to living agents, one can act out one's feelings. One can thank them for favours received and ensure further favours by set rituals and sacrifices. One can pit one's will against theirs by countering their black magic with one's own. In that way, one's own wilful acts help to control the wilful acts of others – whether they show themselves in lightning, drought, the illness or the death of humans – in events later experienced as natural. How is one to know at this earlier stage that natural processes have a structure of their own and that by temporarily controlling one's own emotional involvement, by exploring the immanent structure of these events – in short, by a "detour via detachment" – one may gain a far more reliable and effective control over natural events and may meet dangers with greater assurance than by magical controls?

It is hardly less and perhaps even more difficult for human beings to understand that not only natural but also social processes can be unplanned and can have a structure of their own – it is difficult to understand because the wilful and deliberate acts

of people obviously play a part in these processes. Hence it is easy
to imagine that society, as well as any specific social order, has
been brought about by people's design, by their planned and
intended actions either in the pursuit of their own interests or in
that of their ideals. And if they have been brought about by the
plans and actions of some people, surely they can be changed in
the desired manner by the plans and actions of others?

To comprehend that social processes, like the processes of
nature, can have a structure and dynamics of their own and that,
in this case, too, the effective control or elimination of dangers
requires knowledge of that structure – requires, in this case, too,
a detour via detachment – is made difficult not only by the fact
that the order in which people live with each other depends, up to a
point, on human wishes and goals, but also by the fact that the
order which people form with each other is an order of a different
kind from that of non-living things, often called "the order of
nature".

By and large these two, a voluntaristic and a naturalistic
approach, appear to be the only alternatives which offer themselves if one asks what kind of order human societies represent.
Social processes are either perceived as a medley of individual
acts of will – a medley of actions without a structure of its own –
or else as predetermined by mechanical causal connections that
operate over the heads of individuals regardless of what they wish
or do, thus running their course inexorably, according to
predetermined laws, like other processes of nature.

One can move a little away from this standard polarity of views
by remembering that people are not 'men'-made. Nor are the
societies people form with each other 'men'-made. It is true enough
that societies do not exist if men and women do not exist, and that
they do not function or develop if people do not act and pursue their
goals. Yet from the intertwining of the actions and thus the plans
of people emerges an unplanned order which, as a type of order, is
different from that of what we call "nature". Acts of will,
individual actions and plans are its constituents and, unlike the
order of nature, it would neither exist nor change without them.
Yet individual actions have behind them the unplanned five-
dimensional framework of a human being; they are themselves
determined by the fact that they emerge from the matrix of an
already existing social order – a pre-existing network of multidimensional and interdependent human beings. Every human
being has his or her parents and starts acting in response to them

or their substitutes. His or her acts of will are performed in the service of needs that were not brought about by an act of will. Nor are other human beings, their plans and their desires, which may fulfil or frustrate one's own, brought about by acts of will. Nor is it due to the voluntary action of a person that, as a child, he or she is totally dependent upon others and that, up to a point, people remain dependent on others throughout life. Thus, voluntary actions take place within a network of human interdependencies which, since it results from the unplanned interweaving of the unplanned needs of many unplanned people, is not the result of the action or the plan of any of them. The intertwining of the plans and actions of many people and many groups, in other words, results in social processes that are not planned or intended by any of those who help to bring them about. These processes are structured – they can be explained – but theirs is a structure *sui generis*, different from those of physical and biological processes.

Double-bind processes at the inter-state level are an example. Neither of the great powers tied to each other in this manner by their reciprocal threat intends or plans to form with the other a double-bind figuration. The voluntary acts, intentions and decisions of the representatives of both sides keep the double-bind process going. However, plans and decisions themselves emerge from the matrix of the double-bind process. They keep the process going and are determined by it. At present, as far as one can see, their representatives are only able to perceive the other hegemonial power as an opponent, as a "they" on the other side of a great divide. They are not yet able to ascend the spiral staircase of knowing to the next higher level from which they will be able to perceive themselves ("us") and their antagonists ("them"), as standing together on the platform below as interdependent antagonists tied to each other inescapably by the reciprocity of their menace. Neither of them is as yet able to analyse in a factual manner the roots of their hostility, a hostility the fantasy-content of which is high and the reality aspects by comparison, small – smaller, for instance, than those of the hostility between the Israelis and the Palestinians who are rivals for the same territories.

XXV

One can see why the transition from a voluntaristic or, for that matter, from a naturalistic to a figurational approach is difficult. It requires a considerable measure of detachment from the existing spectrum of antagonists. It also requires standing apart from the idealized self-images and beliefs which provide the intellectual and emotional legitimization of their hostility towards each other. Greater separation and detachment are not easy to achieve while the double-bind circularity is still in full swing. At this level, too, the ever-present danger nurtures a high affectivity of thought and action, a low ability to constrain strong feelings which, in turn, makes for the perpetuation of a high danger level, for an inability to bring these dangers under control. Moreover, this inability is supported by the belief of those who form the double-bind, not only that they are right, but also that they are rational.

Thus immobilized in their double-bind clinch, the representatives of both sides tend to think that one might conceivably arrest the drift towards war of the double-bind process at the inter-state level by an agreement on just one link in the circular movement – by an agreement on a restriction of armaments, on the reciprocal military threat alone. The double-bind model indicates that and why such attempts are not likely to succeed unless they go hand in hand with agreements on the lowering of the cognitive or ideological weapons with which the hegemonial powers continuously threaten and attack each other. This is a more difficult task; for, as a means of strengthening the emotional cohesion of their peoples and their allies, and in particular, of strengthening their readiness to fight and die for a cause, the contestants foster – and are forced to foster, given the reciprocal threat – a hate-picture of the other side and an idealized praise-picture of their own side and its mission and value.

Seen at close quarters, neither of the social systems functions well enough to be worth dying for. Yet, high emotionality of feeling, which is the concomitant of the very real threat which the great powers constitute for each other, transforms two still very imperfect social systems into the living embodiment of eternal ideals and values. Overtly, it is mainly in the name of these ideals and values that they consider each other as enemies. But more fundamentally, the two establishments are driven against each other, like those of Rome and Carthage, like the Bourbons and the Hapsburgs, because they are the most powerful establishments of their age, rivals for hegemonial power in the world. They would probably be antagonists if both ruled in the communist or both in the capitalist manner.

In our age, however, wars are no longer fought with illiterate armies of mercenaries and other sons of the poor, but with armies from educated nations that are reasonably well fed, well clad and inclined to be critical of their rulers. In order to mobilize populations such as these mentally for fighting a war, fairly sophisticated secular beliefs are required which can catch their imagination, hold their devotion − in short, which can command their allegiance as firmly as supernatural beliefs did in former days. The fear and the danger which rival countries constitute for each other, in other words, have to be lifted above the personal level. It is not enough, in order to rouse the populations of advanced contemporary nation–states and to induce them to break through the civilized revulsion against killing humans, to decry specific persons in the opposite camp. That can only be done with the help of very strong beliefs which objectify the extended self-love for their country in the form of impersonal causes. In the double-bind process at the inter-state level, this type of beliefs, social ideals and their disparaged counter-ideals, relatively impersonal love- and hate-pictures, play an indispensable part.

In all these relationships, the threat of the weaponry and the threat of the beliefs which give rise to an uninterrupted stream of reciprocal stigmatization, reinforce each other. Therefore, if the temperature of the self-escalating process is to be lowered, both threats have to be tackled together.[16]

I have tried to indicate that double-bind processes such as that which, in its most virulent form, can be observed at present at the inter-state level, are at work in earlier-stage societies at all levels of their social life. People's relationship with nature was once determined by double-bind processes of a kind similar to that which we still find at work, at the inter-state level, in the lives of differentiated industrial nation–states. It is one of the most significant characteristics of these societies that, internally, the danger which human groups constitute for each other, though it has not disappeared, has been tempered to some extent. Normally, antagonistic groups within such states no longer kill each other. They are forced to constrain their hostility against each other to some extent, because of the existence of fairly effective means of violence-control.

The development of more effective violence-control within states, in conjunction with the development of longer and more differentiated chains of economic and other interdependence, played a very decisive part in the emergence of the personality structure which made possible the transition from the dominance of a magical–mythical to that of a scientific approach. The latter, as it emerged in the European Renaissance, represented the final break through the double-bind processes which previously, to a greater or lesser extent, had kept humans captive in all spheres of their lives. But the fact that the emergence from the double-bind trap took place in some areas of human experience and control but not in others – in relation to non-human nature but not, or not to the same extent, in the relationships between human groups – has had a curious effect on what is often called "modern civilization".

The idealized picture of that civilization gives the impression that its representatives are civilized evenly all round. But that is not the case. The scientific approach to nature represents a high level of self-control that goes hand in hand with a high level of object-control. There, the fantasy-content of people's cognitive processes has been lowered, their reality-orientation increased, and this "rational" mode of thinking has taken root so deeply and has spread so widely through the more developed societies that people have come to regard it almost as an inborn faculty of theirs, as a natural gift shared by all humans prior to any experience.

Earlier-stage societies for whom natural processes constitute a far greater danger – a danger largely beyond their control – and whose cognitive processes show a correspondingly high affectivity and an equally high fantasy level, often appear to members of more developed societies as "irrational", "uncivilized", perhaps as "savage" and "barbarous". Yet, they themselves are not uniformly civilized – or, for that matter, "rational" – in all spheres of their lives. Where conditions are more akin to those of simpler people, their standards of action, and their codes of thinking, too, show greater affinity with the former. The inter-state level is an example. Ways of thinking and acting at that level show particularly clearly that standards of civilized conduct are not all of a piece, that they are divided and contradictory. A relatively high level of self-control, a high capacity for producing more reality-orientated knowledge, have been attained in people's relationship with nature, and their capacity for controlling nature is correspondingly high. Not quite so high is their ability to control the dangers inherent in their coexistence within the framework of states. Still, in the more developed state-societies, the control of the physical dangers which humans represent for each other, the control of violence, is relatively effective, and a correspondingly high level of self-restraint, with a tolerable rate of exceptions, can usually be maintained.

But in the relations between states, the dangers which humans constitute for each other are as high as – if not higher than – at the simplest levels known to us. It is true that people no longer hunt each other for food. Cannibalism, as well as slavery, has become rarer. But the way in which people kill, maim and torture each other in the course of their power struggles, their wars, revolutions and other violent conflicts, is different mainly in terms of the techniques used and the numbers of people concerned. High involvement of thinking, the black and white design of their images of others and of themselves, the belief in the absolute goodness of their own side, and in the absolute badness of the other, and the emotionality of their vituperations – all these and many other characteristics of inter-state relatonships show structural affinities to the more emotive, more involved forms of cognition and conduct of earlier-stage societies.

Needless to say, the fact that standards of civilization are not uniform, that codes of cognition and conduct in intra-state and inter-state relationships differ considerably, raises a great number of problems. What has been said here may help to show that the great unevenness of civilized standards in our age is not accidental. It may contribute to a better understanding of the fact that the contradiction of standards is structured. The differences in the levels of civilized conduct correspond to differences in the level of danger and danger-control in different spheres of life. The difficulty is, as has been shown, that the interdependence between danger-control and self-control is circular. The problem is, thus, how to lower dangers and to raise self-control and danger-control among all concerned at the same time.

XXVI

This, then, as one may see, is at the same time a theoretical discourse about problems of involvement and detachment, and a practical exercise in both. What is distinct about the approach chosen here is, firstly, that processes are consistently conceptualized as such, even though related concepts which are more familiar, but reduce the processes in question to static conditions, may be at hand; and secondly, the fact that traditional process-reducing concepts which represent the processes to which they refer as ontologically independent and inert entities, have been replaced by, or developed into, concepts which clearly show these processes as ontologically interdependent with others. Tradition enjoins us to speak and to think in terms of "subjects" and "objects", and of the related adjectival forms, "subjective" and "objective". This makes it appear as if people as the "subjects of knowledge" first existed in some mysterious way independently of "nature", and as if natural data could have the character of objects independently of human subjects for whom these data become objects in their quest for knowledge. Even at a more popular level, the world of humans, according to a widespread mode of thinking of our age, seems to be set apart from the world of nature. Just as the concept-formation, "subject" and "object", suggests two inert figures standing at a distance from each other at opposite sides of a great divide, so concepts like "men" and "nature", or, for that matter, "society" and "nature", "culture" and "nature", suggest in each case two ontologically independent modes of existence.

The whole furniture of our mind is cut according to the same pattern. Just as in a department store different types of goods are neatly displayed on different counters, all carefully isolated from each other without reference to any possible functional interconnection, so most of our key concepts – symbols of the steadily increasing academic compartmentalization – represent data in isolation. Thus "science" stands on its own without any relationship to pre-scientific modes of cognition which, under headings such as "savage thinking" or "primitive mentality", belong to a different department. Theories of knowledge stand unconnected next to theories of thinking; thinking has nothing to do with emotions, affects and drives. Intra-state power structures

and their development, under names such as "social development" or "home affairs", appear to have nothing to do with
inter-state power structures and their development, which are
dealt with under names such as "international relations" or
"foreign affairs".

Overspecialization – the tendency to represent the functionally
interdependent subject-matters of different departments conceptually as wholly autonomous and independently existing objects
of research – and the conceptual reduction of processes to static
conditions, are closely connected with each other. Hence a
framework of research which aims at restoring the connections
that have been artificially cut and at restoring the flow of streams
that have been artificially frozen, cannot fail to differ from those
already existing.

Within the traditional field of sociology, the unlearning
required for such a transformation may not be too difficult. No
doubt, there is a disinclination among sociologists to say, clearly
and unambigously, that the boundaries of the framework for
most of their research projects, even though they call it "society",
are in most cases the boundaries of a particular state. But it is
perhaps not too difficult to see that it is quite realistic to regard
the state as a specific social formation, more particularly as a
specific level of integration, and to suggest that the bulk of
sociological inquiries, as of those of most other social sciences,
are concerned with problems at or within the state level of
societies. What is perhaps more difficult, at least initially, is to
envisage the social events at this level as a continuous process. It
may be of help if one remembers that states, although they may
appear as such in the mythology of their members, are not an
eternal given of human nature. As a form of human integration
and organization, states developed rather late in the history of
humanity and, once developed, passed rather slowly through a
succession of stages of which the so-called "welfare state" in its
capitalist and communist guises is the latest example.

Also not very easy to understand initially may be the treatment
of people's relationship with nature as a level of integration and
as a process. In that case, too, the tendency towards conceptual
isolation, towards a neatly separated "department store" type of
abstraction, militates against the recognition of human beings,
their societies and their culture, as emerging from within the
natural universe. Advancing urbanization as well as advancing
human control of natural processes have left their mark on

people's outlook. Therefore, the idea that humans and their world are existences set apart from nature has become deeply ingrained in traditional modes of speaking and thinking. In actual fact, by transforming nature people transform themselves. The integration of humans with other humans and the integration of humans with the non-human features of nature are inseparable; they represent, as it were, two levels of one and the same process. As has been shown, problems of danger and danger-control, changes from greater fantasy-orientation to greater reality-orientation, occur on both; and so do double-bind processes.

As a theoretical model, double-binds, with their inescapable circularity, their eventual loosening and their possible break-up, can serve as an example of the advance in reality-orientation which becomes possible if one overcomes the tendency towards departmental isolation and process-reduction in the formation of concepts. As one may have noticed, problems with which one formerly could not get to grips come within the inquirer's reach if attention is focused on connection and integration as well as on separation and isolation, and on processes rather than on fixed and frozen states.

The greater reality-adequacy of relationship- and process-models shows itself perhaps most clearly in the approach to the inter-state level of integration. As one can see, the process of people's relationship with non-human nature, their relationships with each other within states and the relationships between states, can be caught with the help of the same theoretical net. By joining them within a multi-level model, the model itself becomes more reality-adequate. Similar problems – for example, those of dangers and danger-control – and similar tools of thinking – for example, the concept of double-bind processes, their possible relaxation and resolution – present themselves in the exploration of all three levels, as well as in that of a fourth: that of the individual self.

As for the loosening of a double-bind process, the simple model of the fishermen in the maelstrom may go some way towards a solution. However, the example has to be used with care, for it shows a single person taking a decision in a dangerous situation. The processes discussed here are group processes; and, given the reinforcement they receive from being the beliefs of many people, changing group fantasies and beliefs is a much longer, much more arduous task than such examples can show.

Still, to increase the awareness of these problems of involvement and detachment, and, with it, of the nature of double-bind circularities, may be of some assistance in easing the constraint which this kind of process puts upon humans in thinking as in acting. There is no reason to assume that we have yet reached the point of no return in the maelstrom in which we are drifting.

Notes

8. In this book I have used, or rather avoided, as is now more the norm in sociological writings, the term "human" or "people" to replace the term "man" in all contexts, where it does not simply mean "males". We found that our female acquaintances, friends and colleagues felt a good deal of bitterness and resentment about a linguistic usage which, as it were, relegated them to the status of non-humans. Obviously their feelings were justified. We now hope that, in Sociology at least, every effort has been, and is being, made to redress this linguistic bias.

9. One of the shortcomings of most sociological "action" and "interaction" theories is the implied or explicit treatment of actions that involve movements of the skeletal muscles on the one hand, on the other hand, such activities as thinking or reflecting without such movements, as activities on the same level. The representatives of action theories often insist on conceptualizing both types of human activities purely and simply as "actions". Their different function in people's lives and thus their different character, as well as the problem of their relationship, is thus obscured. In the aftermath of the behaviourist fallacy, sociological action theories will tend to accentuate visible actions, evidently following – knowingly or not – the behaviourists' ruling that behaviour which cannot be directly perceived by human observers like the behaviour of pieces of matter, cannot be regarded as an object of scientific investigation, and does not lend itself to investigation in a scientific manner; and that, whatever does not lend itself to investigation in the manner of the physical sciences, simply does not exist or, at any rate, can be regarded as non-existent for "scientists".

    The result is a curious break-up of the sociological tradition into schools of thought which concentrate on "action" and "interaction", with an accent on the directly visible and thus possibly measurable activities of people, and schools of thought which concentrate on the activities of humans which are not directly accessible to the perception of other people, though they are, of course, accessible to observation by other methods. Human reflections, people's thinking activities, the silent manipulation of learned symbols without visible movement, belong to this group of human activities. If they are conceptualized as "actions", they are certainly actions of a different type from actions that involve the skeletal muscles. As part of the personality structure of humans, they belong to a different – a higher level of integration. What we call "reflection" combines and often struggles with drives, affects and emotions in the steering of muscular actions. Tensions and struggles of this kind, as the fishermen example shows, form a normal part of human life. The socio-physiological functions of people to which we refer as "thinking" – again, as this example indicates – are exposed to the pressure of feelings and to that of the wider situation in their struggle for the direction of the coordinating motor centres that steer people's executive organs, their skeletal muscles or, in other words, their actions in the narrower sense of the term.

In actual fact, apart from the level of the cerebral steering and coordinating centres, and from that of the executive motor organs, one would have to distinguish the speech level, which involves a special kind of muscular activity such as those of the lips, tongue and throat. Speaking, too, if it is "action", is "action" at a different level and of a different kind from, say, the lifting of one's legs when ascending a staircase or the movement of the arm and fingers when using a fork.

That sociological theories often concentrate on the representatives of one level of the human personality only – only on "action" or only on "experience" – thus relying on a flat, one-level picture and neglecting the many-levelled character of personality, has far-reaching theoretical consequences. Each of these partial schools of sociological thought treats its own part-aspect as if it were the only relevant aspect of people. Behavioural sociologists see actions in isolation, phenomenological sociologists experiences (to name only these two).

Figurational sociology, on the other hand, is concerned with human beings in the round. It is centred on a five-dimensional image of plurality of human beings that includes the directly visible four-dimensional behavioural aspects and the "experiential", thinking, feeling, drive aspects of humans which, although not directly accessible to people's observation in the same way as bodily movements, are, nevertheless, accessible to human observation – for example, through the examination of linguistic and other symbols that carry meaningful messages from one person to others. Hence, problems of drives and drive-control, of emotions and emotional control, of knowledge and reflection as controllers or, alternatively, as dependents of emotions and drives – in short, the experiential aspects of people – play in figurational sociology no less a part than the visible movements of people's skeletal muscles that are singled out by behaviourists and action theorists. The task is to show their functional interdependence within the many-levelled units of human individuals and within the unplanned social processes that humans form with non-human agents and with each other.

10.   In a series of books, Lévy-Bruhl has presented a comprehensive survey of the different categorial structure of thought and experience of earlier-stage people. In a weak moment, he used – and later withdrew – the concept, "pre-logical", as a generic characterization of their intellectual operations. That was, in fact, a misleading term. Yet his books have considerable merit. They are wrongly neglected today. Even though they do not explain the differences between the earlier modes of thought and experiences and our own, they not only provide a wealth of evidence on these differences, but also succeed, above all, in showing some of the common structural characteristics of the mentality of humans at an earlier stage of development. The philosopher's tradition, which makes "reason" appear to be an unchanging form and knowledge a changeable content, sets up an artificial barrier which prevents those brought up in that tradition from seeing clearly that human beings, at a stage when they knew less, could not help connecting events differently from groups with a larger knowledge

inheritance. As long as this separation of reason as an eternal form and knowledge as a mutable content prevails, the difference between the categorial structure of "the primitive mentality" and that of scientific or "rational" societies will remain inexplicable. Lévy-Bruhl could not quite break through this philosophical barrier. But those who are able to do that can learn a great deal from his work. Although he does not use the term "structure", he has, I believe, shown more convincingly and comprehensively than Lévi-Strauss the structure of "primitive mentality". The latter's attempt to explain "savage thought" appears, by comparison, to be a sophisticated artefact, a riddle explained by a riddle. His evident resentment against any developmental terms deprives him of the chance of arriving at a genuine understanding of human groups that represent an earlier stage in the development of knowledge and danger-control. His fear that the ordering of earlier- and later-stage people in terms of a process, of a sequential order, may imply a lowering of the human dignity of the former, is unfounded. The opposite is the case. Only through understanding and explaining the thought and experience of earlier-stage people in terms of their position in a sequential order can one even hope to arrive at an understanding of, and to be able to explain, those of groups that represent a later stage. In order to explain such differences between earlier- and later-stage societies, one needs, in other words, a developmental ordering of evidence which can only be brought to life by a testable process theory that shows how such processes as the development of knowledge and the closely related civilizing process fit into the wider development of human societies.

11.   Since power is a relationship, I try, as far as possible, to use technical terms which give expression to that fact. "Power ratio", which is one of them, seems quite a handy term, not much more cumbersome, yet more precise, than the usual term, "power".

12.   Henri Bergson touched upon this problem in his book, *The Two Sources of Morality and Religion*, 1935, 1932. It was a useful beginning, philosophical rather than sociological in manner. It may seem surprising that so significant a problem has not been pursued further. Academic over-specialization, which has led to the study of the sociological problems within states and those between states by different academic groups, each with its own unconnectable type of theory, may account for this neglect.

13.   N. Elias, *The Civilizing Process*, vol. 2. *State Formation and Civilization*, Oxford 1981.

14.   See above, p. 48.

15.   L. Lévy-Bruhl, *La Mentalité Primitive*, 15th edn, Paris 1960; see also his *Les Fonctions Mentales dans les Sociétés Inférieures*, Paris 1923. Readers may, perhaps, feel that these books are ancient and, therefore, of no relevance for research and discussion in the late twentieth century. That argument would be valid if one could be sure that the human sciences, like some of the natural sciences, advance steadily in the form of a straight progression, be it unilinear or dialectical; but that is not the case. Lévy-Bruhl's work has suffered from the false sense of professionalism that has developed in some of the human sciences. As part of this, to be wholly "with it", one need not consider the intrinsic cognitive achievement of a book, but only whether it is fashionable at the moment, whether it is new.

This is partly due to the fact that, in most of the human sciences, clear criteria of advance are lacking – unlike some of the natural sciences where such criteria and, therefore, a fairly clear order of succession, do, in fact, exist, even though philosophical theories of science pay little attention to it. Because most human sciences lack criteria of advance, the turnover of published books and, therefore, the wastage of human effort, are enormous. In some fields of historiography, books about particular periods are written again and again, by every generation. With few exceptions, those written by previous generations rest in the libraries unread. Closer examination would probably show that, in some cases, later books do, in fact, represent an advance but, in others, a deterioration relative to earlier books. The latter I believe to be the case as far as Lévy-Bruhl's collection of evidence about "primitive mentality" is concerned. It is a solid and modest body of work with some theoretical flaws. It does not yet suffer from the sophisticated confusion of some of the later books on that subject and, though one can go beyond it, it should not be bypassed.

16. The antagonism between the hegemonial powers of our age receives part of its driving power from tensions and conflicts between working and managerial classes. Beliefs and ideals derived from these class tensions in industrialized countries play a leading part in the contrasting ideals of the hegemonial powers at the inter-state level. Yet, in that respect, too, ideal and reality do not match. It is remarkable how small the real differences are between the conditions of the working classes in capitalist and communist countries – except in one respect: the intergenerational rise from the manual working classes into higher administrative and governmental positions is easier and, probably, more frequent in the East than in the West. Thus the social cadres from the two camps who fight each other are not the working classes on the one side and the managerial classes on the other, but a cadre of party, army, administrative and government officials on the one hand, largely of peasant and working-class stock, and on the other, an establishment of party members and high office holders, largely of middle- and upper-class stock. However, the composition of the Russian establishment in terms of social descent is likely to change, if no major upheaval occurs. Establishments incline towards self-perpetuation. It is likely that, gradually, the proportion of people of peasant and working-class descent will decline and that of the offspring of party, higher administrative and government officials will increase in the composition of the Soviet establishment. Whether the share of non-Russians will increase is another matter.

Part III

Reflections on the Great Evolution

Two Fragments[1]

Part III

Fragment I

I

Both the connection and the differences between the main groups of the theoretical–empirical sciences, that is, between the physical–chemical, the biological and the human sciences, can perhaps best be grasped by pointing to the process whereby the increasingly complex structures, integrated in increasingly complex ways, that make up the fields of investigation of these sciences, emerge from the less complex structures and, in some cases, revert to them. To be sure, this process of the great evolution is, at the present stage of research, only a hypothesis. But findings on the most diverse levels impel us towards a comprehensive process-model of this kind. Our view of it is obstructed only by the difficulty which scientific specialists still have in the present organization of scientific activity, in crossing the mental boundaries of their enclaves. But in attempting to construct a model that does justice to the unity as well as to the multiplicity of the sciences, one simply cannot be the slave of a single science.

In reflections on the relationships between the different sciences today, a not inconsiderable part is played by the idea that originally the entire universe, including human and other living beings, issued from a physical event – the explosion of a highly concentrated primal mass. Among the contending hypotheses, the prevalent opinion among physicists appears today to be inclining towards the big bang. This does not affect the problems under consideration here, and need not be the concern of this discussion. But it is perhaps not quite idle to say that this hypothesis is only one proof among many of how strong the human desire for security in the notion of an absolute beginning remains, and of how difficult it still is for people to envisage processes without a beginning. So people comfort themselves with the myth of the primal egg. This is supposed to have reposed for aeons – where? – in the space of a not yet existing universe. Suddenly, for reasons that are not as yet considered, it explodes. At the seeming zero-point of time the pyrotechnics begin. The hour of birth of the expanding universe strikes. So arises a myth of physics, which is confirmed by more and more observations and calculations, and yet which springs, like so many myths of primeval times, only from the human desire to carry over the category of the beginning from the parts, and particularly from oneself, to the whole, in order to escape the disquieting conception of an infinity without beginning.

Well and good. Anyone who finds comfort in beginnings can be content with this caesura in a course of events which has no beginning. It is more difficult to dispose of another expression of this quest for beginnings. There seems to exist among physicists the notion that the principal key to the problems of the universe, and so the answer to all the problems of science, including those of the biological and human sciences, could be found if the smallest particles, of which everything in the world consists, if the "elementary particles" and their properties, were discovered. Undoubtedly, the knowledge we can obtain by breaking down futher and further the elements of matter is quite indispensable. But whether this can be managed with categories like those of the "particle", belonging to a quite different order of magnitude, is more than doubtful. And the notion of an ultimate "primal particle", of the absolutely indivisible *atomon* on the subatomic plane, is thoroughly problematical. Here, too, is frequently at work the tacit assumption that definition of the properties of the smallest parts of a composite unit is sufficient to explain the properties of that unit. In reality this notion is one of the chief obstacles to an understanding of the diversity of the sciences – particularly of the differences between the physical, biological and human sciences – and so to a theory of the sciences. Does it not sometimes appear as if the claim that physics can serve as a model for all sciences rests, among other things, on the fact that it is physicists who investigate the particles of which everything in the world consists?

II

The widely held notion of the primacy of analysis should also be seen in this context. This takes the dissection and isolation of individual parts as the central scientific procedure, whereas synthesis, if considered at all, is regarded as a second-rank scientific activity or even as non-scientific, a tool of metaphysics. One cannot quite escape the impression that here too the theory of science lags behind the practice of the sciences and the changing conceptions of the processes which they investigate. In the praxis of some sciences – cosmology or "molecular biology", for example – it is becoming increasingly clear that forms of synthesis, that is, processes of integration, play as great a part among natural processes as phenomena of decomposition and disintegration. The implications of the growing knowledge of blind, unplanned and largely self-regulating integration-processes of this kind for the procedures of the sciences concerned, for the nature of their theoretical models, and for the general theory of the sciences, the model of the models, have up to now been scarcely examined. Once we begin to examine them it is not difficult to see that these implications are very extensive.

One of the most obvious symptoms of this advance of knowledge is the gradual change in the cognitive status of laws. Laws were for a long time the highest ranking scientific instrument, the discovery of which was held to be the supreme objective of scientific endeavour. Of course, the symbolic representation of the results of research in the form of laws, or theories having the character of laws, remains one of the goals of the physical sciences. But alongside this goal, in a number of physical sciences, theoretical formations of another kind have emerged, models of temporal–spatial structures and processes. These theories, unlike laws – which can be expressed as mathematical formulae beyond time and space – have themselves a spatial–temporal character, a three- or four-dimensional form. It is certainly no accident that the development of theoretical tools of this kind, that is, symbolic representations of structures and processes in time and space, is to be found particularly in those branches of science which are concerned, like the ones mentioned above, with processes of synthesis, integration and disintegration.

This connection between the study of integration and disintegration processes and the formation of process-models is found in a relatively simple form in the field of cosmology – for example, in the investigation of what we call "stars". Synthesizing processes of a comparatively loose and simple kind are involved here. The composite units with which cosmology is concerned, stars or galaxies, are, as regards the linking and the division of functions of their parts, far more loosely integrated and far less complex in their structure than unicellular organisms or even enzymes, not to speak of fishes – or humans. But even here we find – on a relatively simple level – spontaneous syntheses, such as the condensation of a loosely integrated gas cloud into the early forms of a star, and long, self-activating processes with a regular sequence of stages. On the plane of scientific synthesis this relatively simple process of integration and disintegration was first represented by Hubble in the form of the so-called principal-series model. One could go a stage further and say that Hubble's model represents in cosmology one step in an advancing synthesis. For a time it was only possible to establish a statistical star-catalogue. Within it different types of stars could be distinguished – stars of the type of our sun, and red or white dwarfs. Hubble was the first to succeed in making these different *types* of stars, which were juxtaposed in previously attempted theories in a static and unconnected way, recognizable as phases in a *development* of stars.

If the instruments at the disposal of Newtonian cosmology are compared to those of the present day, it is soon evident how dominant in the former was the notion – represented by the concept of the natural law – of the eternal uniformity and immutability of the universe, and how strongly, by contrast, in present-day cosmology, the accent has shifted to the question of the development both of the universe as a whole and of the diverse celestial bodies forming it. Compared to the present view, the earlier way of seeing appears as a phase in which scientists, with the aid of mathematical formulae and regularities, were still limited to describing recurrent patterns, the How of the relationships between the movements of celestial bodies. In the current practice of cosmology, on the other hand, diagnostic interest in the How of the different stars and constellations is far more strongly combined with an interest in the Why, in explanation, and particularly in explaining the sequence in the transformation of stars, of constellations and of what is accessible to us as the universe. The increasing interest in diachronic sequences –

often enough irreversible sequences following a particular direction – is very closely connected to the growing ability to pose Why
questions.[2] Since the universe and all the part-formations
composing it have for all time been in a process of change and will
continue to be so, immutable laws are not sufficient to explain
their partly self-regulating changes. A process-model, a symbolic
representation of sequence, is needed as a starting-point in
seeking to explain how and why they have become as they are and
not otherwise.

The theoreticians of science of our day have concerned themselves relatively little with the change in cosmological theories
since Newton's time. In some cases the image of classical physics
as an ideal for all possible sciences still plays a determining role,
even for present-day theories.

One might wonder why the majority of modern theorists take
scant notice of the real development of the sciences and the
diverse problems to which it gives rise. The question deserves a
fuller treatment than can be given here. But one of the reasons is
certainly that the philosophical tradition of which the present-day
theory of science is still a part, blocks access to problems of
development, of diachronic sequences – in short, to the very
nature of change. It is tied to a hierarchy of values according to
which it is the highest task of science to disclose immutable
patterns and abstract them from diachronic change, which is
usually devalued as the "merely historical". The adherence of
many present-day theoreticians to the immutable "law" corresponds to the reverence for the idea of immutable "truth" as the
highest symbol of the task of all scientific research.

III

In other respects, too, the development of the model of the
sciences has not kept pace with the development of the sciences
themselves, which has led to an ever-increasing differentiation
and specialization. It is no longer nearly enough to speak of
physics, biology, sociology or history. One can only do some kind
of justice to research practice by speaking of the physical
sciences, the biological, the human sciences. But the theorists of

science itself, the specialists concerned with elaborating theoretical models of science, pay little heed to this growing diversity of the sciences. They sometimes attempt to describe the differences between them. But no explanation of why all sciences are not cast in the same mould is offered. At most they elevate one science, usually physics, to the rank of a prototype of every possible science, and its methods to the ideal form for all sciences. But they practically never elucidate why, for the study of organisms and then of human beings, an increasing number of special sciences have evolved, and why the exponents of these sciences feel the need to proceed differently, in their investigations, from physicists.

In particular, the question is seldom posed of whether the forms of analysis based on the isolation of parts, that is, the traditional method of the physical–chemical sciences, is equally appropriate to the subject-matter of all empirical–theoretical sciences. Closer study shows that this is not the case. The connections existing on the plane of events to which the physical–chemical sciences are adapted have very specific characteristics distinguishing them from those on other planes, and their peculiarity as sciences is closely bound up with this peculiarity of their subject-matter. The way in which, on each of the different planes, composite units of a lower order together form composite units of a higher order – that is, the kind of integration existing on the different planes of events in the universe – can serve as a test case. Indeed, if we picture the areas of subject-matter of the principal sciences as lined up before us, it is not difficult to perceive that the peculiarities of these subject-matters differ in quite specific ways. These variations have sometimes been understood as differences in the direction of increasing complexity. This is not wrong, but it is not enough. The whole manner in which integrates of a lower order are bound together in integrates of a higher order, varies. At the same time, the significance of the behaviour of the component parts as determinants of the behaviour of the composite units also varies. The models and procedures needed to investigate the different planes of events making up the subject-matter of the principal sciences vary accordingly. Corresponding to the change in a particular direction that is observable in the *fields* of subject-matter, if we mentally review them in sequence from the physical through the biological to the human sciences, is a continuum in the *models* of the subject-matter that emerges clearly if these models are reviewed in the same sequence. The theory of science – understood as a theory of the sciences – therefore calls for a synthesis, a model of models.

Moreover, the direction of the change that is revealed by this kind of synoptic view, both on the plane of the subject-matter and on that of the scientific models, is certainly not accidental. It reflects aspects of the great evolution that was mentioned at the outset.

A hypothetical model of this kind shows nature, if this personifying expression can be used once again, from a side which is somewhat neglected in the current image of nature. The image prevalent now is so physicalistically tinged that "nature" appears simply as the immutable world of the eternally valid laws. This is a very comforting view; for many people find salvation from the consciousness of their own transience in the thought of the immutable order of nature, whose symbol is the natural law. But today the problem of the transformation of "nature" or, if one prefers, of the "universe", is moving more and more clearly into the centre of scientific attention. One of the directions of this transformation of natural events is meant when the expression, "the great evolution", is used here.

The great evolution has many interdependent aspects that cannot all be discussed at the same time. It is enough at present to point to one of the central aspects of the direction of the transformation. Simpler structures whose component part-units one level lower are not yet linked by a division of functions, so that their synthesis is reversible without these components changing their properties, become more complex structures whose component part-units one level lower are linked by a division of functions. The structure of these components is therefore adjusted to functioning within the framework of a particular composite unit of a higher order. In this case the parts lose their peculiar structure when the higher unit, the synthesis binding them together, breaks up or decays. Since, in the first case, the components are not specially adapted through integration and the division of functions to the higher unit, but retain their structure whether or not they are integrated in this way, the integration is reversible. In the other case it is not. Furthermore, this line of evolution leads to differentiation and division of functions not only on one plane, but on more and more planes which all interlock in complex hierarchies through divisions of functions. Each small molecule is an example of the first type of integration, the reversible type. Unicellular organisms, for example, amoebae or bacilli, are simple examples of the irreversible type of integration. It is difficult to dismiss the idea that there is a continuous transformation in a particular direction, an evolution leading from natural units with reversible integration not differentiated by division of functions, to natural units integrated by division of functions, such as cells, even though we have as yet very inadequate knowledge of the stages of this transformation and of its conditions, its motive forces. Something similar applies to the stages of the path leading from unicellular organisms to multicellular ones having an increasingly complex specialization of their part-units and a corresponding increase in the complexity of their coordinating central organs. The fact that spontaneous syntheses of a higher and higher order are among the natural processes unplanned by humans is, at any rate, of not inconsiderable importance, not only for an understanding of the multiplicity of the sciences, but for the image of what we call "nature".[3]

IV

Even though knowledge of the path of evolution is still very fragmentary, we have seen that the direction of change, and so the structure of the change process, can be determined quite unambiguously. Knowledge of this direction and structure is quite indispensable in understanding the relationships of the main sciences to each other, and in clarifying the differences and connections between their tasks. The procedure of the physical–chemical sciences is based on the atomistic basic dogma that the properties of all composite units can be determined by the isolation, needed for all measurement, of component parts (or aspects) – that is, by tracing these properties back to those of the component parts. That measurement and quantification are tied to the possibility of observing the parts in isolation is a decisive aspect of the basic dogma. This observation in isolation, however, as has been mentioned, is neither equally possible for all the empirical–theoretical sciences, nor equally appropriate to their tasks.

On the plane of events dealt with by the physical sciences, the isolation of parts needed for measurement and quantification is possible and appropriate because the component parts of the composite objects on this plane are either not at all or only slightly interdependent through division of functions. An oxygen atom remains an oxygen atom whether or not it combines with two hydrogen atoms to form a water molecule. But higher up the evolutionary ladder the validity of the atomistic basic dogma proves restricted. Even a single cell and, therefore, a unicellular organism, be it bacillus or amoeba, has part-units such as nucleus, nucleolus, vacuole or membrane, which are so bound together that they lose their structural peculiarities if they are isolated without at the same time being placed in a medium which fulfils at least some of the tasks of their original functional context. Quite certainly these part-units of a cell on the next lower level consist in their turn of part-units of a yet lower order. These include, for example, large molecules with the function of enzymes which, while tied in the total organization of the cell to certain temporal–spatial positions, can be isolated without loss of structure or properties. They can, by and large, be dissected into their component parts, and, in some cases, re-synthesized into units on the next higher level, enzymes, in imitation of spontaneous natural synthesis. Within the overall framework of a cell that is so organized through division of functions that, on disintegration – that is, when the part-units on the next lower level are isolated – these part-units, with the unit they form, lose their structure together, there are yet lower part-units whose own part-units are not bound together by division of functions and whose decomposition is reversible. They are potential objects of physical–chemical investigation.

The picture of biological units that is being unfolded here is of some significance for an understanding of the relationship between the biological and the physical sciences. It shows a hierarchic order within which, over a number of stages, part-units together form composite units which, as part-units in their turn, form composite units of a higher order and so lead, through a growing number of planes of differentiation and integration, to more and more complex formations. In the case of a simple cell there are estimated to be between ten and fifteen interlocking planes of integration. How many can be distinguished in a human organism is still beyond estimation. But the model of multi-level synthesis that is beginning to emerge here makes a number of things comprehensible that often remain unclear in discussions of the relationships of the main sciences to each other.

All natural formations, including human beings, consist of part-units of the type which the physical–chemical sciences specialize in investigating. But even in the case of a simple cell, the part-units on the physical–chemical level, the properties of which can be very largely determined by examining those of their component parts, are embedded in a composite unit of a higher order, the component parts of which on the next lower level can no longer be isolated in a reversible manner. The disintegration of a cell goes hand in hand with the disintegration of these parts. On this plane the composite unit loses its peculiar structure together with the component parts of the next lower order. In composite units with a large number of interlocking levels of integration, irreversible disintegration is what we call "death". The synthesis of parts on many levels, through division of functions, disappears. What do not disappear – disregarding relatively durable and slow-disintegrating remnants of higher integration levels like bones and teeth – are molecules and other part-units on the physical–chemical level. The irreversibly ordered levels of organization are exposed to decay; when it sets in, we say of the affected units that they die. By contrast, molecules and other reversibly organized units do not die. To do justice to the peculiarity of combinations of events on higher levels of organization, one finds oneself in need of stage-specific terms and context-models that are not applicable to lower levels. Expressions like "birth", "death" and "life" or, to mention stage-specific terms for structural peculiarities of yet higher planes of integration, "consciousness" or "mind", are examples of these.

At this point we observe something of very far-reaching significance. In the course of a spontaneous development process which is unplanned but follows a specific direction, there emerge under certain circumstances from reversibly and thus relatively loosely organized units, irreversibly organized units of integration with more and more specialized part-units and more and more tiers of integration centres. If we advance in thought from one to the other, we discover that the units representing a higher stage of integration possess stage-specific behavioural and functional properties which are not derivable solely from the properties of their component part-units on a lower level, or explicable solely by their functions or behaviour, but must be explained in terms of the peculiarity of the configuration which the part-units of the lower level form together. The expression "stage-specific" refers to this fact. It implies that in explaining the structural peculiarities of more complex formations, it is not enough to know the structural properties of their component part-units. This knowledge is necessary but not sufficient. To explain these structural properties, one needs to know not only the properties of the part-units but how they are organized functionally, how they are adapted to interact. In other words, one needs to know both how the part-units function and how the composite unit they form together functions – that is, their mode of integration.

The higher one moves up this evolutionary ladder from one area of subject-matter to another, the more predominant the pattern of integration becomes as a factor in explaining the properties of a composite unit, as compared to the properties of the part-units observed in isolation. A heart – one might say – is a muscle consisting of muscle fibres consisting of cells consisting of large molecules consisting of molecules consisting of atoms, and so on. The behaviour of the molecules can be explained almost exhaustively by that of the constituent atoms. But with large molecules the organization of the constituent molecules often begins to play a major part, alongside their properties, as an explanatory factor. Even in explaining the behaviour and functioning of the heart muscle as a higher-level order of integration, one cannot dispense with knowledge of the functioning of its part-units on the different levels of integration – the constituent atoms, molecules, cells, muscle fibres, and so on. But the importance of the higher level of organization formed by the heart with other organs and part-units of the same level, as a factor in explaining the functioning of the heart, is far greater as compared, say, to that of the molecular configuration of atoms in explaining the behaviour of the latter.

This example makes clear, perhaps, why it is necessary to introduce the term "stage-specific concepts". Our traditional linguistic habits play a major part in blocking understanding of the autonomy of examples of different levels of organization. To begin with, they obscure the obvious fact that the formations on a higher level of organization contain, as part-units in a hierarchic order, formations on all the lower levels of organization in nature. However, the fact that the higher-level units have stage-specific properties which their part-units on the lower level do not possess, and which cannot be derived solely from the properties of the latter, is usually taken account of only by being symbolically reified and then presented as something attached in a purely additive way to the units of the lower level of integration. So, for example, the difference between the stages of integration forming the subject-matter of the physical–chemical sciences, and those forming the subject-matter of the biological sciences, is expressed by the concept "life". Organisms are postulated in this way as physical–chemical formations to which something further is added, namely, "life". In the same way the integration levels of non-human organisms are distinguished from those of human organisms by attributing to the latter, apart from their animal body, something additional, an invisible thing, a "soul" or, variously, "mind", "consciousness" or "reason". One need not undervalue the emotional function of such reifying concepts; but they have over and over again impaired the ability of people to orientate themselves in their world. It helps towards a long-overdue clarification of this state of affairs if one says that reifying concepts like "life", "soul" or "reason" are nothing other than preliminary forms of a stage-specific set of concepts. They indicate that the picture of an evolutionary process leading to an increasingly comprehensive hierarchy of interlocking planes of integration necessitates a reappraisal of traditional concepts and categories.

The current conceptual apparatus compels thought into a schema of highly unfruitful controversies. It often appears today as if, with regard to these problems, only two, equally speculative, solutions are possible. One is the physicalist solution, whose exponents postulate that one day it will be possible to explain the properties of all higher-order units of nature formed of cells, by those of their physical–chemical components. The other seeks to dispose of the non-deducibility of the behaviour of higher-order composite units from the peculiarities of their constituent part-units, by oracular utterances such as the notion of the whole being more than the sum of its parts. There are situations in the development of human knowledge in which problems remain insoluble because the facts needed to solve them are at that stage unknown. There are others in which society's stock of knowledge offers the necessary facts in abundance; but the prevalent modes of thought, the pre-existing categories and concepts, block the way to a solution. We are concerned here with a blockage of the latter kind.

That no formation exists in which atoms and molecules or their equivalents do not form at least one of the levels of integration, and to the understanding of which physicists and chemists cannot at least contribute, is quite obvious. It is no less obvious that many natural formations that have emerged from a blind development process, including human beings, comprise a complex hierarchy of interlocking levels of integration, the functioning and behaviour of which cannot be explained by those of their part-units on the physical–chemical level of organization. But traditional intellectual and conceptual forms resist an elaboration which would take account of the evolution of natural formations integrated reversibly and without division of functions towards an advancing synthesis of formations with more and more interlocking planes of integration. The simple fact that there is no natural formation that does not *also* possess a physical–chemical plane of integration, continually gives rise to the mistaken idea that all natural formations are to be explained either by reduction exclusively to chemical–physical units, or by the presence of supernatural or extra-natural factors. Our concept of nature itself is physicalistically tinged. The development which would accomodate it to the evolutionary order of planes which is slowly being delineated, still lies ahead.

Furthermore, the direction of this evolution also manifests itself very clearly in other ways. One of its tendencies is to develop towards increasingly comprehensive powers of self-regulation. The simplest unicellular organisms are borne passively hither and thither by the surrounding stream. Flagellates can steer themselves to a slight extent. Fish can manoeuvre and swim against the stream. Amphibia are capable of the far more complex locomotion over land. Humans, in keeping with the unique multiplicity of their levels of integration, possess an apparatus of self-regulation surpassing in variability those of all other natural formations. Neither the idea that they are a piece of matter, governed in their behaviour like atoms and molecules and reducible to them, nor the idea that they are governed by a non-natural, inmaterial substance, is adequate. But this reference to the autonomy of natural formations in relation to others – an autonomy which (if never absolute) grows in the course of terrestrial evolution – must suffice here as an example of the strictness of the direction followed by this development. This autonomy corresponds to the growing functional differentiation and the growing hierarchy of interdependent centres of integration within a structure.

V

One of the key concepts needed to come to grips with these problems is that of advancing synthesis. In this context it is needed on two interdependent planes. With its help one can, on the one hand, account for certain factual connections better than was previously possible. If one tries to picture the long process in the course of which – under certain conditions – large molecules have arisen from small molecules, more highly-organized units and finally unicellular organisms have arisen from large molecules, then organisms with more and more specialized organs capable of wider and wider syntheses, up to the most complex formations – humans – one sees what the concept of advancing synthesis can achieve on the plane of factual connections.

But at the same time this concept refers to the development of human knowledge of the world in which we live and of which we are a part. I have attempted elsewhere to show this with the example of those syntheses which are currently represented symbolically by the concept of time. The span of what can be related by this concept today is extraordinarily wide. It can be applied to all stages of integration – the physical–chemical, the biological and the human–social. The concept of time itself is the expression of a synthesis between two or more continua of change, one of which is usually calibrated, so that with its help one can, as it were, build milestones into the incessant flux of change, and in this way determine the length of the intervals, that cannot be directly grasped, between what happened earlier and what later. At the present stage of knowledge, however, the types of time allocated to the different sciences – that is, physical, biological or social time - are juxtaposed in an unrelated way like the sciences themselves. A model of their connections is lacking. One finds oneself here, therefore, in the front line of current knowledge, where the open problems present themselves. But it is precisely this study of the development of what we today cover by the concept of time that shows how immense was the exertion that humans had to expend over millennia in order to elaborate conceptual symbols for the wide-span synthesis of which the present-day concept of time is an example, and which is now in its turn showing gaps in its front line, unlinked islands of knowledge in the sea of human knowing.

How vast is the scope of the synthesis represented by the present-day concept of time only really becomes clear if its range is compared to that of its predecessors used by simpler peoples. One finds stages of conceptual development at which, whether people were referring to ancestors or to contemporaries, the wide synthesis expressed by terms such as "year" or "season" was still inaccessible. There were (and are) stages in the development of knowledge at which people communicated primarily with signs for discontinuous here-and-now events about what we seek to symbolize by time concepts. So the sight of the new moon, for example, could be an important social event for them, without their being able to form a conceptual sign, a symbolic representation of the relation between the two statically experienced sightings, for the stretch of time between one appearance of the new moon and the next. In a word, their stock of social knowledge and thought did not yet provide them with a conceptual representation of the relatively impersonal synthesis which finds expression today in such apparently simple concepts as weeks or months.

The current concept of the sciences certainly represents a stage of conceptualization at which people are capable of a far more comprehensive synthesis than at the stage when "harvest" stood for "year" and perhaps "new moon" for "month", or when the tides served as a means of defining what we today refer to as "time". But in the long process of advancing synthesis which accompanies the growth of human knowledge, related figures constantly recur. Again and again people at the frontier of existing knowledge find themselves confronted by facts that they cannot relate – often enough without being aware of their inability to do so, of the open problem impinging on them. Their ignorance escapes their notice; it does not occur to them that what for them is still unconnected could be related at all. Then, at the next stage, the problem is solved. The answer to the question of how the previously unconnected facts are related is found, and people have developed in their intercourse a concept which symbolizes this relation, with which they can speak about it and which at the same time so stamps its impression on their lives that they perceive events in terms of the relation symbolized by the shared concept. In former times this was the case with the perception of the new moon. If, for example, a king of Babylon proclaimed that the new moon had been sighted, the notion of a recurring relation between one new moon and the next as a predictable interval of time was not yet intelligible, or at most only evolving.

The case is similar with the relation of the sciences to each other. Today the question of why there are several different sciences and not just one, and the problem of their relation to each other, are still somewhat shrouded in obscurity. Attempts to relate the various sciences, as far as they are made at all, tend to be based on a Linnaean typology. The different sciences are placed side by side, as plant species were earlier, and compared. Their differences are described as those between static types, as those of animals and plants were earlier, but they are described and explained not in terms of an evolutionary frame of reference: which would allow their functional spheres, and then themselves, to be perceived no longer as unconnected types, but as stages in a process. Traditional notions of the relation of the physical–chemical to the biological, and of the latter to the human sciences, can easily give the impression that they all stand side by side on one plane. Our tradition, one might think, accustoms us to a one-dimensional model of the sciences, whether by juxtaposing them in one system or by reducing the different sciences to one. One might suppose that the social organization of the sciences, which – whatever the informal differences of power and status may be – places the disciplines formally side by side, favours this conception. On closer consideration, however, it emerges, as we saw, that a multidimensional model of the sciences is needed to do justice to the peculiarity of the relationships between them, and to represent them adequately in symbolic form. A model of this kind can also correct the idea that the areas of subject-matter of the different sciences exist separately, in the same way as the disciplines themselves, which are divided by high ramparts. The difficulty is that their subject-matter meshes together in diverse ways. We come here upon one of the obstacles standing in the way of interdisciplinary collaboration.

VI

Dispassionately considered, it is evident enough that the sciences are ordered in ascending tiers. But to perceive this it is clearly necessary to rise to a level of detachment which is difficult to attain in social life today. Work on a more adequate model of the relations of the sciences – on a model of the models – therefore also throws light on the attitudes that play a central part in scientific work: on the problem of detachment and involvement.

It is not difficult to recognize that the subject-matter studied by biologists comprises higher forms of organization than that of physicists and chemists. Nor is it particularly difficult to see that the level of events studied by physicists and chemists lies not only outside the levels of integration studied by biologists, but also within them. Indeed, there is no scientific field in this world that does not contain, as one of its levels of integration, phenomena of the order which we call physical–chemical. Physico-chemists work, in a word, in one stratum of a common world. In some fields, for example astronomy, it is, as far as we know, the only stratum. Within it, as we have said, the constituent parts are, with few exceptions, integrated to form the next level of composite units in reversible ways, without division of functions. Within the fields of other sciences, however, the stratum of physical–chemical sequences is only one of several layers. That with higher and higher integrations of part-units on a growing number of planes, structural and functional peculiarities emerge which cannot be explained solely by those of the constituent parts on the physico-chemical planes, has already been said. But a clear, considered set of concepts that does justice to this state of affairs is still lacking. It is clearly difficult to elaborate, and it will be necessary to reflect on the reasons for this difficulty.

That a cell represents a different and higher form of integration, that cells and, still more so, multicellular organisms, represent in the sequence of terrestrial evolution a later stage than the molecular part-units of which they consist, can be taken as fairly securely established. What still seems largely obscured in the current canon of thought is the fact that the atomistic basic dogma is no longer applicable as a guideline for the study of more highly-integrated units. One might say that it has been reversed. The higher one moves on the evolutionary ladder, and the greater the division of functions and the more diverse and comprehensive the hierarchically ordered systems grow, the more necessary it becomes for thought to proceed not from the component parts to the composite units, but from the higher order to the lower. What that implies is the following: even in studying a highly complex system – say, an ape – it is indispensable to lay bare as many physical–chemical chains of events as one can. But all processes on this plane have their specific place and function in the total systems of such an organism. Isolated studies on the physical–chemical plane, however numerous, remain unfruitful until the functions of the lower-order processes are brought into relation to the higher levels of integration by means of a model of the latter. In the praxis of science this reversal of the atomistic dogma is found everywhere. In work on organisms, and not least on problems of human beings, the awareness that in studying higher structures one must proceed from these to the lower part-systems, has in many cases been assimilated as an established practice.

But the importance of this distinction between the exploration of physical–chemical strata and that of higher integration units, for the theory of the sciences, has probably not yet been fully realized. The exponents of sciences concerned with investigating more highly-organized subject-matter frequently develop concepts for relationships which differ sharply from those used in exploring simpler levels of organization. But these differences usually emerge and remain on the level of praxis. They are seldom thought through systematically, and the praxis itself remains half-hearted. We lack a model of the sciences which would make it possible to underpin the differences of praxis theoretically as well, and make the relations between the different fields more comprehensible.

First of all, one needs to show the limits within which physicalist models of scientific work can be fruitful, and to explain why they have only restricted application outside them. The guiding image of hierarchic levels of integration is of particular value in this context. For even though there is no field of subject-matter in which one can entirely dispense with the study of physical connections, in which physical–chemical investigation cannot contribute something to an understanding of the behaviour of composite units within it, this contribution diminishes as the distance between the physical level of integration and the highest level of the composite unit in question increases. And the reversal of the atomistic dogma, whereby one should proceed from the higher to the lower level of organization, becomes all the more applicable. For, as in the course of evolutionary change the autonomy of systems becomes greater and more variable, so all physical–chemical processes are increasingly governed by the order of the higher systems. And however little in such cases one can understand physical–chemical processes without knowing their inherent regularities, no more can one understand their functions in the total context of a higher system such as a complex organism solely on the basis of these regularities.

The higher one ascends the evolutionary ladder to more and more differentiated and integrated units, the more pronounced becomes the difference between the structural properties of the processes one now encounters and those on the physical–chemical plane. We have already alluded to the fact that in the absence of a model of evolutionary stages, the ordered conceptual apparatus developed by people in their attempts to elucidate the specific properties of the higher and highest systems known to us are often shrouded in an aura of mystery. Involuntarily, materialists and anti-materialists alike assume the physical–chemical level of existence – that is, matter – to be the truly real, that which conceals no secrets. The stage-specific properties of the higher structures, and particularly of humans, then appear – as compared to the reality of matter – as mysterious, and often enough as symptoms of an immaterial reality existing outside the physical–chemical sphere, but frequently presented by means of concepts derived from models of the physical world.

Fragment II

I

In the course of the twentieth century, in the investigation of the celestial bodies, the genetic approach has gained precedence over the more descriptive study of their regularities. Of course there have long been speculative hypotheses on the genesis of the cosmic bodies. The Kant–Laplacian hypothesis is one example. But at that time there was no possibility of empirically testing such hypotheses. In the twentieth century this became possible. At that point the genetic approach, the question of the origin and evolution of cosmic bodies, and in this sense of their explanation, entered its scientific phase. From the point of view of the theory of science, it is not without interest to define more precisely the turning-point of this transition to the scientific phase, and so the criteria of what constitutes scientific method in this case.

As in other cases, the turning-point came after a long preparatory phase. In the course of the nineteenth century, and still more in the twentieth, the techniques of astronomy made rapid progress. The star-catalogues grew. At the same time there were increasing efforts to achieve a better classification and typology of the celestial bodies. But up to the early twentieth century these efforts still had the same static, descriptive character as the well known Linnaean classification of plants and animals. To go beyond this, problems needed to be solved that one hardly dared pose, because all basis for a solution was lacking. A prime example is the problem of solar energy. How was it possible that the sun was able to emit energy unceasingly – for example, in the form of light and heat – apparently without exhausting its supply of energy? How was it possible at all to produce energy so extravagantly? One could speculate on such questions, but the answers lay so far over the horizon of knowledge that for a long time they surpassed the human imagination.

The transition from the speculative to the scientific phase came about in this case too because scientists succeeded in developing theoretical models in close touch with experimental, empirical studies. The question of the energy emission of stars only became answerable in conjunction with the experimental splitting of atomic nuclei and the understanding of its theoretical significance. Systematic observation of the sun and other stars confirmed the supposition that energy emission based on a continuous, spontaneous splitting of atomic nuclei was involved. The nuclear fission which was achieved after long preparatory work in the twentieth century and then, for good or ill, turned to practical use, provided the key to the riddle of the sun. The light and heat of the sun and other stars turned out to be by-products of a gigantic process of nuclear fission. What people had succeeded in producing in the laboratory was a miniature copy of a natural process that has been taking place for millions of years and which is among the preconditions of the emergence of organisms, and so of human organisms, on this planet. It remained to be explained how this natural process of nuclear fission had arisen.

The turning-point in cosmology, between an approach concerned predominantly with laws to one primarily interested in processes, was a star diagram called, after its authors, a Danish and an American astronomer, the Hertzsprung–Russell Diagram. A number of behaviour patterns of certain groups of stars are correlated in this diagram – above all luminosity and spectral type or temperature. Tested in this way, stars are not distributed randomly over the diagram, but follow a specific pattern. Attempts to explain this pattern led to the realization that it must represent a stellar evolution. Grouped at one end of the pattern are types of stars recognized as "young" stars, with "old" stars at the other; between them lies the part of the pattern to which the majority of the stars tested belong – including stars of the same type as our sun. This part of the diagram represents the phase in the evolution of stars in which they spend the major part of their careers. This section is now generally known as the "main sequence", and stars in it as "main-sequence stars". This diagram and the theoretical extension it underwent at the hands of other scientists, particularly the American cosmologist Hubble, is a turning-point in cosmology. It marks the transition from a Linnaean to a Darwinian typology of stars, and, more broadly, from the primacy of static law-orientated theories and concepts to dynamic process-orientated ones.

That is not to say that this turning-point marked a conclusion. It was a transition from one dominant approach to another, from a quest primarily for the eternal regularities of structures beyond space and time to one more concerned with their origins and evolution in time. What has changed are the questions and the expectation of solutions. The solution itself is still, for the most part, far off. Nor is it the case that the study of what used to be referred to as laws, that is, constant relations of magnitude, has become irrelevant to the progress of research. That is by no means so. What has changed is the cognitive status of immutable relations of magnitude as an instrument of research. Instead of being a kind of substitute deities, law-like rules of thumb have now become auxiliary instruments in the construction of process models.

E. P. Hubble, whose achievements included being the first to identify the formations known as nebulae as independent galaxies outside the Milky Way, discovered by means such as spectral analyses a simple formula expressing in the manner of a law the relation of the distance of these galaxies to their velocity. He noted that the proportion between the distance of remote galaxies from the earth and the speed at which they seem to be moving away from it is always the same (which does not mean that the solar system is situated at the centre of these receding movements). Considered from any possible observation point, a galaxy recedes at a speed proportional to the distance from the observer. This formula could certainly be referred to as Hubble's Law; today it is usually called the Hubble Constant. It greatly helped the construction of a process-model – the theory of the formation of the existing universe that has become known as the theory of the expanding universe. The pattern of the Hertzsprung–Russell Diagram and its interpretation should also be understood in this way. Its construction depended on a wealth of measurements, and law-like rules of thumb played a part. But in this case, too, they were tools with the aid of which people tried to make comprehensible the process of the emergence of stars, their relative stability as figures in the main sequence, and the last stages of the stellar process.[5]

The image of the stellar process that the current state of knowledge presents is really that of a gigantic chain reaction. In its simplest form, this kind of reaction can be set in motion in any laboratory. It is a reaction the products of which automatically set off and maintain identical or similar reactions, until gradually all the material capable of this reaction is consumed. Even 'man'-made chain-reactions show a clear diachronic sequence of phases within which each later phase necessarily presupposes the earlier phase or sequence of phases. The traditional coal fire can serve as a simple example of such a chain-reaction. Left to themselves the coals emit no heat; but if some are made to glow by an external source such as a wood fire or gas flame, the incandescence is transferred spontaneously from one coal, if suitably arranged, to others, until they have been converted, while emitting energy in the form of heat and light, into cinders and ash, substances no longer capable of such a reaction. A similar sequence is to be observed in the best-known chain-reaction of our time, nuclear fission. It becomes self-activating when, in a suitable material such as a uranium isotope, and after an energy stimulus has been applied, at least one of the particles liberated by the splitting of a nucleus – neutrons – causes the splitting of another nucleus. In stellar processes chain-reactions of a quite different order of temporal and spatial magnitude are involved; they therefore differ from terrestrial reactions in particular respects. But the allusion to the latter can perhaps simplify understanding of the peculiarity of these – by human standards – immensely long natural processes.

According to the current conception, accumulations of gas and dust particles, observable as a kind of cloud in certain places between stars, form the starting-point of this cosmic chain-process of star formation. If such a cloud attains a certain density, the effect of gravity can cause it to contract further. Temperature and density increase. The formation begins to emit a faint reddish glow. In this phase the energy giving rise to the incandescence of the mass results from its increasing conglomeration through gravity. When the internal temperature rises still further, to a few million degrees kelvin, nuclear reactions of a particular kind are triggered as an energy source, and after a series of intermediate stages the formation takes on the structure and form characteristic of a main-sequence star. The time it needs for this contraction and the attainment of the main-sequence structure depends on its mass. Within certain limits one can say that the larger the mass, the more quickly the formation reaches the temperature which sets the self-activating nuclear fission process in motion and maintains it as a chain reaction, and the more quickly the star process passes through its different stages.

At the present stage of research, such a process is certainly far from being understood in all its details. The chemical composition of the sun, for example, is not yet clear. What is of interest, from the point of view of the theory of science, is in what respects the procedures used and the solutions expected in the case of these problems differ from those of classical physics and the philosophy of science based on it. One of these procedures is the construction of a series of mathematical models of the sun, representing different possible types of chemical composition. One can then test which of the models agrees best with relevant observations. But such models cannot perform their task unless they take account of the preceding stages of the chain-reaction process up to the present one – in other words, unless one pays regard, in constructing such models, to the diachronic aspect of the nuclear process that we refer to briefly as the "history of the sun". In this, measurements are as indispensable as ever; advanced calculating machines make it possible to process a large amount of measurement data very rapidly; but the object of the exercise, as we have said, is not the discovery of a timeless law but the construction of a four-dimensional process-model. Without reference to the dynamics of the preceding phases, the attempt to define the structure of the sun, or of any other star, would go astray.

The central feature of a main-sequence star, as it appears at the present stage of research, can be expressed by a relatively simple formula, even though as regards details there are many different possibilities and countless unsolved problems. The enormous energy discharge of main-sequence stars results from nuclear fission processes that constantly and spontaneously produce new nuclear fission processes. Hydrogen atoms, above all, serve as fuel. The splitting of their nuclei and the fusion of nuclear particles release energy. What is left as a kind of waste matter is helium. A star twice as big as the sun uses up its combustible material in a period of about 3000 million years. A star only slightly bigger than the sun uses up its supply of hydrogen in 5000–6000 million years. When about 10 per cent of the hydrogen has been converted into helium, the structure of the stellar process changes. The first spate of energy discharge and the longest phase of the process are over. The helium core contracts and grows hotter. As this happens, the helium itself becomes a fuel. It is in part converted into heavy elements with a new but smaller release of energy, which comparatively quickly consumes the energy sources. The star inflates. Depending on circumstances, it turns into a red giant or bursts its outer shell and explodes in the form registered on earth as a supernova explosion. What is left behind condenses into a white dwarf or a neutron star, and perhaps then into a black dwarf, a sluggish reacting mass of extreme density, relatively small size and low luminosity. That is the end of this chain-process.

II

Even this short survey may serve to show that the unit with which a process of this kind is concerned on the level of atoms and molecules, that is, the physical–chemical level, is different in kind from the units involved on higher levels of integration. Even a simple unicellular organism is generally isolated from the surrounding world by a membrane, and possesses within it an active autonomy. But the stellar process possesses at most a passive autonomy. It can really only take place over millions of years as a unified process, because the universe is so large and it, by comparison, is so small – so that, in many if by no means all cases, the distance between such cosmic processes is correspondingly large. Linguistic tradition accustoms us to speak of these cosmic processes as if they were things – understandably, for at an earlier stage of knowledge they appeared indeed as immutable objects, if not as divine entities. Although we might hesitate to speak of a coal fire as a thing, we shall undoubtedly continue to speak of the cosmic chain-processes as we are accustomed to, as stars and suns and the eternal, unchanging heavenly bodies. For a human life is short, cosmic processes are long and, measured by the former, are indeed practically immutable and eternal.

It is nevertheless worthwhile to reflect on the meaning of the change which began in science, when not only organisms or human societies but stars, the sun and the solid earth itself were set in motion, so to speak, and turned out to be, instead of immutable objects, changing phases in a long process. Fundamentally, this assimilation of certain physical–chemical areas into the dynamics of development represents a simplification of the picture of the world in which we live. It allows a wider synthesis than was possible up to now – the synthesis referred to as the great evolution. With its help it is easier to take account of the fact that the different process areas with which the separate sciences are concerned, such as cosmic, biological and, within the latter's framework, social development, are levels or phases of a comprehensive development process. If one keeps this in view, it is easier to determine the relations between the various areas of subject-matter, and between the models of them used by the different disciplines concerned with exploring this subject-matter. The different sciences can then be understood as each contributing to solving the problems which the different stages of an evolutionary process pose, their respective theoretical models as symbolizing different stages; and the model of the great evolution, which is emerging here only in rough outline and will only take on the shape of secure knowledge gradually in the work of future generations, can be seen as a symbolic synthesis of their subject-matter, as a model of the models that is itself in the process of developing towards a greater proximity to reality.

The cosmic processes, like physical–chemical processes in general, represent a relatively simple type of order. The loose sense in which physicists often use the concept of order impedes understanding of evolutions leading beyond the physical–chemical level. For even in the simplest cell one has to do with a type of order which differs from that prevalent on the level of atoms and molecules, even if genetically derived from it. In physicists' usage, "disorder" frequently means merely non-reactivity, incapacity to do work. Perhaps the problem of entropy, that points to a hypothetical ultimate state of absolute "disorder", should be treated as an open problem. If one does so the question arises whether the use of the terms "order" and "disorder" on the physical–chemical levels is anything more than an anthropocentric distinction. From a human standpoint the gigantic explosion at the end of a star's career that we call a nova may appear as catastrophic disorder, and the regular circulation of the planets around the sun year in, year out as the diametric opposite to this chaotic event, the epitome of natural order at its most beautiful and eternal. But such a distinction merely expresses the evaluation of the two events by humans. Within the framework of physical–chemical occurrences themselves – that is, in terms of the chain-reaction of a star process described earlier – the phase of a nova explosion represents exactly the same order or disorder as the circulation of satellites around a main-sequence star like the sun. Applied to this level of natural events, the distinction between order and disorder is meaningless.

The situation is different if one reflects on the process of the great evolution and asks what the terms "order" and "disorder" mean when applied to higher levels of integration, to organisms like bacteria, flies, carp or mice. In relation to the level of integration of any kind of organism, the distinction between order and disorder has a far more precise meaning than in relation to physical–chemical events. Even in the simplest unicellular organism a very complex functional interdependence of constituents can be observed. There are specialized organs which cannot function, or cannot function properly, if other organs do not function in a corresponding way. There are control mechanisms of one kind or another which maintain the unity and integrity of such a system within the surrounding world, and assure its survival in a constant interchange of products with this world. Such systems represent, therefore, a type of order which is different from and – one is surely justified in saying – of a higher and more complex kind than that prevalent on the physical–chemical plane. Corresponding to the degree and stability of the functional integration of composite units on this level of natural events are forms of disintegration which have no counterpart on the physical–chemical plane. For them we have names such as "illness" or "death". A fly is swatted. It lies motionless. If one were able to take a complete inventory of its physical–chemical components, there is a high degree of certainty that, to begin with, there would be no difference between the living fly and the dead one. What has changed is the organization of the physical–chemical processes, their integration to form systems on a higher level of organization, such as tissue and organs, and their self-regulating adaptation to each other – just because organisms represent a specific organization of physical–chemical processes and therefore a type of order which does not exist on the physical–chemical plane. This is precisely why there are forms of disorder and disintegration on this plane which lack equivalents on the physical–chemical plane.

III

If one reflects on what has been said, one comes to a curious conclusion – though perhaps only curious in the light of a traditional way of thinking and the theories of science guided by it. The behaviour of a fly, unlike that of a chemical compound or a molecule, so it appears, cannot be explained solely by its chemical–physical composition, by the properties of its chemical–physical part-units examined in isolation. It is the arrangement in which chemical–physical processes are bound together and interact, the organization, the integration pattern of these processes, that has explanatory value on this level. To understand this is simple enough in itself. But deeply rooted intellectual habits – and the control which their exponents are able to exert on the mental habits of our society – obstruct this understanding.

The discussion on how to explain the difference between the functioning and behaviour of molecules and the connections between them, on the one hand, and those of representatives of the next higher level of integration, that is, unicellular organisms, and then organisms in general, on the other, has been stuck fast for some time. The paradigms common to the opposed parties make it appear as if there were only two possible answers to this question. Either one can assume that unicellular organisms like protozoa, or the somewhat more primitive bacilli and the more complex organisms derived from them, owe the quality which distinguishes them as living entities from the chemical compounds of which they consist, to a special agent of a non-material nature, an invisible "vital force", added to the physical–chemical composition of unicellular as of multicellular organisms as a distinguishing attribute. Or one can assume that the distinguishing qualities of all living beings will one day be traced back to the properties of their chemical–physical constituents in exactly the same way as the properties and connections of molecules can be derived from their constituent atoms and their particles. In short, hardly has one escaped the idealists in this discussion than one falls into the hands of the materialists. Undoubtedly, the consensus of those researching in the relevant disciplines today inclines strongly towards the latter. The idealist vitalists have clearly lost the battle. But the physicalist solution, for its part,[6] and the expectation tacitly contained in it that, sooner or later, one will be able to explain the functioning and behaviour of complex organisms like human beings exhaustively on the pattern of physics by the properties and behaviour of their constituent parts, and so finally by the molecules, atoms, electrons, and so on, forming them, is scarcely convincing.

Perhaps in thinking and speaking about this problem one should be more concerned with intellectually assimilating what can be observed all around us. The petrified clinch in which physicalist biologists perceive as the only alternative to their position that of the metaphysicians and vitalists, and vice-versa, obstructs the view of the evidence. The available factual material shows quite unambiguously that the functioning and behaviour of more highly organized units cannot be explained solely by the properties of their part-units studied in isolation. They are explained also, to a greater or lesser degree depending on the level of order in question, by the organization of the parts, the configuration they form together – in short, by the way they are functionally interdependent. On the physical–chemical plane such functional interdependence of part-units is not encountered. For this reason scientists elucidating these levels can very successfully develop procedures aimed at deducing and explaining the properties of composite units from those of their constituents studied in isolation. In the study of different biological units, too, procedures and explanations of the physical–chemical kind can be indispensable, since organisms after all consist of atoms and molecules. But it is a vain hope of physicists and chemists (and at bottom only an assertion of power), that organisms will ever be adequately explained in their manner, by reduction to the integration level of molecules and atoms. It is a vain hope not because some extra-physical vital force is at work here, but because in this case the organization and integration of the parts have a determining influence on the properties and behaviour of the composite units, and often enough on those of the constituent parts as well.

Here one can perhaps see somewhat more clearly why the intellectual assimilation of what distinguishes the areas of subject-matter of the different sciences is essential for an understanding of the relationships of these sciences to each other. It is one of the special difficulties encountered in trying to clarify the relationship between these different areas, that existing terminology and concepts are not equal to the task. It is sometimes said, for example, that the distinguishing property of living beings is that they are able to create more order out of less. This does indeed point towards a central aspect of the difference between living and non-living units. But the manner of expression is not particularly clear. The development of linguistic and conceptual symbols clearly lags behind that of knowledge; and this discrepancy hinders or blocks the latter's progress. The concept of order proves to be too static to express what is observable in detail if, for example, a vegetable organism is studied in relation to its nutrients. Through the action of solar energy and the mediation of their own chlorophyll, plants are able to convert substances poor in energy and of relatively simple organization into more highly-organized, energy-rich substances. In food-chains there is a whole series of steps whereby what is eaten belongs to a relatively low level of order and is assimilated by the eaters, partly converted, to their own, higher level of order.[7] Traditional linguistic usage really only allows us to use the term "order" statically, with the equally static concept of "disorder" as its counterpart. But what can be observed if we mentally ascend the evolutionary ladder from the level of subatomic particles, atoms and molecules to large molecules, unicellular and multicellular organisms, is not only an order of stages, but stages of order, transitions from units made of parts hardly linked by division of functions, to units with parts more and more functionally interrelated on more and more levels of integration. The dynamization of the theoretical model to encompass the great evolution therefore requires that static dichotomies like "order" and "disorder" be abandoned. In their place concepts are needed that make it possible to symbolize the interlocking levels of order that can be observed, and to communicate about them unambiguously.

IV

It is partly, if not solely, this weakness of conceptualization on the higher levels of symbolic synthesis, in contrast to the development of detailed knowledge, that currently makes it difficult to perceive and express the co-determining function of the configuration of part-units in the behaviour of composite units above the molecular level. Of course, on the level of individual sciences, the idea of a hierarchy of the stages of integration of forms of existence, corresponding roughly to the sequence of development stages, is now by no means alien. But the study of the theoretical

Table 1   shows some of the stages of integration as they can be presented today.

	Most highly differentiated and integrated organisms (human) with multi-level neural centralisation, uniquely high learning capacity, with inter-generational knowledge transmission, with a biological potential for forming permanent social units which, however, have no biologically predetermined structure, are, therefore, not species specific and can change in accordance with learning processes and other external or internal levers of change.
from these	More highly differentiated and integrated organisms with multi-level neural centralisation, higher though still very limited learning capacity, forming transient or permanent social units with species specific structure.
from these	More differentiated and more closely integrated organisms with one or two levels of neural centralisation and some learning capacity forming loosely integrated mostly impermanent social units with species specific structure.
from these	Multi-cellular organisms loosely integrated without or with rudimentary neural or hormone centralisation, no or little learning capacity, no or loosely integrated social units.
from unicellar organisms	unicellar organisms
from large molecules	large molecules
from small molecules	small molecules
from atoms	atoms
from sub-atomic particles	

implications of such findings, and of their significance for a theory of science, is blocked.

The facts on which table 1 (see p. 151) is based are very simple. One might suppose them to be widely known. Nevertheless a provisional synopsis sharpens perception of problems that often merely vegetate in the margins of awareness, or are beyond its horizon. One of these problems invites reflection.

Problematic is, for instance, what the preposition "from" refers to. It can mean both "composed of" and "developed from". The ambiguity could have been avoided, but it draws attention to the question of whether the hierarchy of interlocking levels of an organism, as it can be observed today, duplicates the hierarchy of development stages – that is, the diachronic process whereby relatively simple integrates, atomic and molecular units, gave rise to more complex ones. For the time being the question will remain open. It will be rewarding to come back to it somewhat later.

Another problematic aspect, unfamiliar in this context, is the concept of a "society of organisms". The distance between biology and sociology is at present so great that biologists use the concept of society only in quite specific cases – for example, in studying the social life of anthropoid apes or ants. The habit of speaking of "the" organisms in the singular is still deeply ingrained in them. When they wish to speak of a plurality of organisms, they use expressions like "populations" or "species". Often enough the individual organism in its environment serves as the biologists' model. However, at least in the case of all species that reproduce sexually, the relation of the individual organism to others cannot be simply subsumed under the concept of "environment". In many cases the individual organism is constitutionally dependent on living temporarily or permanently with others of its kind. This is especially the case with humans, who only attain the human level of experience and behaviour through learning a social communication system, a language.

Expressions like "genus", "species" or "population" give the impression of a merely statistical agglomeration of individuals. They are characteristic of an atomistic canon of thought: each individual organism, so it appears, can exist like an atom totally independently of others. It is enough to count the heads or determine the properties and behaviour of many individual organisms, to be able to make reliable statements about populations or species. In some cases this procedure is also sufficient on the level of organisms; but in many others it is not. Traditional habits of thought often blind us to the obvious. One says, for example, that a species is a multiplicity of populations of similar individual beings that can together produce offspring of the same kind. But the very fact that an individual organism is dependent by nature on producing the next generation with another organism of its own kind gives a peculiar character to the relationships between members of a species. There are associations between such members – for example, herds, households or hordes – that outlast the rutting season, with emotional ties limited primarily to members of the species – associations of a social kind, the survival value of which undoubtedly lies above all in protection against attacks by non-members. There is strong reason to believe that, precisely in the evolution of hominids who possess no inborn weapons like claws or powerful teeth, the forming of groups played a central role in the struggle for survival with other species or with other groups of the same species. The development of many species-specific peculiarities in humans is hardly understandable without this fundamental adaptation of individual humans to live communally with others.

In many cases, therefore, the species and the population do not consist of isolated organisms. The individuals are linked in social unions of the most diverse kind – in societies whose structure, in the case of non-human organisms, is fairly immutably established in conjunction with genetically rooted instinctual and behavioural structures. In the case of humans, by contrast, owing to the far greater plasticity of their instinctual and behavioural structures, the social structure is malleable and, in conjunction with the growth of knowledge over generations, for example, highly capable of change.

In this way, in the form of the intellectual tradition which induces biologists to perceive the unit of species simply as a unit composed of individual organisms, a political preconception, the image of society as a plurality of independent individuals, may be misleading thinkers. For the simple desire of a single individual for sexual association, and beyond that for a wide range of intense and subtle emotional relationships, together with the need for protection already mentioned, impels the individual to form social structures. The tendency to generate social formations of one kind or another, whether in congenitally fixed or largely learnable form, is biologically anchored in practically all higher organisms and in many lower ones. In the hierarchy of integration stages, therefore, one cannot ascend directly from the isolated organism to the biological unit of genus and species. Between them, as an integration level of a specific kind, comes the grouping of individual organisms into social units, whether they be families or herds as in the case of lions and elephants, or tribes and states, villages and cities as in the case of humans. Even in speaking of humans and their environment one scarcely does justice to the facts. One can really only speak of the environment of villages and towns, tribes and nations – that is, of human societies of specific kinds. The relations of people to their fellows, social relations, have a different character from their relations to rivers and rocks, plants and animals – to their "environment". The society they form together, one might say, is the primary sphere of humans.

The habit of many biologists – and of many physicians – of placing the isolated organism at the centre of attention and of neglecting the fundamental sociality of organisms – their need to live, whether temporarily or permanently, in interdependence with their fellows as a particular form of integration – originates in part in an intellectual tradition which was most pronounced in the seventeenth and eighteenth centuries. In accordance with the state of knowledge at the time, all that was really regarded as structured and therefore accessible to scientific theory was "nature" and the individual with his or her "consciousness" and his or her "reason", that is, only the "object" and the "subject". What lay between them, particularly the social groupings of individuals, of "subjects", appeared as devoid of order and structure and was therefore consigned to the sphere of practical life that existed in the anteroom of science and philosophy, but was not really a part of it. The gradual rise of the social sciences, and particularly sociology, in the nineteenth and twentieth centuries, for all the frailty of these disciplines, made the scientific exploration of the social level of integration of humans a tangible possibility. Nevertheless, many scientists, especially biologists, not to speak of philosophers, still really hold fast to the old ideal of the isolated organism in its environment, the human individual as opposed to "nature", the "subject" as against the "object". Sociologists, on the other hand, always beset by anxieties over status and autonomy, have developed, after a number of bad experiences in the past, a kind of traumatic aversion to all attempts to elucidate the relationship of the level of integration they themselves study to the preceding levels, and particularly to the biological. They fear reduction to this level, and the propensity of many biologists to explain human society and behaviour entirely on the pattern of pre-human integration levels contributes in no small way to the exaggeratedly defensive attitude of sociologists towards biology.

But it is not really an answer for those afraid of reduction, whether it be of sociology to biology or of biology to physics and chemistry, to abstain from asking whether and how far the sciences exploring the different integration levels of the universe are justified in claiming autonomy. Is this claim by different groups of scientists merely a by-product of the social organization of science, which allocates separate and more or less autonomous departments and institutes to each group of specialists, and so unintentionally provokes competition for status, finance and power between them? Does the demand by the different academic groups for autonomy in their relations to each other result solely from the desire of different professorial establishments not to be interfered with by other groups in their investigation of their field, or even to be forced into the position of client to another group? Or are there objective reasons founded in the nature of the subject-matter itself which prevent the great disciplines working on different levels of integration from simply dissolving into each other?

The schematic representation of the levels of integration set out earlier offers a good starting point for a discussion of this question. Some aspects of it are very instructive in this context. Considered as social organizations, the different disciplines stand side by side, so to speak, in the same plane. A one-dimensional model outside space and time appears to be enough to symbolize their relations to each other. And as it is often presented today as if the relationship of the different sciences to each other is representative of the relationship between their areas of subject-matter, one unwittingly thinks of the subject-matter of the physical, biological and human sciences as if they too existed side by side in the same plane. On closer consideration one readily sees that their relationship is considerably more complex. They are representatives of an advancing synthesis, an integration process within which, above the level of molecules, each stage of a higher and, in evolutionary terms, later integration contains representatives or descendants of all the earlier stages as part-units. Humans, too, consist of atoms and molecules. They too consist of cells which in their basic structure are practically identical to those of many, if not all, unicellular organisms. The assumption that all living beings are descended from unicellular organisms thereby gains probability. Humans, too, consist of tissue, organs and systems of organs like bones, muscles, nerves and viscera. But in their case the differentiation of organ systems, like their integration, their centralized regulation and control, has attained a degree and a structure unique among the forms of life known to us: humans are the highest units of integration that we know. In brief, the simple picture of the subject-matter of the sciences based largely on the horizontal juxtaposition of departments gives way to a vertical continuum of levels of integration representing the sequence of stages of an evolutionary process, and within which representatives or descendants of earlier stages are either subordinated to later ones or, as in the case of younger and older brain centres, form with them a complex equilibrium.

This implies at the same time that the idea that the relations of the sciences to each other can be grasped by a model representing them as simply juxtaposed is misleading. Here too a multidimensional model is needed which, among other things, takes account of the hierarchic interlocking of different levels of integration, and so of the subject-matter of different sciences.

V

It was emphasized above that the modes of behaviour of organisms, of units integrated by division of functions, cannot be adequately explained, on the pattern of molecules and atoms by the properties of their constituent part-units. To say this in no way contradicts the fact that the more organized units have *developed* from molecules. In the course of this century the probability of the assumption that all multicellular organisms have arisen from unicellular ones, and these from non-living tissue, has increased very considerably. As early as the twenties the Russian scholar A. Oparin elaborated the first model of a "primal organism" which could be in part experimentally tested. Since then the idea has gained increasing authority that the form of organization which gives a system the character of a living being – that is, to begin with, the form of a cell – has emerged from simpler large-molecule structures which did not yet have the character of living beings. This emergence is thought to have taken place in conjunction with stages of the earth's development which were different from the one familiar to us.

The search for intermediate links and processes between molecules and cells has made considerable progress. We should imagine ourselves transported to a world in which plants and therefore photosynthesis did not yet exist. We must suppose that these early systems, which in terms of development antedate the differentiation of living beings into plants and animals and can be considered as ancestors of both, were not yet able to use chlorophyll to convert solar energy into nutrient chemical energy. It is therefore usually assumed today that these transitional systems drew nutritive substances from energy-storing compounds in their environment, which, like themselves, had come into being in connection with certain cosmic events, such as repeated electrical discharges or protracted ultra violet radiation. Laboratory experiments have confirmed that more highly-organized organic compounds, that we know as constituents of cells, can come into being in this way. The early terrestrial atmosphere was very different from the present one. Water, carbon monoxide, nitrogen and hydrogen – pure or in combi-nation with chlorine – were predominant, and free oxygen was absent. So the earliest forms of the integration stage that we call organisms may have been anaerobes – unicellular creatures which need no free oxygen and usually perish when it is present. What is fairly certain is that a very special sequence of circumstances – an improbable sequence – was one of the preconditions for this early synthesis, and for the next stages as well. The presence of free oxygen with its reducing effect would probably have made the earliest levels of organisms impossible; and the absence of free oxygen, the later ones.

At any rate, the discovery of fossilized remains of primitive unicells in geological formations without other traces of life have lent weight to the supposition that such simple unicellular organ-isms formed, among the ancestors of the polymorphous organ-isms, one of the transitional stages between the groups of objects that we classify as inanimate and animate. It may perhaps help in imagining these remote events to call to mind the timescale over which such processes take place. The geological formations in which fossil traces of these early organisms have been found are about 495 million years old. But these early unicells were already relatively complex and specialized creatures. If one attempts to calculate the timespan within which large molecules combined to form these simplest, yet in comparison to them far more complex, cell systems, one must envisage far longer stretches of time as the framework for this life-forming process. Estimates vary between 1500 and 3000 million years. So far back lies the period of transition from systems we today consider as inanimate to those regarded as animate.

The fixed language of our day impedes understanding of this process. We are fond of formulations like "the origin of life" or "the earliest form of life". But concepts of this kind obscure the actual character of what happened – its character as a process. Traditional habits of speech and thought impel us to seek the "beginnings" of life. But there are none. Our concepts, and so our imagination, are attuned to a sharp distinction between animate and inanimate entities. This makes it difficult to take cognizance of transitional forms. It impedes the imagining of pre-animate entities that cannot be accommodated in the familiar categories of "animate" and "inanimate", that are no longer merely physical–chemical molecular systems and not yet bio-logical cellular systems.

In our day too, of course, there are related entities – for example viruses – of which some are no more than sacs full of large molecules, of genetic material. They derive all other materials from host cells which they permeate and infect with their genetic material, so that these cells, as if under a changed command, produce entities of the same kind as the invading virus instead of their own kind. But whether such simple organisms of our time are counted, like bacteria and blue algae, as direct descendants of the early unicellular organisms that are among the ancestors of all living things, or whether they are seen as regressive forms of more developed unicellular organisms – only an enlargement of our temporal awareness makes it possible to understand the processes that are involved. Our immediate consciousness of time is largely conditioned by the length of a human life. A hundred years – broadly speaking one's own lifetime and that of one's parents and grandparents – are for many people within the range of their imagination. A span of ten thousand years takes us to the limit of what we consider as history; a million years are beyond normal apprehension; 3000 million abolish it entirely. But if the desire for knowledge is great enough to open minds at all to the problem of the great evolution, and within it to questions about the processes by which living beings have emerged, it may be hoped that the ego-related, involved awareness of time will succeed in subordinating itself to a more detached one.

For many hundreds of millions of years, therefore, the process lasted which led from the emergence of large molecules – which now no longer arise spontaneously outside organisms – to the protists, the early unicells. This, as one can see, was a process of natural synthesis. One might think that the use of the term "nature" today is not very readily associated with processes like this one – that is, the formation of more highly-organized units distinguished, from other units representing a lower level of differentiation and integration, by a higher form of functional differentiation and integrating control. For many people "nature", it seems, is represented essentially by simple mechanical cause-and-effect relationships and general, timeless laws for an unlimited number of particular cases. But problems of synthesis, on the level of integration of "cells from large molecules" just discussed as being on higher levels, are no less to be counted among normal natural phenomena than, say, the gravity pulling bodies thrown in the air back to earth, or the valencies binding two hydrogen atoms to one oxygen atom in a water molecule. But this perspective on nature, as was seen earlier with regard to the evolution of stars, is now still further removed from "nature" as the epitome of the unchanging and everlasting. Nature is only so when seen in the light of the human longing for immortality, for a still pole in the flux of appearances – that is, when seen through the lens of involvement. With greater detachment, the character of nature as process emerges more sharply even here, in the study of the transition of the natural levels of organization that we register as inanimate to others that we classify as living beings. And as always in the great discoveries of humanity, with the joy of seeing a veil drawn aside and a growing synthesis which slowly makes visible connections that were unseen before, is mixed a feeling of regret and disappointment: the beautiful sun – an episode in a blind chain-process, a meaningless fire consuming itself; the human beings who demand meaning – descendants of very small unicellular creatures that formed on a wholly inanimate earth, like minute scraps of jelly in a thin broth of larger molecules.

VI

At first sight a scientific development in the direction just described appears to confirm the widely disseminated physicalist–materialist thesis on the explanation of living beings. But if the argument used in this thesis is considered more closely, it loses its power to convince. That it has retained this power so long can only be explained at all by the fact that the eyes of its exponents have been fixed on the vitalist thesis as the only alternative. From the obvious wishful thinking of their opponents, the supporters of the physicalist argument derive their strength. The central point of this argument is simple enough: since biological units, organisms, have emerged in all probability from physical–chemical units, molecules, their properties too must be explainable by those of the constituent molecules and, further, by those of the atoms forming the molecules. This conclusion is itself questionable. It becomes still more so when applied to humans. Human beings, too, are made up of molecules and atoms. Therefore, the physicalist argument runs, one can expect that sooner or later the distinguishing characteristics of human beings as well will be explained by those of their constituent chemical–physical units.

The inadequacy of the physicalist argument does not lie in its exponents' insistence on the idea that the properties of composite units, in this case human beings, could be explained by those of the constituent parts, but rather in the fact that they regard this kind of explanation as quite generally sufficient. It is sufficient, as far as can be seen, only on the level of phenomena where the constituent parts, the integrants, are bound together to form the integrates of the next level in a way which involves no division of functions and is therefore reversible. It is indispensable, but no longer sufficient, for elucidating levels of integration where the integrants are joined functionally and irreversibly in integrates. The contribution which physical–chemical investigation on the level of molecules and atoms can make to an understanding of the functioning and behaviour of a more highly organized unit diminishes – without reaching a zero-point – as this unit becomes more highly organized, with a correspondingly greater hierarchy of interlocking centres of integration. The contribution of a study of molecular structures to understanding unicellular organisms such as bacteria is relatively large, though not sufficient even here. The great successes of physicalist microbiology are thus quite understandable. The contribution of a study of molecular structures is relatively slight, if not entirely dispensible, when the functioning and behaviour of higher organisms, and especially human beings, are to be explained. In these cases the explanation of the behaviour and functioning of a unit in terms of the *configuration* of the parts – of their organization and integration – is joined to the explanation in terms of the properties of the constituents as an indispensable, central element; and this mode of explanation, explanation by synthesis, as against explanation by analysis, takes on increasing importance the further one moves up the ladder of evolution, of interwoven levels of integration. Physical–chemical studies of human beings are indeed essential and very useful. But they contribute relatively little, and can in fact be misleading, unless they are incorporated into a model of humans which shows their structure and the many interlocking levels of differentiation and integration above the physical level.

What is preventing discussion from advancing beyond the materialism–vitalism debates is a number of specific habits of thought which have now largely been left behind by recent developments in research. To be sure, it is not long since analysis – dissecting into parts and determining their properties in iso-lation – was regarded not only as the most distinguished instru-ment of scientific research, but as the only one that could legitimize systematic investigations as scientific. It sometimes seemed as if the adherents of analytical methods regarded analysis not merely as a scientific instrument but as the innermost property of nature itself, the scientific procedure that most closely matched the normal processes of nature. In the meantime, awareness has grown that syntheses, too, are among the normal processes of nature. As long as the study of integration levels without division of functions was taken as a model for the study of all levels of integration in the universe, autonomous syntheses of simpler units to form more complex ones played only a small part among the phenomena investigated by science. But in the course of the last century understanding of autonomous natural syntheses has increased visibly. The higher we go up the evol-utionary ladder, the more decisive becomes the role, and the more complex the pattern, of self-regulating processes of organiz-ation and integration.

The task and methods of scientific research are changing

accordingly. Analytic methods aimed at determining – and above all at measuring – isolated parts remain fruitful and necessary. But the more science endeavours to elucidate higher levels of integration, the more the function of the isolating method, and its contribution to problem-solving, changes. The fact that it has been possible to develop physical–chemical methods continuously, from their application to atomic and molecular processes to the elucidation of organic molecules synthesized from living entities, can easily obscure the functional change they have undergone in the process. In studying parts of a cell, and still more in studying parts of a multicellular organism, it is no longer possible to explain and understand their structures unless one simultaneously attempts to determine their function within the framework of the higher level of integration, and the organized configuration of their own parts corresponding to this function.

A cell is a highly complex organization of part-units. Investigation of, for example, the cell nucleus, the locus of genetic information, or of the small cylindrical bodies, or mitochondria, which regulate breathing and produce enzymes, certainly entails studying the molecules and atoms forming them, including their nuclei and electron shells. But in this context, studying them in isolation is only of significance if it helps us to understand what functions cell nuclei, mitochondria and other parts of cells may have in the total operation of the cell, and how their composition and organization make it possible for them to perform these functions. This is more true the higher the level of integration being studied. Investigation of the atomic and molecular composition of liver or brain is necessary, but not sufficient, for an understanding of their functions. One would go considerably astray if one approached the problems posed by such organs with the expectation that physical–chemical investigation could supply the final, fundamental answer to these problems. However indispensable knowledge of the atomic and molecular composition of such organs may be for understanding their functions within the organism, the final, the fundamental task in this case is to determine these functions, and the hierarchic organization of molecules into cells, cells into tissue, tissue into organs, that enables the latter to perform their functions.

To sum up, where processes of natural synthesis have led to more complex forms of the organization of matter and energy, the problems arising can never be solved solely and adequately by chemical–physical investigation of the matter that has been organized. The results of purely physical–chemical studies of the atomic structure of liver or brain remain meaningless until they are seen in relation to the functions of these organs in the context of the whole organism. The patterns of biological organization and integration therefore provide, in this case, the framework of reference for investigating physical–chemical part-units. That is why the procedure needed here is in certain respects the exact opposite of the one appropriate to the subject-matter of the physical sciences. In the latter, it is possible to obtain very precise information on the properties of integrates by studying their parts observed in isolation. Here, the process of research leads from the understanding of the smaller constituent parts to that of the larger composite units. In the former, the representatives of higher levels of integration, it is necessary to dig tunnels, as it were, on the various levels of integration and to coordinate the findings in a model of the highest level. It is from these models, the construction of which necessitates work on the tunnels at different levels, that this work derives its direction and its purpose – they define the problems to be solved on other levels, and give meaning and relevance to the results of research. The patterns of organization on the highest level provide the framework of reference: by moving up or down between levels of integration within this framework, whether alone or in collaboration with specialists in different levels, one works towards a goal – to understand and explain how the integrate on the highest level has come into being in the process of evolution, and how and why it functions in this specific way. As long as one is dealing with units not organized by division of functions, it is appropriate to proceed from the integrants to the integrate. Even in studying the behaviour of large molecules – for example, the long chains of nucleic acids – this procedure is no longer enough. But the transition from the study of smaller molecules to that of large ones took place so gradually in science that those who brought about the change were hardly aware of the different procedure that was being introduced.

Thus Crick and Watson, for example, in discovering the structure of the large molecules which bear the genetic codes of all organisms, clearly believed they had followed the traditional procedure of physical–chemical science. This procedure was indeed indispensable to their success. Countless measurements of isolated parts of these large molecules were needed to solve the riddle of the genetic codes embedded in them. But what was decisive from early on in the task the scientists set themselves was a question that could not be answered by the traditional procedure of physical reduction, the tracing back of the properties of a composite unit to those of its constituent parts. The central problem was, precisely, which organization of the parts could explain the autonomous replication of the relevant large molecules, and so finally, too, the resemblance of parents and children. The measurement of isolated parts alone, although essential, could not lead to the intellectual synthesis that was needed to reconstruct the natural synthesis in thought; it alone was not enough to tell the scientists that the organization of parts in the form of a double helix could provide the best answer to the question of how genetic information is transmitted by chromosomes.

VII

The fact that even in a living cell, and then in all organisms without exception, the part-processes are governed by the integrate they form together, has a number of aspects the presentation of which requires particular circumspection. As has been stated, in the hierarchy of integration levels there is a transition from the constituent parts to the form of organization as the prime explanatory factor. This transition cannot be properly grasped until one realizes that it is a process in which relationships of power and dominance play a part. Caution is indicated in the use of such terms, since it is not uncommon in our world for the ideological conceptions which a scientist has of power relationships between people to be projected on to nature. It is perhaps useful, therefore, to point out briefly that the relations between integrants and integrate encountered on the different levels of integration are found to alter not only in the transition to animate systems, but also in the transition from pre-human organisms to humans. Much could be said on the way in which, for example, the relation of individuals to the groups which they form differs between pre-human organisms and humans. But the difference is much greater in the case of the relation of the individual cell to the "society" of cells, or of the organs to the organism. On all rungs of the ladder there are relationships between integrants and integrates. The specific nature of each deserves to be studied, for on many levels they differ ontologically. Likewise, the nature of dominance on various levels differs. But to gain a picture of the process of the great evolution we cannot entirely do without a concept of this kind, and related ones such as the power struggle and the balance of power. Perhaps human beings can only attain full awareness of the human task in contemplating the unmitigated savagery of the struggle for existence of far-off creatures without awareness.

A few examples may help. Among the evidence for the process character of the transition to the level of integration characterized as "life" is the discovery that there are, among living things, a number of simple forms with low differentiation in their cell structures – procaryotic cells. All other organisms, without exception, have the more developed type of eucaryotic cells – amoebae, like humans, possess these cells. Procaryotic organisms include bacteria and blue algae, very early organisms which have remained largely unchanged over aeons. Procaryotic organisms lack an internal membrane system. Consequently, they lack the small "organs" that are found at the later stage as clearly defined separate formations, such as the cell nucleus in which the genetic information is embedded, or the small cylindrical corpuscles known as mitochondria and specializing in functions such as enzyme synthesis and gaseous exchange. Precursors of these specialized corpuscles in the less complex cellular organisms are simply incorporated in or attached to the inside of the surface membrane. That the more complex cell form has evolved from the less differentiated one can be considered probable. As to how and why this happened, there are at best hypotheses. It is surmised, for example, that the stages of this development include the union of two cells of the older type. One of them was transformed in the course of time into an organ of the other. The mitochondria of the more developed, eucaryotic cells possess, indeed, a number of structures in common with the older procaryotic cells. They alone, of the parts of the eucaryotic cells, synthesize their own proteins; they reproduce themselves. They form, on the one hand, parts of the eucaryotic cell having certain special functions with regard to their total economy; on the other, they possess peculiarities of an independent organism.[8]

Here, therefore, we have an example of a process that escapes understanding if we rely on the traditional, unrefined concepts usual in this context. A concept of the organism that takes no account of the evolution of organisms can easily suggest that within organisms the subordination of the parts to the command of the whole, the degree of integration, is the same at all stages of evolution; but that is not the case. At present the concepts at our disposal are not sufficiently developed to express in a clearly understandable way the observable differences not only between stages but between degrees of integration in the course of development. For this reason one must first refer to specific empirical observations, and use them as models to make clear that the natural process of integration is also a process with many stages and degrees. The example of the mitochondria shows one of these stages. Whether or not the hypothesis is correct that the path of development from the simpler procaryotic organisms to the more complex eucaryotic unicells included a union of two procaryotic cells, leading to a limited predominance of one over the other – the example of the mitochondria remains in the memory as a model of a transitional situtation in which, while the predominance of the total economy of an organism over the constituent parts is already partly established and genetically anchored, nevertheless a particular organ has retained functions which in the total structure are performed by other organs.

Precisely this relinquishment of functions by one part-unit to others – that is, the extent of functional interdependence – differs on different levels of organic evolution. On the level of unicellular organisms, the extent of differentiation is certainly great as compared to that of their supposed abiotic predecessors, the freely existing large molecules such as protein or nucleic acids. It is also greater than in the most complex machines so far produced by human beings. But it is relatively small if a eucaryotic unicell is compared to a multicellular organism of higher levels – for example, a mammal. On the level of mammals the functional differentiation of organisms is so advanced that there are special systems of coordination, integration and control. The system of endocrine glands and the nervous system are examples. On the level of unicellular organisms, there are as yet only the beginnings of a specialized central control. To a high degree the functionally interdependent organs regulate each other, although there are clearly balances of power of widely differing kinds. In speaking of the total economy or the total structure of a cell, one does not refer to a "whole" existing beyond its parts or which, as is commonly said, is "more than the sum of its parts". One refers to the mutual dependence of the functionally divided special organs of the organism, in this case a cell. The more exact study of its genetically rooted balances of power and their failure is among the somewhat neglected tasks of biological research. The underlying physicalist attitude of many biologists, and the idea that any deviation from it must betray vitalist leanings, so concentrates scientists' attention on the study of individual organs, of their composition and functioning in isolation, that the investigation of power relationships among part-units in exercising their interdependent functions suffers.

One example is the main direction of cancer research. In carcinomas a cell growth that is normally controlled by an organ's function in the overall structure of the organism becomes autonomous. The subordination of cell growth to the demands of a functionally differentiated structure may have been preceded at earlier stages by other balances of power and a kind of power struggle – different power balances that proved less successful. Unlike human societies in which people without biological differences are bound together by division of functions, and within which the distribution of power can be changed without the people changing biologically, composite units on the biological level comprise functionally interdependent part-units which themselves differ genetically, biologically, in accordance with their functions. And changes in the balance of power over generations – such as increasing cerebral dominance in the course of hominization – depend on changes in genetic structure.[9] How the mutual adaptation of all part-units is actually maintained in an organism, and secured against deviations, is not quite clear at the present state of research. But cancer is at any rate an example of such a deviation. In this case, by a sort of revolt, cells throw off the control that adjusts their growth to the functional needs of an organ, and grow as if they existed freely and independently of the organism within which they help to form one of the specialized organs. In this way they lead the organism of which they are a part, and so finally themselves, to disintegration and destruction.

VIII

Human beings comprise cell structures so highly differentiated and so firmly integrated that any autonomy among cells has the character of an illness destroying the total structure. In simpler organisms, in which the functional independence of the constituent parts is less, these parts, even including individual cells, sometimes have greater autonomy and freedom of movement. The contrast is instructive. It perhaps makes it easier to understand the peculiarity of the subject-matter of biology, as compared to that of physics, and also the differences between biological units themselves resulting from the direction of evolution.

One of the basic peculiarities of eucaryotic cells – that is, of the more highly developed cells of which all living creatures except the very simplest consist, from amoebae to humans – is their mutual adaptation. They possess a kind of ontological sociability which – so it appears – is lacking in the more primitive type of cells, and certainly in molecules and atoms. Cells are predisposed to certain forms of interdependence, such as material exchange, contact, communication. Accordingly, one frequently encounters cell societies or, to use the technical term, cell colonies.

Even bacteria form colonies. The earth is covered with them, as are human beings externally and internally – millions of bacteria in a drop of saliva. Of the theories seeking to explain how multicellular organisms arose from unicellular ones, the theory that they are derived from cell colonies is among the most convincing. Most of the transitional forms between unicellular and multicellular organisms have naturally disappeared; like many other links in the evolutionary chain, they have been superseded and suppressed by more efficient descendants. But a few such transitional forms still exist. A frequently mentioned example is the colonies of a slow-moving or stationary protozoan called volvox. They form small, spherical societies. In them can already be observed the beginnings of the change that unicells can undergo when they start to form a unit on the next higher level of integration. This union clearly offered advantages when it went hand in hand with a certain division of functions. But here and in other cases the biological division of functions signifies a transformation of the unicellular individual in keeping with its functions in the overall context of the society it forms with others, that is, the next higher level of integration. Particular cells develop relatively large eye-dots – spots which are light-sensitive. Other cells specialize in reproduction.

Matthias Schleiden who, together with Theodor Schwann, propounded in the first half of the nineteenth century the view that cells are the "elementary particles" of vegetable and animal organisms, expressed the idea that a cell leads a double life: it has some features of an independent entity, and others that identify it as an integral component of a composite unit of a higher order. This too is best expressed in terms of equilibrium. At the stage of colony formation, individual cells can still for a time exist independently of the society they form with others. Possibly the specializing transformation they undergo in the interests of the whole volvox colony can be reversed. In the balance of power between the function of the individual entity for itself and its function for the social integrate it forms with others, the two sides are at this stage quite evenly weighted. As the division of functions grows more complex and the transformation of the single organism in the interests of the multicellular one becomes more radical, the balance of power slowly inclines towards the higher level of integration. It gains the upper hand as the matrix determining the form of the part-units which compose it.

In scientific research too, therefore, it is less and less possible to proceed from the individual cells and independent units to the more comprehensive unit. Instead, it becomes increasingly necessary, in explaining the form and structure of individual cells, to proceed in the opposite direction from their functions within the mechanism of the composite unit, and so from this higher-order unit itself, to the lower-order units. Cells become specialized in accordance with their functions in the structure of the organism of which they are a part – for example, as muscle or nerve cells, vascular or epidermic cells – without ever entirely forfeiting their activity for themselves. Accordingly, the significance of the model of the higher-order unit as a factor in explaining the form, structure and behaviour of the lower-order units increases – without, as has been said, the explanatory significance of the latter's structure ever disappearing. The colony-forming unicells represent an early phase of the evolution of firmly integrated organisms with high division of functions. They therefore make visible a central aspect of this process. As we go up the ladder of biological evolution, we find that the balance of power between the representatives of different stages of configuration shifts in favour of the higher level, without the lower-order units' power potential ever being lost. Their function for higher levels of integration influences their structure and form increasingly, without their own structure and the power potential founded on it disappearing. What is decisive is that such balances of power are clearly anchored in the genetic material, the chromosomes. But for the present one only knows *that* this is the case; one knows only that gene mutation and natural selection in the struggle for survival play the central role in this transformation of part-units in the direction of greater stage-specificity. One knows less about *how*, in detail, the process operates, that leads increasingly to a transformation of less specialized but more independent ancestors into less independent but – in terms of a more comprehensive unit – more specialized part-units, and at the same time makes this transformation, over many intermediate stages, inevitable and irreversible.

One further example from the early stages of the evolutionary trajectory may make the direction of this transformation easier to visualize. The relatively simple organisms that we call fungi, some varieties of which have a protective skeleton that is sold as a bath sponge, are considered today as organisms that have evolved from colonies of a certain kind of protozoan, the flagellates, in all probability through amalgamation with a different, amoeba-like form of unicell. In the tightly knit contact-society of a fungus which they form together, the flagellate cells, through the combined movements of their small, whip-like projections, fan nutritive micro-organisms to the fungus, while the amoeba-like cells take over functions of digestion, gaseous exchange and reproduction. Here, therefore, an early form of the division of functions probably emerges from the union of two different types of unicellular organism to form a multicellular organism. On the level of development known to us, however, the inter-adaptation of cells of different origins is clearly already firmly anchored genetically. One perceives this if the integrating organization is destroyed – for example, by filtering the fungus through a cloth – and the behaviour of the now separate individual cells is observed. The single cells show a distinct tendency to reunite into fungi on the pattern of the destroyed organization, provided a flagellate-like cell can combine with an amoeba-like one. The part-units are therefore already programmed to integrate functionally to form a higher-order unit. Moreover, not only unicellular organisms but multicellular ones can form colonies. Jellyfish and sea anemones are examples: they exhibit a very tight integration of small multicellular organisms to form a larger and more complex unit. On this level there are again different types of division of functions. Some of the part-organisms change into organs serving to obtain and digest food, for example, and others into organs of propulsion and defence.

Through tissue cultures – the cultivation of isolated cell tissues and parts of organs in artificial nutrient material – one can examine more closely the behaviour and structural development of the more specialized cells of higher organisms. These experiments show, among other things, how far in many cases the genetically inbuilt functional specialization of the cell goes – a specialization that is sometimes rather misleadingly called the predominance of the organism over its parts – and how far the specialization of a cell is bound up with its interdependence with other cells, and so with its incorporation in the more comprehensive association of cells constituting the organism in question. The ability of cells as a tissue culture outside the organism to preserve the special function and structure they possess within the living organism, varies. It disappears most readily, it seems, in highly specialized cells whose special function is very closely bound up with the overall metabolism of the organism. Isolated cells of the mammary glands, for example, relatively quickly lose their ability to synthesize milk-producing enzymes. But on the other hand one finds that cells which normally – that is, within the "power structure" of the living organism – do not divide, regain the tendency to divide when isolated from it. The regulation of individual cell behaviour in keeping with the cell's function in the total structure appears in this case to include the suppression of a latent tendency to divide. In the case of a carcinoma it re-emerges.

IX

These few examples may be enough to make clearer how different the relationship between constituent parts and composite unit on the integration level of organisms is from the corresponding relationship on the level of atoms and molecules. The atomistic basic hypothesis of physics, the assumption that the properties of the smallest part-units can explain those of the higher units formed by them, finds its justification in the fact that on the levels of existence investigated by physicists the part-units have no stage-specific peculiarities. They are not transformed and specialized in conformity with the functional structure on the higher level, the integrate to which they belong as integrants. The levels of existence explored by biologists include at their periphery physical–chemical subject-matter; subatomic particles, atoms and small molecules constitute some of the levels of part-units of any organism. But in the living organism their behaviour is regulated by a type of order differing from that governing them on the physical–chemical levels. Their behaviour is regulated in accordance with their function within the framework of an overriding organization. They unite to form cells, which in turn form multicellular organisms; loosely integrated multicellular organisms form tightly knit, complex organisms. But the internal organization and behaviour of atoms and molecules remain unchanged, despite their integration into these higher-order formations. Only the regulation of their behaviour in keeping with the higher-order integration changes. This integration and organization of atoms and molecules is the reason why the behaviour of these higher-order units cannot be explained solely by the properties of the constituent atoms and molecules. When this organization disintegrates, when the integrate dissolves, molecules and atoms composing it are finally left behind. Only the configuration, the order which previously held them together, has disappeared. They lose thereby precisely those characteristics we refer to by terms such as "life" or "organism". The failure and finally the collapse of the organization of molecules in the form of cells, organs and organisms, we call "death". The small molecules and atoms which are bound together in this organization and regulated in accordance with it, but are not transformed stage-specifically in their structure, are therefore preserved on the death of an organism, but without self-regulating organization. Only from the integration stage of cells upwards are part-units formed in a stage-specific way – that is, in keeping with their functions in a higher integrate; and in this case their stage-specific structure is lost when this integrate decays. The cells that together form a human being die when the human being dies; the atoms forming the human being hardly change.

I have already said that the synthesis whereby molecules give rise to large molecules, and these – over many intermediate stages – give rise to cells, and cells to multicellular organisms, is a natural process. It is a natural process which is just as autonomous as that of star formation, discussed earlier, although, of course, of a different kind. Star formation is a chain-reaction within the same level or order, whereas we are here concerned with syntheses the results of which, integrates on a particular level of order, are combined by further syntheses into integrates of integrates, and so, through a whole series of interlocking planes of integration, into more and more complex and differentiated structures. To develop more appropriate symbols, more adequate concepts for these forms of existence – organisms – which would allow people to come to terms with them better, and beyond that to evolve more appropriate, stage-specific procedures of scientific research, is certainly not simple. But the difficulty is reduced if the task itself is clarified; for the difficulty in this case, to state it once more, does not lie in a shortage of detailed knowledge – the extraordinary progress which has been made at this level in the last generations, particularly as regards the significance of natural syntheses, has long called for a more comprehensive intellectual synthesis. What is blocking further development in this direction at present is a dominant array of mental habits, an outmoded system of categories which obstructs access to these connections and masks the connections themselves – partly, no doubt, because they run counter to human wishes. In addition, these mental habits are so familiar to people today that they seem self-evident; a deviation from them is almost inconceivable.

Among these mental habits, as has been said, is the idea of the all-embracing explanatory potential of atoms or, in more general terms, of the smallest part-units, with the concomitant idea of the precedence of isolating and dissecting procedures, of analysis, over model-constructing synthesis. How often one reads sentences like: "As the smallest structural and functional unit of the organism, the cell is the fundamental unit of life."

That from a certain level of subject-matter upwards, thought must proceed from models of the more comprehensive unit to its part-units, in order to gain more adequate knowledge – knowledge that does better justice to its object – is not, in itself, difficult to understand. But discussion, it appears, is stuck so fast in the struggle between false alternatives, that considerable effort is needed to steer the ship between Scylla and Charybdis – between the atomistic reductionism of the physicists and the holist or vitalist speculations of the metaphysicians – into clear water. This cannot be done convincingly by philosophizing, or at any rate not by being content with general reflections devoid of contact with relevant empirical facts. Even if these facts are only presented as if on the wing, this constant empirical relation, in conjunction with the corresponding steps of theoretical synthesis, is an indispensable moment in the effort to break out of entrapment by the present polarities.

X

What has been said so far has taken the argument up to the early stages of function-division and specialization in the formation of organisms. It would not be difficult to pursue the development of organisms from this aspect. It could be shown how organs are differentiated: certain tissues develop – in the form of muscles – into special organs for the conscious or automatic performance of movements, motorial organs; other cells are specialized to receive sense impressions, others again become specialists in digestion. Within each of these special areas, the organs become differentiated and organize themselves into systems of organs. It must be enough to point to this process of the increasing differentiation of organs in the course of evolution (which certainly goes hand in hand with shifts in the opposite direction), and to elucidate it by a single example.

The example relates to a peculiarity of the natural make-up of human beings which, as evidence of the increasing differentiation of organisms, has perhaps not received the attention it deserves. If the faces of higher apes are compared to those of human beings, there are certainly a number of resemblances. But the differences include a peculiarity that on a purely factual level could perhaps be most simply described as the greater mobility of the human face, and the greater fixity of the ape face by comparison. This is confirmed if we go further down the evolutionary ladder. The parts around the mouth, nose and eyes become more rigid. Even fish may in human eyes have faces with a certain expression, but really the area around the eyes is entirely fixed. That humans, among all the higher organisms, have the least rigid or, as people say, the most "expressive" faces, can, of course, be attributed to the fact that the face is the mirror of the soul. But if the question is pursued somewhat more precisely, one finds that humans are by nature equipped in the frontal part of the head with a more highly differentiated system of cutaneous muscles than any other living being. The muscular movements that people coordinate in order to produce a smile, to name only this, go far beyond those of the higher apes in terms of differentiation. The same can be said of the musculature of the human hand, particularly the fingers. No other kind of organism possesses the differentiated muscular system that is needed to play a piano sonata by Beethoven or Liszt. People pride themselves on the agility of their minds. But whatever the word "mind" may mean in this context, this agility would be useless if people were not also equipped with equally agile executive organs, with the highly differentiated motorial apparatus of front feet which have developed in them into hands.

XI

One cannot speak of the increasing differentiation and specialization of organisms in the course of evolution, without speaking at the same time of the similar increase in the special apparatus of coordination and integration. Growing differentiation and a growing capacity for coordination and integration are complementary processes in the bio-organization. Neither of them can advance from one phase to the next if the other does not keep pace. If in the following, therefore, a few aspects of the evolution of biological coordination and integration mechanisms are pointed out to make clear the peculiar nature of this area of subject-matter and knowledge, one is at the same time pointing to the continuation of the process of increasing division of functions in the course of biological evolution, the earliest stages of which have been elucidated by a few examples. In this context it will be sufficient to refer primarily to the development of one of the two forms of coordination and integration that come into being in organisms – integration through nerve cells (neurones) and nervous systems. The other form of integration, coordination by chemical means, the best-known example of which is the system of the endocrine glands and their products, can by and large be left aside.

A brief review of the evolution of the nervous system gives a vivid picture of the way in which the increasing specialization and functional division of organs and systems of organs finds its complementary counterpart in the formation of special organs of integration, with an increasing tendency towards a highly centralized control of all the particular processes of the organism. In brief: the more differentiated an organism, the more pronounced is the centralization of control over all the processes within it. However, the elementary structure and function of nervous systems are finally the same in all organisms. They provide connections between organs specialized in receiving sense impressions and other specialized organs, executive organs, that are able to react appropriately, in terms of the organisms, to information received from the sense organs by way of nerve channels. This elementary structure of the nervous system can be readily understood. For a living being which, whether amoeba or human being, possesses to a certain degree, unlike atoms and molecules, an individual, that is, self-regulating existence of its own – an existence that it can maintain by the constant absorption of somewhat less highly organized nutrients from its environment – needs information in order to continue its existence and to preserve its integrity; and it needs mechanisms that enable it to react appropriately to this information, in the interests of prolonging its existence and maintaining its integrity. Even unicellular organisms, whether bacilli, blue algae or flagellates, are organized on this pattern. But, naturally, unicellular organisms need no specialized organs to coordinate impressions received and reactions to them. However unicellular creatures bring it about, they are at any rate capable of orientation in their world and of appropriate adaptation of behaviour to it on the basis of an inbuilt automatism – we are concerned here with adaptation without awareness.

To make clear the process of increasing centralization, it is perhaps best to begin with a relatively simple multicellular organism. The starfish is a good example of incipient, relatively slight centralization. In this process, too, specific kinds of balances and shifts of power are involved. That in a starfish centralization is still comparatively slight is seen in, amongst other things, the ability of its arms to react relatively autonomously. Each arm can react to a stimulus it has received independently, to a degree, of the other arms. The nerve paths are in part laid out so that the information which one of the arms receives through a local sense organ, a receptor cell, can be transmitted directly – without being first fed to a central control – to a muscle of the arm, a local executive organ. The arm concerned may then bend without the other arms moving. But there is also at the centre of a starfish a simple network of conduits that connects the nerve paths of the different arms with each other. Even though the autonomy of the part-units is still relatively large *vis-à-vis* the centre, there are situations in which the movements of all the arms are coordinated. Only there is as yet no hegemony of the centre in relation to the part-units. This hegemony develops slowly.

Notes

1. These fragments are taken from the workshop. As a result they contain occasional repetitions and other deficiencies that further revision would have removed. Moreover, they are not complete; they are in the full sense fragments. It nevertheless seemed important to append them here in this provisional form. They contain ideas that merit discussion. Just because they represent work in progress, they make in their way a not insignificant contribution to understanding the mode of thinking and working that underlies the preceding essays.

2. By "Why questions" here I mean genetic questions. Philosophers have often tabooed them as unscientific. In sciences such as cosmology, biology and sociology they have become common practice.

3. One might suspect that the reference to automatic syntheses and the constant, irreversible division of labour that they entail is not entirely irrelevant to understanding the problem of entropy.

4. Cf. N. Elias, "Über die Zeit", *Merkur*, vol. 36 (1982), no. 9 (= no. 411), pp. 841 – 56; no. 10 (= no. 412), pp. 998 – 1016. A complete version of this study will appear shortly as vol. 3 of *Arbeiten zur Wissenssoziologie* by N. Elias.

5. "Development" is perhaps not the right word here; and terms like "young" and "old" stars, when referring to the chemical–physical level of integration, i.e. to integration units such as molecules, atoms, electrons or neutrons, have no more than a metaphorical meaning. Strictly speaking, all these are stage-specific categories that refer to processes on a higher level of integration.

6. The monopoly of materialist and reductionist assumptions finds expression here in attitudes such as the custom frequently encountered in recent times

of referring to organisms as systems of molecules – as if one could really expect one day to explain their characteristics adequately by those of the constituent molecules.

7. It might perhaps be useful to introduce the concept of the "stage fall" here, to come to terms with this problem; for it is repeated at all descending stages of biological evolution. Thus plants are able to absorb and synthesize chemical–physical compounds of a lower stage of integration that the human organism is unable to synthesize and convert into its own substance directly, but only by absorbing plants and animals.

8. One could imagine that there were preceding power struggles, that several forms of coexistence by two cells of the older type came into being in a kind of blind experimentation of the natural process, and that finally one of them, the eucaryotic, that stabilized a particular balance of power and division of functions between the two united cells, proved successful in the struggle with other forms, multiplied quickly and so became the ancestor of all other organisms. The less successful experiments left no traces.

9. It should be noted in passing that the dominance of gene structures, their power to command as the highest centre regulating all organic processes, does not perhaps possess the absolute character ascribed to it today.

Index

Compiled by Eric Dunning